How to Computerize Your Small Business

How to Computerize Your Small Business

Patrick D. O'Hara, PhD

John Wiley & Sons, Inc.
New York • Chichester • Brisbane
Toronto • Singapore

In recognition of the importance of preserving what has been written, it is a policy of John Wiley & Sons, Inc., to have books of enduring value printed on acid-free paper, and we exert our best efforts to that end.

This publication is designed to provide accurate and authoritative information in regard to the subject matter covered. It is sold with the understanding that the publisher is not engaged in rendering legal, accounting, or other professional service. If legal advice or other expert assistance is required, the services of a competent professional person should be sought. From a *Declaration of Principles jointly adopted by a Committee of the American Bar Association and a Committee of Publishers.*

Library of Congress Cataloging-in-Publication Data

O'Hara, Patrick D.
How to computerize your small business / by Patrick D. O'Hara.
p. cm.
Includes index.
ISBN 0-471-57870-3 (cloth). — ISBN 0-471-57869-X (paper)
1. Small business—Data processing. 2. Microcomputers—
Purchasing. I. Title.
HF5548.2.O43 1993
658.02′2′0285416—dc20 92-14972

Printed in the United States of America

10 9 8 7 6 5 4 3 2 1

Acknowledgments ⸺⸺⸺

I wish to express my appreciation to my wife Betty for her acceptance of the sacrifice of our time together while I wrote this book and for her suggestions, and those of Robert Swersky and Arlene Johnson, in improving its presentation to fit the uninitiated computer novice. Through their suggestions I avoided many areas of confusion from the inadvertent use of computer jargon.

I also want to express my gratitude to Mike Hamilton and Elena Paperny at John Wiley & Sons for their support and encouragement of this project. I hope my efforts here meet their expectations.

Trademarks

Apple and Macintosh are trademarks of Apple Computers, Inc.
AT&T is a trademark of American Telephone & Telegraph Corp.
Central Point and PC Tools are trademarks of Central Point Software Corp.
CompuAdd is a trademark of CompuAdd Corp.
CompuServe is a trademark of CompuServe Corp.
dBASE is a trademark of Borland International.
Disk Optimizer is a trademark of SoftLogic Solutions Corp.
FAST! is a trademark of Future Soft Engineering Corp.
Fastback Plus is a trademark of Fifth Generation Systems, Inc.
Fax-O-Matic is a trademark of Tall Tree Systems, Inc.
FaxConnection is a trademark of Extended Systems, Inc.
FAX96 is a trademark of Fremont Communications Corp.
FoxPro is a trademark of FoxPro Corp.
IBM and OS/2 are trademarks of International Business Machines, Inc.
JetFax II is a trademark of JetFax Corp.
LaserJet is a trademark of Hewlett-Packard Corp.
LaserScript is a trademark of Everex Systems, Inc.
Lotus 1-2-3 is a trademark of Lotus Corp.
MS-DOS and Windows are trademarks of Microsoft Corp.
Norton Utilities is a trademark of Symantec Corp.
Paradox is a trademark of Paradox Corp.
QEMM-386 is a trademark of Quarterdeck Office Systems, Inc.
Quicken is a trademark of Intuit Corp.
Stacker is a trademark of Stac Electronics Corp.
Superstor is a trademark of Addstor Corp.
WordPerfect is a trademark of WordPerfect Corp.

About the Author

PATRICK D. O'HARA has been involved in managing and marketing computer and related technologies since 1965, working for organizations such as the EDP division of Honeywell, Computer Systems and International Divisions of Hewlett-Packard, as well as many technology start-ups in the Silicon Valley. He is President of O-TEK Enterprises in Fremont, California, a management and technical consulting company, lending his expertise to such companies as Scrib-Tech, Inc. of Menlo Park, a magnetic printing technology company, the Information Systems department of the City of Fremont, and Strategic Computer Solutions, a retail security software development and custom software/systems development company in Fremont. He is the author of *The Total Business Plan* and *SBA Loans: A Step-by-Step Guide* and *The Total Sales and Marketing Plan,* all published by John Wiley & Sons, Inc. Dr. O'Hara received his PhD in business administration from Columbia Pacific University in 1983.

Preface

This book is written for the small business owner or serious home computer user. The primary purpose of this book is to allow a small business owner and computer novice to be able to purchase, configure, install, and begin to use a basic personal computer system, without difficulty and confusion.

The products mentioned by name for the purpose of this book are examples only. They are neither recommended nor discouraged for your particular situation. They are, to my knowledge, the most popular items available on the market today. And their installation and setup procedures are fairly typical of the IBM clone segment of the personal computer industry. However, the author and publisher assume no responsibility for any person's loss due to the use of the information given here. There are just too many manufactured variations of hardware and software in this industry for a general text to be totally accurate. Always refer to your supplier and your equipment and software documentation for specific information.

This book is written with the small business owner in mind: That person whose business takes his or her full-time effort to keep in operation and who doesn't have time to "study" the intricacies of computer technology and/or terminology, yet is fully aware that computerizing the business is necessary if it is to grow or even possibly survive. It does not presuppose any knowledge of computers. And it does not expect a person to become a computer "expert" merely by reading it.

The book is meant to give a computer novice a basic understanding of what computers can do and how to make them do it with the tools currently available. It is expected that by first briefly reading through this book the reader will gain an acquaintance with computer systems and their general application. A second reading will walk you through the selection and purchase of your system. And a third more detailed reading during and after acquiring your system will enable you to talk to and generally understand any so-called computer expert when you ask for information about your system. It will also help you in the buying process to not be "snowed" by salespeople's free use of computer jargon, which is primarily meant to confuse and impress you with their knowledge.

This book is not necessarily written for the large corporation that has many expert resources available, though some corporate managers may learn from it.

As you read through the book you will probably notice certain redundancies. This is done to familiarize you with the use of the same terminology in different contexts. And it gives you familiarity in the opposite sense: same context with different terminology meaning practically the same thing. This type of "word play" is common in the industry. The two most common areas of this are in the subject areas of data storage and communications. Although confusion was not the intent of the industry, it happens when multiple discrete technologies are brought together to form a singular science—such is the case with "computer science."

My purpose in writing this book is to present the information in such a way that the computer novice can understand and make sense of it. I've used as little jargon as possible and explained the jargon you should know in "layperson's" language. If I'm successful, I'm happy. If not, I apologize. Either way I sincerely hope you enjoy reading the book and get some benefit from it.

Contents

1

Why You Should Computerize Your Small Business

Computers are everywhere you look today—banks, businesses, stores, schools, and homes. With the help of personal computers, people are improving productivity, increasing market share and profits, sending electronic messages to other computer users, making their own airline reservations, and even shopping from home!

Computerizing your business can be one of the best business decisions you'll ever make, but it's also one of the trickiest. Just finding the appropriate software or hardware can be a long, slow, anxiety-filled process—and then you have to learn how to use it. When done with patience, preparation, and careful planning, however, going "on-line" can make a world of difference in the efficiency and profitability of your business.

One Businessman's Computerization Story

Some miles north of the border of New Brunswick is a woodworking shop. It is a compact, well-considered space, incorporating a wealth of practical ideas. The shop evolved gradually, as most small businesses do, on a modest budget, over the past 13 years. Its owner is in it to make a living. The owner builds a wide variety of furniture and cabinets in the shop. But the key to his flexibility (and to his living) is not in the shop, but in his living-room office. The office, the owner is convinced, has "something to do with woodworking—and everything to do with staying alive in woodworking." If it takes up almost half of his living room, it composes fully half of his business.

According to this woodworker, you build a business like you build a piece of furniture. It goes together one piece at a time, and you make plenty of mistakes along the way. This businessman speaks from personal experience. After several years in business—"working my tail off and not making any money"—he hired a small-business consultant. The first two meetings produced no tangible results, and by the third he was desperate. "Can I afford to hire someone?" he asked. After studying the business's books, the consultant replied, "Not only can you not afford to hire somebody, you can't afford to stay in business past noon."

The owner dates the birth of his business from that point. The consultant introduced planning, long-term goals, ongoing evaluation, and focus—all the tasks that the owner previously thought were reserved for "the big guys." Shortly thereafter, the woodworker set out to buy a typewriter and came home with a personal computer (PC). Many small business owners choke on the price tag of a computer. Many also never get beyond the stigma of automation. But, according to this owner, "In this day and age you can't afford not to have one. The computer absolutely will not lie." He now uses his computer as a project management tool, to plan and to forecast work flow and cash flow.

The consultant taught the woodworker the "miracle of spreadsheets," and he began to play "what if?" What if I make 10 of these? What if I take a week off? How much do I have to increase my hourly shop rate to buy a new jointer by December? In short, he explains, "I took control of my business."

In a short time, he upgraded his computer system with a 286 computer (an IBM clone), color monitor, a daisy-wheel printer, and a dot-matrix printer. He uses the dot-matrix printer for all business and accounting functions and the daisy-wheel for presentations. Its clean, crisp type conveys the professional image that he considers a necessity for conveying the idea of a quality product. The new system cost approximately $9,000, about four times the price of the original computer, which his son now uses for school work. The later addition of a plotter and a fax machine increased the system cost by another couple of thousand dollars.

For software, the woodworker uses five programs: a word processor for correspondence, a spreadsheet program for "what if" analysis, a database program to index photo negatives (it takes him less than a minute to locate any photo on file), a project management program for shop scheduling, and an accounting program to track his professional expenses. He also does most of his design work on the computer, using a three-dimensional CAD (computer-aided design) program, which allows the same sort of flexible manipulation of graphic lines as word-processing programs do for text.

As the woodworker became more familiar with his system he began to explore the interplay between the work he did on computer and the work that goes on in the shop and achieved intriguing results. For example, the CAD program enables him to work the bugs out of a project simply by powering on the computer, loading the CAD program, and creating a draft of the project. On the screen, he can enlarge or reduce the image and play with curves and details. Then he can print out the modified image and tack it above the lathe for reference. All the refinements are performed without ever making dust. "It's almost better than the lathe," he comments. "I'm more productive downstairs if I've gotten as much design work as possible done up here in the office."

As you can see, the computer has become a real help to the woodworker in running all aspects of his business. In a more general sense, the benefits computerization offers are dramatically clear:

- Quick, reliable, down-to-the-penny financial and sales data
- Neat, well-organized records that you can access in a matter of seconds
- Reduced transaction time with bar code and laser scanners
- A modern and professional business image
- Minimized paperwork time
- Cost effective advertising and promotions because you can easily track results
- Reduced transaction errors and shrinkage
- Improved employee productivity tracking
- Improved inventory control
- Improved cash flow from minimizing inventory
- Effective purchasing and marketing decisions based on actual sales data and customer preferences
- Repeat business from marketing to your customers
- Remote control of your business, via a modem, from the comfort of your home

Sounds good, doesn't it? Better information makes you a better manager. Inventory turnover and repeat business ensure that you earn more. Businesses run efficiently generally translate into those run more profitably.

These are not mere marketing claims. Several industry associations that have surveyed their members conclude that businesses that run on computers run in the black. The old saying that this is "one investment that will pay for itself" has a solid basis. Nevertheless, there remains a big BUT. When it comes to choosing and implementing the right business management system, "What you don't know CAN hurt you!"

How a Computer Can Make (or Save) You Money

The business concerns discussed here are some key ways in which you can use a computer to raise your profits.

Inventory Management

Having a computer enables you to "turn" your inventory more often. It enables you to purchase more intelligently. For example, a manufacturer's salesperson offers you a 5 percent discount on the purchase of 10 cases of blue widgets. You can look up blue widgets on your computer to see how many cases you sold last year. Say you sold 10 cases of blue widgets. Do you really want to carry what could be a year's worth of widgets? Do you want them cluttering up your storeroom?

The computer keeps track of purchases and sales and makes the information accessible in a matter of seconds. You may check your inventory and run a report that gives a list of items that haven't been sold in over six months. (It can be very depressing if it shows too many items!) You can run a sale on items that haven't sold in more than six months. This enables you to clear shelf space and free up inventory dollars for other, faster-moving goods.

Policing Your Profit Margins

Why is it necessary to guard your percentages? Sometimes you may not be aware that your profit margins have fallen. If you have an average profit margin of 34 percent and an average net profit (pretax) of 6 percent, a 6 percent increase in your gross profit margin means a 50 percent increase in your *net* profit. Expressed another way, you will stop those pennies from falling through the cracks.

Sample of What It Takes
For example, assume that you have a business grossing $2 million a year and that your average profit margin is 50 percent. Also, for the sake of simplicity, assume that your expenses are similar to these:

Sales	$1,000,000	
Cost of goods	– 500,000	
Gross profit	500,000	(50% margin)
Payroll and taxes	250,000	
Advertising	80,000	
Utilities	5,000	
Rent	35,000	
Other expenses	70,000	
Total expenses	440,000	
Net profit	$ 60,000	(6%)

Now, assume that by carefully watching your inventory and by reviewing the management reports, you can increase your profit margin to 53 percent. What will this do to your net profit? The profit picture will look like this:

Sales	$1,000,000	
Cost of goods	470,000	
Gross profit	530,000	(53% margin)
Payroll and taxes	250,000	
Advertising	80,000	
Utilities	5,000	
Rent	35,000	
Other expenses	70,000	
Total expenses	440,000	
Net profit	$ 90,000	(9% = 50% increase)

You have witnessed a 50 percent increase in the bottom line because of an increase in the profit margin from 50 percent to 53 percent!

Why You Should Expect to Increase Your Profit Margin
When you are busy taking care of everything from leaky faucets to advertising, it is impossible to spend the time necessary to follow up on every detail. A computer can do this for you.

There are many ways profit margin dollars fall through the cracks. Here are a few:

1. Clerks enter wrong prices when goods are received.
2. Clerks enter the correct prices, but prices rise subsequently.
3. Some merchandise has been on the shelf so long that its selling price is no longer valid. Your original cost may have been $5.00 and you are selling it for $10.00, but the replacement cost is $7.50. (By repricing here you are not "increasing your margins" but merely acting intelligently.)

4. Some items prove to be such good sellers that they could command a better margin if repriced.

5. By knowing the *exact* volume of items you will move over a given period, you could take better advantage of manufacturers' discounts. For example, a certain manufacturer always pushes for sales at the end of a quarter (every three months), so he always calls you with some type of special offer—generally an additional 10 percent to 20 percent off. To capitalize on this, you see what you sold in the prior three-month period and use that information to determine your next order. You try to order a three-month supply. This reduces the number of times you turn the inventory per year to four, which most experts will agree is very low, *but* you get an extra 20 percent off the merchandise, which justifies carrying that extra inventory. Without the recent sales information at your fingertips, you are just guessing. Purchasing that inventory at 20 percent off can enable you to slightly underprice the competition and capture additional sales.

6. You can expect your shrinkage to decrease. Employees know when inventory is not being accurately watched. Some reports today show that over 50 percent of shrinkage is due to internal problems. Can you watch every sale? Are you tied to your store 24 hours a day? When your employees ring up a sale, is it at the right price? Do they give a family member or friend a "special discount"? A computer system that tracks these items greatly discourages theft and abuse. No computer system can eliminate employee dishonesty, but it can produce improvement. How will employees steal? The same way they do now, by not ringing up the sale. Will you know whether they do this? Yes, because comparing inventory levels tracked on the computer against your shelf inventory will reveal the discrepancies.

Generating Letters, Mailing Labels, and Postcards

At a recent users' group meeting someone asked, "How many business owners send out reminder mailings?" Almost everyone raised their hands. "What kind of response do you get?" The answers ranged from 30 percent to as high as 80 percent. Many users were in the service business, where reminder mailings are an excellent way to keep customers.

Physicians and dentists have known this for years; that's why they mail reminder cards. Recently, the more aggressive business owners have begun to use mailing lists for all kinds of promotions. Most frequent are special sale announcements, "for past customers only" announcements, service reminders (tune up, oil change, inspection), and new product announcements.

The Bottom Line

There are many ways that a computer will increase the profitability of your business. These include uses such as word-processed correspondence; customer information databases; payroll, accounts receivable, and accounts payable spreadsheets; invoice generation; sorting lists; faxes and modems for quick data transfers; and business graphics preparation. A good computer system (hardware and software) should get you a minimum of 300 percent return on your investment over time.

However, remember that all too often small business owners seek computerization as though it were something that could be acquired "off the shelf" from a local computer store, as though it were an entity that could be chosen, financed, and installed on demand. Computerization is an objective and an evolving process.

Planning for Computerization

Computerizing your business is best accomplished in stages. When one area begins to run smoothly, go on to the next. It must be a gradual process, with one area running well before you tackle the next. Over time, as you see what a computer can do, you'll begin to see the possibilities unique to your business. As each area is automated, your understanding of your computer needs will increase.

The entire process will be much easier if all of the individuals who will use the system support your decision to purchase the system. When you have your first thoughts about computerizing, share some ideas with your staff. You will be amazed to see how even the most competent employee can be deathly afraid of a computer. New technology frightens some people, and others may be afraid the computer will replace them. You also may find employees who have experience with personal computers; ask these people to help you sell the idea to the others and possibly help you with some of the necessary research. Allow yourself six months to a year to initially implement your new computer system.

What a Computer Will Not Do

Before you see what a computer can do for your business, it's important for you to understand what it cannot do.

Turn a Bad, Disorganized Business into a Thriving One

If your business is in a state of disarray, matters will become more confused after computerization. It's sort of like getting off an out of control bicycle and into an out of control car. The car travels faster, so you can cause more damage.

Reduce Your Workload Immediately
Your workload may temporarily increase when you convert to computerized techniques. Usually, the businessperson invests a considerable amount of time up front but as a result spends less time later on retrieving the information or compiling it into useful reports.

Run the Business for You
Computers are merely tools, albeit powerful ones, that require commitment and a high degree of consistency to attain useful results. If you are sloppy about the information you enter into the computer, the results you get out will be of questionable value. Or, as the old saying goes, "garbage in, garbage out."

What a Computer Can Do

If the computer doesn't get you organized, immediately end your paperwork, or run the business, what are its benefits?

Free Up Your Time
This probably is the most important reason for purchasing a computer. A business owner's time is valuable. If you could reduce the amount of time spent on day-to-day tasks, imagine the possibilities. As well as providing you with more information, a computer will help eliminate many mundane tasks, such as counting inventory; addressing postcards; preparing account statements; writing purchase orders; calculating employee commissions, sales, profits, and tax payments; and typing the same form letter over and over.

Provide You with Important Details About Your Business
A computer can give you a far more precise and instant view of your operation—everything from profit margins to daily sales, from expense breakdowns to items that have sold poorly. Each day you can see an account of what your business has done for the day. These figures can reflect the exact sales, service income, taxes, employee sales, gross profit, and gross margin. Other sales reports can break down the same information for any period. This flexibility of views enables you to see exactly how your business is progressing.

Do you need to find out which merchandise lines bring in the most profit? No problem. You can find the exact sales and profits by line, department, time period, or individual unit and see the percentage of business that each of these categories contributes to the total store's business. Some programs even enable you to define exactly what information you would like to look at. For example, a spreadsheet can reveal slow-moving inventory or profitable merchandise lines.

Keep the Books
Many point-of-sale programs link to accounting programs or include features such as accounts receivable, accounts payable, and general ledger. If you understand double-entry accounting (debit and credit entries), you may wish to do your own ledgers.

Help Control Theft
With a computerized inventory system, you always know the exact number of each item you should have in stock at any given time. With quick "spot checks" of inventory counts (especially of popular items), problems can be found quickly.

Calculate Sales by Employee
Many programs can figure the exact sales levels by employee for productivity analysis or commission purposes. You can also track sales by geographic region or by some demographic information you're interested in.

Keep You in Touch with Your Customers
With most point-of-sale programs you can quickly follow up each customer for overdue rentals, accounts receivable, open layaways, missing shipments, and so on. You can send reminders for services due or notify your customers about upcoming sales events. Whatever you need to contact your customers about, it is much easier when you can automatically customize postcards, letters, or simply print mailing labels.

Replace Your Cash Register
With the use of "point-of-sale" software (so called because it tracks your business at the point of sale), the computer can print a complete, legible receipt or invoice for your customers. If the item is marked with a bar code label, a bar code reader or "in-counter" scanner (like the grocery stores use) can read the label. The regular or promotional price will automatically appear on the screen with the description.

   If the item doesn't have a bar code label, you simply type a stock number. Some systems calculate change and enable you to charge a balance due to a customer account. With the right software, it doesn't take much longer to ring a transaction on a computer than it does on a register.

Do you have different pricing levels, such as retail and wholesale? A computer can track multiple pricing structures and automatically charge each customer the proper price. If an item is on promotion, the system will automatically use the discounted price when calculating an order. All this adds up to less guesswork and fewer mistakes at the checkout counter.

Track Your Inventory

Before you start using an on-line inventory system, you'll enter your inventory items into the computer with a beginning on-hand count and assign stock numbers to items. As items are sold or returned, their inventory counts are automatically reduced or increased. At any time you can get an "up-to-the-minute" report containing the amount of inventory on hand that can be spot checked against the physical inventory.

Calculate Your Reorders

When you have set up an inventory system, as you enter subsequent orders the reorder levels are established for the items stocked. When the on-hand quantity for an item reaches the trigger level, it appears on a reorder report. Some programs also generate purchase orders for the items you choose to order. This feature alone will save you so much time and energy that it will pay for the system. Many business owners waste two or more hours a day running around the store looking for everything to be reordered.

Understanding the Computer

If you're in the market for a personal computer for your business, whether that business is in your home or an outside office, the experts all agree on one thing: Know what you want the computer to do and do not buy a computer until you thoroughly shop and test the variety of software and hardware models out there. The investigation can save you both time and money. You should also take time to become familiar with some of the computer basics, such as the hardware terminology, before you shop.

The computer you're using right now (if any) is probably thousands of times more powerful than the first personal computer developed in 1975. That primitive machine, the Altair 8800, inspired the revolution that has brought personal computing to you and 25 million others in offices, dens, and dorm rooms. On the pages ahead you can read about some personal computers that became milestones in this revolution. First, though, because computer talk swarms with acronyms and buzzwords, you need some clear standards for comparison.

Four key elements determine what really counts in a computer: computing power, memory, storage, and ease of use. These four elements define a computer's performance. Performance is considered here to be the relative ability of a personal computer to help get something done. This book considers these elements from the point of view of the small, "mom and pop" business.

Allaying Your Fears

Put aside the belief that computers are used only by the most sophisticated businesses and children. Those keys, pushbuttons, and "joy sticks" can do much more than balance accounts payable and receivable or direct yellow, moon-faced cartoon characters to gobble blue-colored ghosts darting swiftly around a screen.

Also put aside any fear you might have about understanding computers. The actual mechanics of computer operation will astound you by their simplicity and logic. If you can hunt-and-peck on a typewriter keyboard and are willing to spend some time discovering what hardware does what and learning which software can help you, you can operate a personal computer with success. And what's more, the learning experiences can be both fun and rewarding.

Let's look at the short evolution of the computer and in the process become familiar with a few of the basic terms used in that industry.

Under the Computer Cover

The *microprocessor* (the heart of the computer) inside today's computer is often described by its raw speed measured in *megahertz* (millions of cycles per second, abbreviated MHz). The processor's actual horsepower also depends on the size of the highway it uses to shuttle data in and out. The Altair's highway was 8 lanes or bits wide. (A *bit* is the smallest data element used in a computer.) Later computers advanced to 16 bits, and 32-bit machines are here now.

The size of your computer's main memory or *RAM* (*random-access memory*—a short-term data storage area where the data can be modified and prepared for permanent storage) determines how big a program you can load. A simple word processor, for instance, might require 64K bytes of RAM or 64,000 bytes (1 byte equals 1 typed character, such as an *A*) of RAM to run properly.

Memory expansion has been swift. Back in 1975 the Altair offered only 256 bytes of RAM, although later machines packed at least 640,000 bytes of RAM or 2,000 times as much. Today the minimum memory is 1 megabyte (M byte) and is expanding.

When programs and data are not in use they need to be stored in some form of auxiliary memory; usually they are recorded on diskettes or a hard disk. The first diskettes held just 160,000 (160K) bytes or about 30 pages of double-spaced text. Today's high-density marvels hold up to 1,400,000 (1.4M) bytes, or about 700 pages. Similarly, hard disks once were considered huge at 10M bytes. Today they can hold hundreds of megabytes.

The final key performance element, ease of use, is only partly a hardware issue. A well-designed system or program makes learning to use a computer easier and mastering new programs much faster—and that counts for a lot. After all, even state-of-the-art horsepower, RAM, and disk storage won't deliver performance until you figure out how to use them.

Where Is Hardware Heading?

As the progression from the Altair to the Next (the newest personal computer system design) illustrates, personal computers are evolving at an extraordinary pace. Hardware trends already under way suggest a future with greater processing power, abundant memory, new interfaces, massive storage, multitasking systems, and increasing connectivity in a smaller and smaller physical package at a lower relative cost. If raw processing power continues to become more affordable, we can look forward to machines that help us to manipulate speech, pictures, and music as easily as we manipulate numbers and text today. When combined with mass storage devices such as optical disks, that power is already spawning *multimedia* products such as electronic books with moving illustrations, games with animation, and even movies on disk.

The powerful laptop and notebook computers popular today may lead to even smaller computers that become integrated into the dashboards of our cars, the heating and cooling controls of our houses, and the credit cards in our wallets. Today's keyboard and mouse will be joined by scanners, voice recognition devices that act on spoken command, and even gesture-driven interfaces. The desktop multitasking computers will bring new levels of productivity as they run more than one program at once. For instance, you could type a memo, download a file from a remote service, and print a document all at the same time. Or your database and spreadsheet could be continuously updated by information arriving over your modem.

All of these advances will become increasingly interconnected by telephone, cable TV, and satellite networks. Electronic publications, information services, and mail systems will proliferate. As this electronic future spins its web around us, we will be asking ourselves again and again whether all these devices bring new controls to our lives or new complications.

Software Essentials

Like a turntable without records or a cassette player without tapes, the fanciest computer is useless without software. Despite its smart image, a computer by itself is just a helpless hunk of silicon, plastic, and steel. *Software* provides the instructions (programs) that unlock the power of the hardware and put it to work for you. The programs that process words, build spreadsheets, and do specific jobs are called *applications programs.* Some common ones are described on the pages ahead. It's important to note that applications rely on *system software,* a category of programs that directly control your hardware. You might say applications piggyback on systems software functions.

Every computer needs an efficient housekeeper—an *operating system*—to manage memory and files. This software handles such chores as formatting hard disks and diskettes; creating, copying, and erasing files; and controlling ports (connections) used by your printer or modem. The machine you're using now, if any, probably runs one or more of these operating systems, such as MS-DOS, the Macintosh System 7, or IBM OS/2.

As operating systems keep house, another layer of system software, called an *operating environment,* is controlling how you communicate with the machine—the *user interface.* Environments can be character-based, as in MS-DOS, or graphical, like the Macintosh, which popularized the *graphical user interface* or *GUI* (pronounced "gooey"). GUIs such as "Windows version 3.1" are quickly spreading to other systems, too. Each application program—whether it's a spreadsheet, game, or communications package—is created for use with specific system software. That's why programs written for MS-DOS normally won't run on a Macintosh and vice versa.

One other type software is worth noting—a diverse group of *utility programs* that have sprung up to extend the functions of operating systems.

Software is published in a variety of forms:

- The commercial package that you purchase from a vendor
- Shareware or user-supported software that you can download from bulletin boards or obtain from user group libraries
- Public-domain software or freeware published in magazines or on bulletin boards.

Before you choose a program, make sure it works with your operating system and environment. Also, because software is seldom self-explanatory, check the documentation and the types of support offered. Some publishers/manufacturers provide on-line help, tutorials, special bulletin boards, or tollfree help lines. Others offer far less. Finally be sure you get the latest version of the software.

To Buy or Not to Buy

Personal computer owners report that the reality of using a computer can be different from what the advertisements would lead you to believe. A computer is not a panacea for all problems, but there are many things it can do.

Consider the computer as a multiuse tool similar to an adjustable wrench—you adjust the jaws of the wrench to fit its application to a nut or bolt. The personal computer is adjusted by the programs used to fit your needs. You realize more from your investment when you use the computer to perform many tasks. If you want it to perform one job, perhaps you should look into a simple system that may be plugged into a television set. Or if you want a computer for games only, you can buy a machine that only plays games. It sells for a fraction of what a personal computer costs.

Buying a computer may cost more than you might first think. The initial cost for the hardware (basic equipment) may not be the final cost. The software (programs) can be expensive. And don't overlook computer maintenance and possible add-on hardware purchases.

Computers do not run themselves. They only perform as well as the person running them. Remember, the information you put into a computer is what determines the accuracy of the information you will get out of the computer.

The alternatives to buying a computer system are renting, leasing, or sending your computer input data to a service bureau for processing (this is a form of what's now called "outsourcing data processing"). And, last but not necessarily least, you may elect to buy used equipment—this is not recommended for the novice computer user, however.

If you lease a business computer system for $3,000 per year, you should look to gain about $10,000 worth of additional income per year. It is possible to achieve a 300 percent return on investment for systems installed for small businesses.

Regardless of how you implement the purchase of your system, the following information still applies and is to your advantage to know.

Personal Computer Components

Buying a computer is not unlike buying a car. There are the basic models and many add-on accessories. This section describes the hardware or physical equipment making up the computer. You can mix and match these components to fit your specific needs.

Central Processor Unit or Microprocessor

As part of the processor unit, a computer will have both a *central processor unit (CPU)*, which is built on the capacity of the microprocessor, and main or random-access memory (RAM). Information is temporarily stored in RAM, not in the microprocessor. Most computers are packaged with a keyboard that acts as an input device. Some computers include a disk drive and built-in monitor. There are other combinations available.

Early personal computers were equipped with 8-bit microprocessors. Now most machines have 16-bit and 32-bit microprocessors. These larger-capacity processors give you more power and speed in computer operation.

With the least-expensive models you get just the processor, the keyboard, and limited memory capability. As the prices increase, more RAM and other components, such as a screen or disk drive, are added.

Screen (or Monitor)

The monitor, which resembles a television, displays your typing, graphic images, and the computer's calculations. If the computer doesn't come equipped with a screen, you may be able to use the screen of a television set. To hook up the computer to the TV, an RF modulator is used. It sells for about $5 to $70, the wide price range reflecting the sophistication of the part.

Many who own a personal computer report that a television screen lacks resolution and that a regular video monitor is best. The green or amber phosphorus screen is preferred by many because the letters and numbers appear clear and the colors are easy on the eye. Also, the computer-designed monitor puts more characters per line on the screen, as a general rule. At the high end are color monitors, which are useful for using graphics programs, for customizing text displays in word processors or spreadsheets, and for games. These color monitors are the most common on newer systems.

If your computer functions are limited to games and very light word processing (typing) chores, a television screen may work satisfactorily. But be mindful that a computer hooked to a television set must be disconnected when you want to watch TV. You can't operate the computer and the TV at the same time.

Disk Drives

Disk drives permanently store the data you enter and can retrieve that information almost immediately. There are two types of disk drives.

Floppy disk drives are mechanisms that function like a phonograph. They store and retrieve information using a removable flexible magnetic disk, which looks much like a bendable 45 rpm phonograph record. The capacity of a single disk ranges from 360K bytes (thousand bytes) to 1.44M bytes (megabytes or million bytes).

Hard disks, as the name implies, are rigid and usually not removable. The drive mechanism and disk are a unit. They have much greater capacity for storage (commonly 40 megabytes to 100 megabytes and more) and provide much faster access to stored data than do floppy disk drives.

Printers

A printer does what the name says: prints the material the computer retrieves onto paper for a "hard" copy. The printer works like a regular typewriter, but automatically.

A variety of printer technologies are available, including daisy wheel, dot matrix, ink jet, or laser. *Daisy-wheel printers* house the actual characters on a wheel- or ball-shaped head, much like Selectric typewriters use, to strike the paper. In fact, in some cases typewriters are modified with a connection for cabling to a computer. *Dot-matrix printers* use very tiny dots to form the letters and numbers. *Ink jet printers* spray ink onto the paper. *Laser printers* use a process like photocopying.

There are two types of paper feeds for printers: continuous fan-fold and single-sheet. Most dot-matrix models will handle both types, but you should check this feature as you decide which type is right for you.

Software

Software includes all the programs that tell the computer what to do. They are contained on plug-in cartridges or floppy disks. As mentioned earlier, software ranges from operating systems (MS-DOS, OS/2, UNIX, and so on) to applications such as text-editing, financial analysis, and educational programs.

Modem

This term stands for modulator/demodulator, a hardware component that changes computer signals into signals your telephone can use, so that they may be sent over telephone lines to link your computer to other system components or other computers.

Database Management

This is the process of organizing and storing information on your own computer system. Software packages exist for home computers to accomplish this. You could use a database management system to store Christmas card lists and phone numbers, for example.

Computer Terminology

Following is a brief, but essential, glossary of computer terms to help you become a smarter personal computer shopper:

Input. The data being received by the computer. You can tell the computer what to do by pressing keys on the keyboard or by programming it with a disk that has been "prerecorded." You also can hook up the computer (using a modem) to a data bank to receive data and programs.

ASCII. American Standard Code for Information Interchange, a coding system that allows the computer to internally represent letters, numerals, punctuation marks, and graphics characters as series of binary digits (bits).

Bit. An acronym for binary digit. This is the smallest unit of information for the computer.

Byte. A unit of eight bits, the equivalent of one typed character.

Word. The number of bits the CPU handles as one unit. Example: If the computer has an 8-bit CPU, the length of the word is 8 bits; if the computer has a 16-bit CPU, the word is 16 bits. A 4-bit word is called a *nibble,* and a 16-bit word is a *double-byte.*

Memory. The computer's temporary storage facility, which is measured in bytes and is usually described in K bytes or M bytes. (1K byte = 1,024 bytes, 1M byte = 1 million bytes.) There are two forms: RAM and ROM.

Random-access memory (RAM). Memory location in which the instructions are stored for the particular task you want to perform. However, if the power to the computer is switched off or goes off during computer operation, all data in RAM is lost.

Read-only memory (ROM). Permanent memory location for the initial instructions the computer uses to start its operation. These are set (programmed) by the manufacturer and are used each time power is applied to the computer or when the computer is "booted."

Menu. A list of what is available on a computer or in a specific computer software program. After you call up your program from memory, the computer will sometimes show a menu on the screen. Here's an example of a menu from a popular computer program:

YOU MAY CHOOSE FROM THE FOLLOWING—

(E) EDIT FILE IN MEMORY

(N) INITIALIZE NEW FILE

(L) LOAD FROM DISK

(S) SAVE TO DISK

(P) PRINT FILE

(Q) QUIT

TYPE LETTER OF YOUR SELECTION:

You choose the *option* from the menu that represents the task you want the computer to do. If you don't want what you see, you push the Q key and the program stops running and control is returned to the operating system.

Word processing. Computerized storage and manipulation of typed data, which increasingly is overlapping *desktop publishing.* Using the keyboard and the screen, you can write and edit, making changes as you type, inserting words or moving paragraphs. Using the printer, you can obtain a "hard copy" of what is on the screen.

Shopping and Comparing Prices

Personal computers are available at general merchandise catalog stores, outlets specializing in computers, office equipment stores, and office machine retailers.

Most retailers that sell computers have demonstration models set up in their showrooms. Do not be bashful about asking for a demonstration and, most important, asking to operate the computer yourself. Only by actually trying your hand at word processing and using other programs can you really understand the workings of a personal computer and make an informed buying decision.

Make sure you check the following items.

Equipment Warranty and Service

If something goes wrong with the computer, where is the nearest service center? What does the warranty cover, who honors it, and for how long?

Hardware and Software Availability
Are all the various components and programs for the computer readily available? Can they be updated if new versions come on the market?

Computer Support
Does the retailer offer classes and instructions for computer training? Does the retailer offer any type of telephone service so that you can get answers to questions quickly?

Computer Clubs (Users' Groups)
Many communities have computer clubs and meetings at which owners get together and discuss problems, learn techniques, and trade software. The club may be under the sponsorship of a retailer, or it may be owner organized. Check with the retailer for information on these clubs. Some retailer-sponsored clubs receive computer merchandise discounts. (Keep in mind that it is against the law to duplicate programs already copyrighted.)

Access to Commercial Databases
Telecommunicating enables you to use your computer to access information from data banks in large computer systems that store a wide range of information. To hook the computer to such a system, you need a telephone line, a modem, and communications software. Charges vary widely according to the data bank source, the area in which you reside, and the type of equipment and information on the computer.

If you plan to hook up your computer to a data source, shop around and compare prices of the various services offered. The computer store or your local telephone company can provide you with additional information.

Access to Noncommercial Bulletin Board Systems (BBSs)
Many computer professionals and amateurs operate their own private database and message center bulletin boards. Most are free or available at a low fee. Most computer stores can provide the telephone number of at least one BBS. That BBS will probably have the telephone numbers of many others.

Total Cost
After you narrow down your computer needs, be sure to find out what the full price of the equipment is. Keep in mind, always, what you want the computer to do right now and anticipate what you would like the system to do in the future. The more sophisticated the computer, the more expensive the hardware and software.

Tips to Remember:

Following is a summary of what you need to know when you shop for a personal computer.

- Have a good idea of what computer applications you want: word processing, data management, entertainment, education, budgeting, telecomputing, desktop publishing, and so on.
- Know the functions of the basic computer hardware.
- Check with friends and colleagues who have recently purchased a computer and with computer clubs for information and recommendations.
- Shop among several different stores, models, and manufacturers. Call the Better Business Bureau for a reliability report on a specific company.
- Obtain information brochures, which are usually free, about each model. Study them to make careful comparisons.
- Be sure to test the demonstration model and programs the retailer has available. Are the instructions easy to use and to understand?
- Does the program do what you need? Is it more complex than you need?
- Obtain firm prices on the computer equipment and software. Ask about the costs of expansion. Are both hardware and software readily available?
- Know the terms of the warranty and service arrangements.
- Ask about computer training and clubs.
- Is special furniture necessary to support the equipment?
- Check the refunds and exchange policy before you buy.
- If the computer will be used in a home office or professional arrangement, find out if its use will be tax-deductible.
- Also, check your homeowner's or business insurance policy to determine whether you are covered should the computer be stolen or damaged.

The remainder of this book expands on these thoughts and gives specific procedures that will make your learning process easier and, hopefully, enjoyable. Unnecessary jargon will be eliminated and necessary jargon will be fully explained in common terms.

2

Selecting the Right System for Your Needs

Today's personal computers are such capable and appealing devices that you might think you can get big gains just by buying one and keeping it around. That just isn't so! Before you expect to profit from computerization:

- Understand the unique capabilities of personal computer technology and learn to view computers as a storehouse of resources that can bring big payoffs in specific areas.
- View computerization as an opportunity to simplify, streamline, and improve the way you do business or work.
- Focus on one sharply defined task that's critical to your business mission or home automation.

Plan, define, and purchase the system to meet all your computerization needs but start computerizing with just one application—and make it a relatively modest one, such as responding to routine business correspondence or setting up a mailing list. Don't try to tackle two or more areas simultaneously.

21

Determining What Functions to Computerize

If you ask a computer science expert what computers do, you may be told something like, "Computers process information." But this definition isn't very helpful. Strictly speaking, computers are machines that run programs. Usually, computers run the programs that have been successful in the market. It follows, then, that a computer can help you—if a program is available that genuinely addresses your business needs.

What kinds of programs have proven to be successful in the market? All the successful personal computer applications—word processing, electronic spreadsheets, database management, desktop publishing, and telecommunications—are little more than electronic versions of letters, reports, accountants' pads, index cards, artists' layout tables, and memos. And what's more, people are using computers not just to represent such documents on-screen but to print ever-mounting numbers of computer-generated paper documents, such as letters, essays, memos, reports, charts, newsletters, fliers, bills, price lists, and more.

The success of such programs astounded the experts, who confidently predicted at the beginning of the computer era that computers would eliminate paper documents. In the 1950s and early 1960s, computer pundits predicted a "paperless society," in which computers would replace all those inefficient, old-fashioned checks, invoices, letters, reports, forms, file folders, and cards. While these authorities talked, businesses bought systems that enabled them to deal with paper documents more efficiently and to print them in ever-increasing quantities. All the basic software functions—word processing, electronic spreadsheets, database management, graphics, and telecommunications—not only represent paper documents, but they also print them—and the result is a stunning explosion of paper usage.

So what do these facts mean? For the most part, the best place to look when you are contemplating computerization is your "out" box, correspondence, and trash can. What kind of paper-based documents are you producing? Which ones are gobbling up huge amounts of your time? Could you improve your business by using the computer to create documents you can't afford to produce now?

Even though most people are using computers to crank out more paper documents than ever before, you should remain alert to applications that make printouts unnecessary, such as electronic mail, computer-generated presentation slides, and online database research. Many computer experts still believe that the greatest productivity gains with computers lie in the future, when people finally break their paper habits. For now, though, most of your applications will involve pushing paper more effectively, efficiently, and cheaply.

Understanding the Benefits of Computerizing

Businesses use computers to help simulate, automate, and enhance the operations people once performed manually. To realize the benefits of computers in your small business, you should concentrate on the tasks that slow you down and cost the most money.

Computers bring five potential benefits to your business:

1. Acquiring new skills
2. Automating tasks
3. Reducing errors
4. Making your work more efficient
5. Producing more attractive output

Remember:

- Computers don't replace paper. Instead, they simulate, automate, and enhance operations you perform on paper.
- To select the tasks that you want to computerize, examine the paper-related tasks that you perform in your business.
- The biggest benefits from computerization come from streamlining the way you do business—not just from using computers.

Acquiring New Skills

The first major benefit of computerizing lies in the capacity of computers to spread skills throughout society that were formerly possessed by only experienced specialists. Consider the task of using a typewriter to type a document with centered headings and footnotes. You had better get ready for some arithmetic! How many spaces do you backspace? How much space should you leave for the footnotes? It takes a professional typist to type a document with beautifully positioned footnotes. But just about any full-featured word processing program can perform the necessary computations automatically—you just insert the words of the note, and the program takes care of the rest.

This benefit makes available to nonspecialists the skills and competence of experts. In so doing, the computer saves you the money you otherwise would pay to hire experts.

With a spreadsheet program, for example, you can choose from many built-in formulas for performing complex financial analyses—the kind of analyses (such as computing the net present value of an investment) that you would learn if you were to study finance at a business school. In a desktop publishing program, you can use many layout techniques that would otherwise require years of experience with layout boards, T-squares, and sharp blue pencils.

A personal computer can help you acquire some of the skills of an accomplished professional typist, financial analyst, graphic designer, or professional business writer. But you still must make sure that the results meet the highest professional standards. Not all programs can ensure that such standards are met.

Automating Tasks

The second benefit of computerization enables you to make money by concentrating on the tasks with high profit margins—and you can be sure that summing and alphabetizing aren't among those tasks.

Task automation can save you time. The best applications provide task automation with a minimum of user input, keyboard fussing, and command memorization. Look for programs that perform such tasks as summing up numbers, alphabetizing lists, sorting in numerical order, and making identical copies, thus allowing the computer to do these tasks while you concentrate on the more profitable tasks of your business.

Reducing Errors

Many programs come with features that can help you avoid embarrassing or costly errors, such as spelling mistakes, calculation errors, misfiled records, and incorrect data entry. Just bear in mind that these features aren't foolproof and don't replace human thought.

Making Your Work More Efficient

If you have ever worked with tools around the house or a shop, you know that power tools—drills, pneumatic hammers, power sanders, power saws, and all the rest—dramatically improve your efficiency in carpentry. Using power tools, you can frame a basement in a fraction of the time it would take with hand tools.

Personal computers provide power tools for your paper tasks. You can store thousands of client records and print hundreds of bills just by choosing a command from a menu. You can search a 100-page technical report for spelling errors just by choosing a spell-checking option; your only role is to confirm the corrections.

Power tools are useful, but buying and using a computer system does not guarantee that you will do a better job of running your business with a computer than you did before. A power saw doesn't guarantee a good carpentry job; if you start with a bad plan, you get bad results.

A poorly designed PC system used as a point-of-sale terminal at a computer store illustrates this point. Such a system requires the sales clerk to ask every customer for his or her name, work address, home address, telephone number, and future purchasing plans before it is possible to compute the sales tax and total. Obtaining this information from computer purchasers makes sense, but it only serves to irritate customers who drop in just to buy a magazine or some other small purchase. After undergoing several minutes of interrogation just to pay cash for a box of diskettes, some customers will decide to go elsewhere.

Producing More Attractive Output

Like it or not, your competition is probably using computers already—and these scoundrels are producing very attractive, well-designed price lists, brochures, letters, and fliers. Worse, the public is increasingly accustomed to professional-looking output. Your typed letters (complete with clumsily whited-out mistakes) and mimeographed price lists may be sending the wrong message about your firm.

Changing the Way You Work

You can't put PCs on everyone's desk and somehow expect productivity to zoom upward. To computerize effectively, you must target the most promising application areas; choose the right software; train yourself and your employees to use it; and guard against computer-related catastrophes, such as accidental data loss.

But if your business is a mess now, when you automate it's going to be an automated mess. The biggest productivity gains you can realize from computerization stem from changing the way you do business, not from buying machines.

Personal computers have the potential to benefit your business, but the key word is *potential.* With a pencil and paper, you can produce an incomprehensible three-page proposal that no one will read. With a personal computer, you can produce an incomprehensible one-page proposal; joining the unread text will be page after page of meaningless and unanalyzed spreadsheet figures.

Businesses all over North America are learning the hard way that the real benefits from computerization don't really come from the technology at all; they come from changing the way you do business. As you ponder your computerization strategy, consider some of the ways that you can change the way you work.

Because the big payoffs from computerization really come from changing the way you do business, bear in mind that you may be able to reap huge gains by skipping computers entirely and concentrating on improving the way you do business! Computers can play an important role in this process if they can provide the foundation, the staging ground, or the communication linkages that make such improvements possible—but they are not the only means of reaching the end. Noncomputer solutions—combining forms, moving people's desks closer together, eliminating redundant work, and so on—may produce the same rewards with far less cash outlay.

You can spend the productivity benefits of technology two ways. You can reduce the amount of work you're doing, or you can put in the same amount of work and raise the quality or quantity of your output. Both goals are possible and entirely legitimate. Even if you can't prove a bottom-line gain from computerization, it's still worth doing if you can improve the quality of the goods or services you deliver to your customers.

This section places first things first by introducing you to the different types of software available. This may be a little overwhelming at first. For now, just browse through the list so you can get an idea of what each type of software can do. You will see as you read this book that it is important to do in-depth research before you purchase software to run your business. Eventually, you probably will need to learn more than what is contained here.

Software Categories

For nonprogrammers, the world of software can be divided into two categories:

1. *System software:* Also known as the "operating system" or "operating environment," system software includes all programs used to control and maintain a computer system. Commonly used system software includes Microsoft Corporation's DOS for IBM and IBM-

compatible PCs, and Apple Computer's System 7 software for its Macintosh computers.

2. *Application software:* All programs that enable computer users to apply computer technology to their own ends (such as writing a business report or analyzing financial data). Utility software is a subset of application software but is within the operating system category.

Operating Systems

The operating system controls the computer's operation and is divided into three categories:

1. *The operating system:* The housekeeping environment includes all processes essential and indispensable to the computer's proper functioning. It allows the system to read application software; to accept input from the keyboard, a mouse (a pointing device), or other devices; and to transfer information for storage purposes.

2. *The user interface:* The portion of the system software that displays messages to the user and handles the user's commands. The user interface provides tools to perform tasks such as preparing disks for use (formatting), copying and deleting files on disks, and starting applications.

3. *System utilities:* These are programs for day-to-day system maintenance (such as backing up files or formatting disks) that are provided with the operating system.

The operating system controls the system maintenance functions. If you will be using one computer, you will need a single-user system. When two or more computers are linked together, a multiuser (network) operating system is necessary. Operating systems and application software must be compatible. In other words, they must be able to communicate with one another.

Operating systems also must be compatible with the computer itself. Application software and operating systems that run on one brand of computer do not necessarily work on another. Such are the differences between IBM compatible computers and the Apple Macintosh series computers. The IBM compatible (DOS) systems are designed as "text-based" or "command-line" systems. The Apple Macintosh has a "graphics-based" design. This is also known as "graphical user interface" or GUI (pronounced "gooey") design.

The Macintosh was originally designed for the home user and game market but found great acceptance in the graphics art world of business.

The IBM (DOS) system was designed for the business world of text and calculations. Currently there is a development movement of the Mac and PC worlds toward an integration of the best features of both of these systems, such as the Windows 3.1 environment. Today if your needs are for graphic art production, the Macintosh will probably best fit your needs. If your needs are primarily business processes, the DOS (IBM compatible) computers are for you.

There are many different types of operating systems other than those issued for IBM and Apple computers.

DOS (Disk Operating System)
Also known as MS-DOS or PC-DOS, the latest version of DOS is 5.0. For single-user computer setups, DOS is without a doubt the operating system of choice. It has its limitations, but with over 50 million copies in use DOS is considered the standard personal computer operating system. It is recommended that you choose DOS as your operating system. Other alternatives will be far more costly and do not provide special features for single systems that you need and are able to have with DOS.

OS/2
This is an operating system codeveloped by Microsoft and IBM. It is an environment that will permit multiple software programs to run simultaneously (a process known as *multitasking*). OS/2 has been available for several years, and its current version is 2.0. It has yet to catch on. Relatively few programs are available to run in OS/2, and it is more expensive to buy and use than DOS. It is possible that in 5 to 10 years this will be the operating system of choice, but at this time it is slower, far more costly, and complicated to use.

XENIX and UNIX
UNIX and the spinoff system, XENIX, are multiuser operating systems that require special program versions that are more costly than DOS-based programs. They offer no real advantages for small businesses. The support of these systems is more costly, because fewer consultants work with them and those who do can charge more. These systems have a real place in medium to large businesses where they can be cost effective, but not for those of you who are just getting started.

Commodore/Amiga/Atari
These systems are not popular enough in small business to consider purchasing. Because fewer units are sold, fewer vendors write software for them and fewer manufacturers develop the *peripherals* (other hard-

ware, such as printers) for them. These have a following in specialized areas of graphic applications, such as movies/video special effects.

Application Software

Application software is any program that allows the computer to do specific tasks. Although computers are being used to accomplish an amazing variety of tasks, six fundamental computer functions exist for business users:

- To enhance the user interface to the operating system
- To write
- To calculate
- To store and retrieve data
- To illustrate
- To communicate with other computers

Software that enables you to perform these functions certainly isn't the only kind of programs you can buy for your computers, but these functions are what business owners do most often. Following are specific programs that accomplish these business functions.

Microsoft Windows: Enhancing the User Interface

This is a graphical user interface (GUI) system that makes the DOS system more user friendly. It was created so command-line computers like the IBM PC could provide a user-friendly "front" like that of the Apple Macintosh. GUIs overlay the operating system and make it easier for the user to implement commands to the computer. Rather than using the DOS command line, you select pictures ("icons") to start programs, copy files, and perform other system tasks. GUIs are easier to learn and use and provide other attractive features.

Because of this, GUIs are gaining great popularity in the business applications world. Many existing applications could not run well "under Windows," however, so in the early 1990s applications developers scrambled to market versions of popular word processing, spreadsheet, and database management programs specifically designed for the Windows environment.

Word Processing and Desktop Publishing:
Automating Writing and Layout

Word processing programs are used to write, edit, save, and print documents (very versatile typewriters). You would use word processing software to type a letter or any other type of correspondence. Some word processing software allows you to take letters that you type and print them as "form" letters, automatically dubbing in a list of names. This feature is called a "mail merge."

Word processing programs automatically format text as you are typing the document. Margins, page sizes, and other specifics are set up at the beginning, but they may be changed at any time. Once you have printed and proofed the document, you can go back and add, delete, or move any text without retyping the entire document. The program will automatically reformat text for you. Most word processing programs also include a spell-checking feature and even a thesaurus to help you revise your word choices as you create a document.

The most popular word processor for DOS-based systems is WordPerfect version 5.1. An early leader in systems that use the Windows GUI is Word for Windows version 2.0.

You can purchase separate *grammar- and spell-checking programs* to reveal typos and grammatical errors in your documents created with word processing programs. Grammar-checking programs such as Grammatik version 5.0 should be used as guides—not all recommended corrections should be used as the program advises because you can wind up with unnecessarily formal and stilted text. Your own judgment should take precedence.

Desktop publishing programs are the most complex word processors used to design and lay out almost any type of publication (newsletters, flyers, advertisements—even whole books). Desktop publishing programs such as PageMaker create "camera-ready" printouts, meaning that you don't pay the printshop that reproduces the printouts to do expensive layout work. Desktop publishing programs may be relatively simple or extremely complex.

When you are using word processing functions in a program, you are working with text, and your primary objective is to create a well-written, letter-perfect, and pleasingly printed document—a letter, a memo, a report, or some other piece of written work destined to be printed on paper. You use four procedures to achieve this objective: entering text, formatting text, editing text, and printing text.

1. *Entering text:* You can think of a word processor program as a typewriter-television, because you type the text at a keyboard (typewriter), and the text appears on-screen (television). The big advantage of this approach is that you can get the wording just right before printing.

2. *Formatting text:* To format text is to use commands that instruct the printer to print text in an aesthetically pleasing way on the page. You can format documents as you type them or go back through

once text is entered to create the formats. You can attach emphasis to the text (boldface, italic, or underlining), reset margins, indent text, change line spacings, and add page numbers. In a what-you-see-is-what-you-get or WYSIWYG (pronounced "wizeewig") program, you see the results of your formatting choices on-screen. Less desirable is the use of embedded commands—formatting commands you place in the midst of the text, the results of which don't show up until you print the document.

3. *Editing text:* Every word processing program provides tools for inserting text within text you have already typed. With a feature called *automatic reformatting,* the text is adjusted to make room for the text you insert. Automatic reformatting also removes the gaps left by deletions. When deleting text, you can make use of commands that delete a character, a word, a line, a paragraph, or even a whole section of text at a time. A major benefit of word processing for writers is the ability to move blocks of text from one place to another; you can use this feature to improve the organization of your written work.

4. *Printing text:* After you create, format, and edit the text, you need to print the document. At this point, the operation is all but automatic. The program prints the document within the margins you choose and with or without page numbers.

These word processing operations are rudimentary. A full-featured word processing program is likely to include many more features that enhance these operations: spell-checking; an on-line electronic thesaurus; automatic hyphenation; on-screen outlining; the capability to sort lists; and the capability to add footnotes, headers, and footers.

Electronic Spreadsheets

An electronic spreadsheet or worksheet is a computerized version of an accountant's ledger sheet. When you use spreadsheet functions in a program, you work with numbers (as well as with explanatory text, called *labels*). Spreadsheet software performs mathematical calculations. It has rows and columns that intersect to form a grid of *cells.* Cells may contain text, numbers, or equations that can calculate a relationship of the numbers in the cells. The beauty of computerizing the spreadsheet is that when you change one cell, it can cause all other related cells (like one for the column totals) to change, too. For example, you might have a list of expenses in a column and have the spreadsheet total the column. Then you discover you forgot one expense item. When you add the missing figure, the total at the bottom changes automatically. Spreadsheet software can compute sales forecasts, track budgets, figure payroll tax deductions, itemize and total travel expenses, or any other task that requires many calculations.

Each cell of the spreadsheet has a distinctive cell address to express its precise location on the worksheet. Cell B4, for example, lies at the intersection of column B and row 4.

In each cell, you can place a value (number), a label (text), or a formula. *Formulas* are what make spreadsheets so powerful. A formula can contain *constants* (such as 2 + 2), but creating formulas using cell addresses (such as A2 + A3) is better, because you can refer to the values in other cells by using cell addresses in a formula. You can create a worksheet in which all the values in the whole worksheet are interlinked to automatically update all the totals when any values change.

The following is an overview of the main operations you perform with spreadsheet software:

- *Entering data and labels:* You type the numbers and headings in cells. You can edit the data you typed, and you can change the alignment (flush left, centered, or flush right) within the cell. More recent programs, such as Microsoft Excel for Windows and Lotus 1-2-3 Releases 2.3 and 3.1, enable you to use distinctive typefaces and type sizes (fonts).

- *Entering formulas:* You can create simple addition formulas and complex financial calculations. Formulas can reference cells so that when you change the cell, the formula is recalculated.

- *Copying formulas:* After you enter a column or row of formulas, you can copy them to adjacent columns or rows in such a way that the formulas are adjusted automatically to suit their new location. If you write a formula that sums all the figures in column C and then copy the formula to column D, for example, the copied formula sums column D. This feature frequently saves time by eliminating the need to retype complex formulas.

- *Choosing formats:* You can define how you want the numbers displayed; you can choose among displays for currency, percentage, integers only, fixed number of decimal places, and other options.

- *Performing what-if analyses:* The point of creating a worksheet isn't just to track existing numbers. When you want to project future income and expenses, you can type in new values, experiment with different (what-if) scenarios, and the spreadsheet recalculates totals almost instantly. With such what-if analysis, you can explore the impact made by changing key variables to see how profit results change.

- *Using a worksheet as a template:* You also can set up a spreadsheet to serve as a generic worksheet, called a *template,* for performing a calculation you must do repeatedly, such as estimating costs. Every time you have some new data to work with, you just read the generic worksheet from the disk file in which you have stored it, type in the new key variables, and in seconds, you see the answer on the bottom line. Creating templates is also useful when you begin fresh spreadsheets for expense items at the beginning of each business year.

- *Graphing:* Included here, rather than under the later discussion of graphics, are business graphs (such as bar graphs, column graphs, line graphs, and pie graphs) because these graphs are generated from tables of numerical data. Many spreadsheet programs—including 1-2-3, Microsoft Excel, and Quattro Pro—can generate these graphs almost automatically after you define the areas of the spreadsheet that contain the necessary data.

- *Printing:* You can print the entire worksheet or just one area. You can "hide" certain columns so they don't print with the rest of the spreadsheet.

Database Management

Database software creates an electronic filing cabinet where information is stored in a specific order and retrieved. A *database* is a meaningful grouping of data stored in a type of *record* that uses a format you design. This information may be sorted in many ways and retrieved later. For a simple example, think of your phone book. Addresses, phone numbers, and possibly birthdays are listed below the names of your friends, relatives, and associates. If this information were stored in a database, at the beginning of each month you could print a list of all people having a birthday that month. Or you could print a list of all the names and telephone numbers only. In more complex databases, you enter data in on-screen forms that can be linked together to reuse the data in different ways. Thus, you can type shipping information in one database form and share the information with another database used to generate invoices.

Leading software packages for database management are the dBASE and Foxpro product lines as well as Paradox version 4.0.

Database management provides computer assistance for the kinds of tasks librarians perform in maintaining a card catalog, such as creating the card format, alphabetizing the cards, deleting old cards, cross-referencing topics, and finding a card on a specific subject. When you use a program's database management functions, your primary objective is to store and retrieve information from a database. Because the database rearranges related information, you can not only easily retrieve information but you can compare it in different ways, draw conclusions, and make decisions.

The basic unit of information in a database is the *record,* which is a complete unit of information about something, such as a book in the library or an employee. In each record, you see *fields,* or areas in which a particular kind of information is stored.

The following is an overview of the basic operations you perform in database management:

1. *Creating the database:* To create the database, you begin by defining the number of the data fields (items) you want to use, with specifications for their length and the type of data you want to place in them (alphabetical, numeric, or alphanumeric).

2. *Entering data:* To help you enter the data, the program displays a blank data form that includes the headings and explanatory text you have chosen as well as the data fields in which you type the required data.

3. *Browsing through the data:* With many programs, you can view the data in two ways. In Record or Edit mode, you see each individual record on-screen, one at a time, as if you were looking at a five-by-eight card. In List mode, you see several records' worth of information expressed as a columnar table. Most programs enable you to enter data and edit data in all of these modes.

4. *Retrieving data:* After you enter the data, you can retrieve it in two ways. You can search for an individual record that contains information you want to see, or you can perform a query. When you query the database, you specify the criteria by which you want to group two or more data records. You can tell the program, for example, "Show me all the customers whose bills are more than 30 days overdue."

5. *Editing and updating data:* You can modify the information in any data record. Particularly useful, however, is a form of data modification called an *update* that uses a query. When you perform an update operation, the program finds all the records that meet the criteria you specify, and then the program makes the changes you request in just those records. You can tell the program to find all the records that contain the text Ace Products, for example, in the data field called MANUFACTURER and to multiply the price in the PRICE field by 1.25.

6. *Deleting data:* For data deletion, you remove the records you no longer need. Because data deletion can have adverse consequences if done accidentally, most database programs make it difficult to accidentally delete records.

7. *Printing data:* When you print a database, you produce a report that compares fields across multiple records. Ideally, a report re-

duces the welter of information in the database to just the information you need for your specific purpose. For archival purposes, it's wise to periodically print all the contents of every record as a single printout.

Graphics

The graphics function of an application program is concerned with the creation, alteration, display, and printing of graphic images of some sort, such as a hand-drawn picture, a technical illustration, a map, or a business graph. The image you create can be printed by itself or included in a document, worksheet, or even (with some programs) a database.

You can use two types of graphics: bit-mapped and object-oriented. Bit-mapped graphics are made up of small squares. Enlarging or reducing this type of graphic is difficult. It is also difficult to edit the drawing, because each addition you make merely adds more squares to the pattern. Removing a line or a background pattern may be impossible. Object-oriented graphics are defined by a mathematical equation. You can easily change the size and shape of an object-oriented graphic. Furthermore, each object you create, such as a line or a circle, can be independently selected, sized, moved, or deleted, so it is easy to edit the drawing.

The following is an overview of the basic operation you perform when you use a program's graphics functions:

1. *Choosing a tool:* Graphics programs present a toolbox in which you can choose from a variety of tools that enter distinctive graphic elements. For a bit-mapped program, you are likely to find a pencil, a brush, and an eraser; a spray can (which sprays a pattern or color); a line tool; a simple word processor for entering text; and tools for entering rectangles, circles, arcs, and polygons. In object-oriented programs, you find fewer tools: a simple word processor, as well as tools for entering lines, rectangles, arcs, ovals, and circles.

2. *Painting or drawing:* With a bit-mapped graphics program, you create the illustration by choosing from the wide variety of painting tools; you build up the tapestry of dots on-screen so that it achieves your goal. Fixing big mistakes can be difficult, however, because you cannot manipulate separate parts of the drawing independently. With an object-oriented program, you draw the illustration using the tools that enter geometric shapes. You can easily edit the drawing so that it meets your objectives just by selecting an object and moving or deleting that object.

3. *Printing or importing:* When you finish the graphic presentation, you can print or import it (transfer it) into a word processing document.

Communications

A program's communications function enables you to exchange information with other computers. The communications function of an application program makes network or telecommunications resources available to you; it does so by transforming your computer into an electronic version of a walkie-talkie: you send messages to other computers, and you receive a response. The closest comparison that can be made between the world of paper and the world of electronic communications is between mail (in electronic mail, you send and receive memos and letters) and database management (when you access a central database or an information service, you send queries and receive views).

Telecommunications uses your computer's serial port (connection) and a modem to send and receive messages over telephone wires. A *serial port* enables your computer to exchange data with other computing devices, including printers and optical scanners (which "read" or digitize drawings and photographs). A *modem* modifies the signals coming from the serial port so that they can be transmitted via the phone line, and it also demodifies the signals coming from the phone line so that the serial port can accept them. Telecommunications is slow; it is used mainly for applications such as exchanging data files and accessing on-line information services. But, equipped with a modem, the entire world's telephone system is open to your computer, as long as another properly equipped and expectant computer is prepared for the exchange at the other end of the line.

Leading stand-alone communications packages for IBM compatibles are Crosstalk (available for either DOS or Windows) and Procomm Plus version 2.0.

Communications software enables you to link with on-line data banks; unlimited amounts of services, including shopping-at-home, airline reservations, the ability to do advanced research, and more. A wave of the future, for sure. Prodigy and CompuServe are examples.

Tip:

The American Small Business Association (P.O. Box 612663, Dallas, TX 75261, telephone 1-800-880-2722) has developed a computer bulletin board to help solve a widespread problem: the isolation that owners of tiny businesses feel who have little opportunity to network or attend educational seminars. The organization, which is based in Grapevine, Texas, represents firms with fewer than 10 employees. It offers a private electronic network to its 155,000 members. The service, offered in connection with CompuServe in Columbus, Ohio, includes a networking forum, a marketplace, databases of government contacts, information on doing business with the U.S. Navy, on-line help from business experts, legislative updates, and the like.

The association doesn't know how many of its members own computers, let alone modems. But marketing surveys generally indicate that as many as 80 percent of small companies use computers.

Requiring more equipment is a *local area network (LAN)* that directly wires from a few to a few hundred personal computers into a network capable of high-speed data exchange. To create a LAN, each linked computer (or workstation) must be equipped with the necessary network interface circuitry and network software and must be directly wired to the other computers. Most LANs also require that a single computer, equipped with a huge hard disk, be set aside as a file server, a machine that contains the computer resources that all the workstations share. Communications resources in LANs include electronic mail, the creation of common databases for storing and retrieving information vital to an organization's functioning, and computer conferencing.

LANs are communication networks that operate in a specified area, such as a business or a department within a business. In a typical LAN arrangement, all the computers within the network can communicate with each other. Also, peripheral technologies such as image scanning, storage, transmission, editing, and high-quality laser printing can be shared among the computers on the network. Networking is a simple concept, but behind it is a complex, sophisticated technology that requires a dealer who is well trained.

Several industry sources identify LANs as the fastest-growing segment of the PC industry. And increasingly, LANs are being sold by traditional office-machine dealers.

All in all, the impact of these technological advances on today's offices is bigger than Texas. The office isn't just changing its appearance; its efficiency and productivity are changing as well.

The following is an overview of the basic operations you perform when you use a program's communications function:

1. *Choosing communications settings:* No single, set standard is followed for telecommunications, so you frequently must choose a pattern of communications settings (called a *protocol*) before you can use a communications system effectively.

2. *Logging on:* You choose the commands that activate the modem (or give you access to the network).

3. *Choosing an action:* In most systems, you can pursue more than one course of action after you log on. If you're using a local area network, chances are the prompt looks like a DOS prompt (such as F>), and you can treat the network as if it were a gigantic hard disk (you can run programs, copy files, and so on). If the system has E-mail (electronic mail), you choose the command that gives you access to the E-mail software, and then you can read your current messages, reply to them, delete them, and write and send new messages.

4. *Logging off:* You choose the command that disconnects you from the communications link. From this point, you can log on to another network or quit the communications function.

Accounting

Accounting software, which is really a subset of database management, performs accounting functions such as accounts payable, general ledger, and payroll. This, of course, is used by bookkeepers, accountants, and others who work with debits and credits. Accounting software is very similar to keeping a set of written books. Getting an accounting system running without having a written set of books is almost impossible. If you intend to use accounting software, be sure that you arrange to get competent professional advice when you set the software up.

Point-of-sale or *business management* software (a subset of accounting) enables you to use a computer as a cash register and to collect customer, sales, and inventory information. The software uses this information to produce reports that can help you run your business. Purchase orders, reorder reports, sales tax reports, profit margin reports, and activity reports are just some of the information that this software can provide. All of this data is accumulated as you ring up each sale and can be produced at the touch of a button and transmitted to the main accounting system.

Bar code printing software prints merchandise price tickets that include bar codes, stock numbers, descriptions, and prices. This is usually linked with point-of-sale and accounting software.

On-line credit card processing (which combines accounting and communications) along with a modem, processes credit card authorizations automatically. It also credits the funds directly to your account.

Portfolio management software (again, database management related) can help you manage all of the assets you own. Not intended for use only by the members of the Forbes 400, you can benefit from an independent assessment of the level of risk and return in your asset base.

Stock market analysis software (database and communications related) provides trading recommendations and some track the progress of the stocks you own.

Income tax preparation software can help you generate your tax return, if you are the daring type that prepares your own tax returns. Information is calculated within the program and prints right on the government forms.

Check writing software automatically prints checks and keeps your checkbook register.

Parcel shipping programs automatically print shipping labels and complete the required forms for shipping companies such as UPS.

Time Management
Scheduling/appointment programs can electronically schedule employee hours and client appointments. Schedules can be printed in various formats including daily, weekly, and monthly. Also included here are the more complex project management programs.

Utility Software

Utilities perform basic, essential functions; no one should be without this kind of product. Programs such as PCTools and Norton Utilities can help speed up your hard disk, can recover files that have been erased (either intentionally or by accident), and much more. These programs can also give you a good introduction to how the basic functions of DOS work.

Backup Programs
Backup programs speed up the process of hard disk backups. The program usually compresses the data stored on the hard disk so fewer floppy disks are used for the backup. A "backup" is a duplicate copy of the data that you have worked so long and so hard to put in. It has been said that the average hard disk contains $50,000 worth of data. Keeping a copy of your data at home suddenly seems like a good idea, doesn't it? Why would a hard disk go bad? Wear and tear, fire, floods, smoke damage from a fire in the restaurant two doors down, and so on.

Miscellaneous, Fun Products

So far you've read about the essential operating system, business applications, and utilities that you'll purchase to streamline your business methods. The categories of programs listed in this section, on the other hand, are computerized training (either about software or a wide range of other topics, from geography to typing tutorials) and after-hours diversions for you, your colleagues, or your children.

Educational Software

This is software that can stimulate your intellect while helping you, your employees, or your children learn important skills, such as drills for college tests like the SAT or GRE exams, reading, writing, and math.

Educational software can range from primitive-looking and somewhat boring products developed in the early days of personal computers, whose sole function was to do on-line testing or drill-and-practice exercises, to sophisticated teaching tools with stunning graphics, lively soundtracks, and peppy prose. Buyer beware.

Games

Games make up one of the most popular areas of personal computing software. Game software brings a new dimension to personal amusement. Many popular games are available at your local software store or, more cheaply (usually), from mail-order catalogs such as CompuAdd, for under $20.

"Recreational" software runs the gamut from preschoolers' graphics/game products like Kid Pix to the truly educational-as-well-as-fun Where in the World Is Carmen San Diego, to the escapist Global Conquest.

Purchasing Versus "Borrowing" Software

This is the type of discussion that is not ordinarily found in a book about computerization. It is, however, an extremely important subject and one you should take seriously.

When you open a software package you will usually find a manual or two, several floppy diskettes, a registration card, and other assorted papers. When software sells for anywhere from $19.95 to more than $2,000, some readers might ask, "What am I paying for?" Others may feel that because of the exorbitant price, it's okay to share software with a friend. There are many good reasons why this is not okay.

- *It's illegal.* It is illegal to copy software unless you have permission from the developer or distribution company. Take a look at the software license agreement. It should state the company's policy. As a rule, you may not give a copy to a friend.
- *It's immoral.* When you look at the end product, software may not seem like much. What you don't see is what goes into the product before you purchase it. Here is a sample:

o Research and development—Before a programmer develops a program, he or she must have an idea and then understand the business. For example, if you owned a software company that was about to develop a general ledger program, you would need to learn exactly what goes on in each column of the ledger. You would also need to know about different types of accounts and how they affect the ledger. If you were really smart, you would also try to find out what existing users of general ledger programs liked and disliked about the current competing programs. Of course, you would also have to hire an expert programmer. The research and development process could take months or years. The program is then updated on a regular basis to keep it current.

o Testing—Once the program is written, it must be tested. Software is put through its paces to help ensure that it works properly under all circumstances.

o Technical support—Once users purchase a program, they expect to have help available should they have a problem. Most software companies employ a staff of technical support personnel to assist users during the installation and use of the program.

o Other—Obviously software companies have all types of expenses (some that are the same as yours). Packaging and duplicating the software, shipping, advertising, rent, heat, light, and payroll are just a few.

• *It's dangerous.* When you copy software from someone else, you run the risk of subjecting your system to a computer virus. A *virus* is a program that can destroy some or all of the data on your hard disk. If you don't already know, you will soon find out how catastrophic the loss of data and the time lost in computer operations could be to your business.

• *It could be devastating.* Suppose you "borrow" a spreadsheet program from a friend. You have just spent three or four hours setting up a spreadsheet to track projected sales and expenses compared to actual profit and loss statements. All of the sudden, the screen blinks and you have no spreadsheet. Any number of things could have happened, but suppose (because you don't have a manual) you pressed a key that erased all of your data. What now?

When you own a legal copy of software you have a manual and you usually have access to the company's technical support personnel. The company will also notify you when it releases enhancements to the products or fixes "bugs" that may have slipped through during the first release. If you intend to base your entire business on a software product, paying for it is certainly worth the investment.

The bottom line is that the software developer is entitled to his or her profits, just like you are. Also, just like any other type of theft, the losses incurred by the software publisher will be passed on to the users.

The Decision Process

Let's assume you are convinced it's time to computerize. Where do you go from here? The process, from the day you decide to computerize to the day you begin using it to improve productivity will take some time. (As mentioned earlier, you should allow at least six months.) It is important to remember this and try to keep from rushing into something you're not sure of . . . you could be making an expensive mistake.

To computerize your small business successfully, forget about hardware for the moment. Concentrate on choosing the right application software for the critical application areas in your business—the areas that must operate efficiently and productively if you hope to turn a profit and keep your customers.

Remember:

- Choose application software first and then worry about the hardware for the software you have chosen.
- Application programs are designed to run in specific system environments, such as the Macintosh System 7, DOS, and Microsoft Windows. Although some programs are available in versions for two or more system environments, most of the programs useful for your business probably will run under DOS or Windows.
- Although people do many things with computers, there are six fundamental applications: to provide a user-friendly interface, to write, to calculate, to store and retrieve data, to illustrate, and to communicate with other computers.
- Four kinds of application programs are available: single-purpose application programs, integrated programs, special-purpose programs, and vertical-market application programs.
- Come up with a plan to pinpoint the areas in which you want to use a computer. Find the appropriate software to accomplish the tasks you want by developing a list of the features and capabilities that the software must have to suit your business's needs.
- Select a dealer that will provide the necessary help and the support you need to implement your plan.

Steps to Follow

The following is a list of steps to follow during the decision-making process.

Step 1. Learn as Much as You Can

There are many ways to learn about computers. Many local schools and organizations offer free or inexpensive courses to get you started. Computer dealers and hardware manufacturers also host informative seminars. Computer magazines or libraries are also excellent starting points. Your industry's trade publications and associations may be able to direct you to reputable vendors that specialize in computerizing your type of business. Perhaps you are fortunate enough to know a computer buff who can give you a few pointers. There are many places to find information and the more you know, the better off you will be.

One of the best possible sources for information can be other business owners in your industry. If you own a flower shop, and you are looking for software for the florist trade, you could start by visiting all of the other florists in town. You probably know them already. You may have met them at conventions or industry seminars. If you are uncomfortable about visiting a nearby competitor, try going to the next town in your county. Most business owners are only too glad to talk about their computer systems. Ask them about their experiences, both good and bad, and see if you can learn from their mistakes. Ask them what they would do differently next time. Perhaps they have a consultant they can recommend.

Step 2. Determine What You Want from the System

The next step is to analyze your business and determine what you want the system to do for you. How are functions currently performed? Who performs them? Make a list of all the things you would like the computer to handle, bring it to the dealer, and make sure he or she hears you when you explain what you really want. Jot down notes as new thoughts occur to you. This list will grow as you do more research. Your analysis can serve as a hedge against early obsolescence of the equipment as your business grows, or against getting sidetracked in the maze of conflicting features you will inevitably encounter as you scout the market.

Although it is tempting to believe that the best program is the one with the most features, you can probably reduce your computer investment considerably by realizing that features you don't need or probably will never use are luxuries you can ill afford. Too many features can be just as undesirable as too few if they make the program too cumbersome to use and difficult to learn—or too expensive.

Be realistic. With different types of software a computer can do many different things. However, when you are purchasing a system for your business, that must be your top priority. Business owners have purchased systems for their business yet were unhappy because their children couldn't print four-color Christmas cards like their friends. Just about anything you want to do can be accomplished with the proper software and peripherals. For now, concentrate on one thing at a time.

Step 3. Select Software: The Key to Success

Some business owners make the decision to computerize and rush out to purchase a computer, only to find out it doesn't make their problems go away. What these business owners failed to realize is that a computer is only as good as the software that runs it. Until you have found a program that seems to suit your business needs, don't worry about the hardware.

Selecting the right software is a process that will take some time if you are serious about what you are doing.

There are several things you should consider before you make a software purchase. First, see the program in action. Companies and consultants that truly believe in the value of their product should have no problem sending or lending you a demo. Often this version has all the features of the complete program but has restrictions on the amount of data that can be entered or on how long the program can run without shutting down. This is an offer that is worth accepting, even if you have to pay for it. Put the program through its paces. Ask about anything you don't understand. Do the features on your list match up to the ones included in the program?

Some food for thought:

- Make sure applications can be accessed quickly and easily and that you don't need to move through an endless series of screens to get to the application you need.
- How easy is it to find an item?
- Can you add another peripheral device, such as a printer, bar code reader, or scanner?
- Is any one of these added peripheral devices required for the system to be used properly?
- Can you enter data quickly?
- If you are currently using custom printed forms, must you change?
- Does the output provide you with all of the information needed?
- Does the output meet any required state and local regulations? If not, can it be modified?

It is reasonable to expect that accounting, tax, and other government-form-dependent software sold in your state should meet state requirements. You should not be charged extra when you buy the software. It your state changes its laws later on, it is reasonable for the software company to charge a fee to modify the software. Most software companies will take care of updating a program to meet state regulations during the course of their normal "version update."

Recommendation:

Updates by the software company usually occur at least once per year, and you can expect to be charged between 15 percent and 25 percent of the original cost of the software for the update. You should always buy the update. Many software companies will not support older versions.

Following are some other considerations during your examination phase:

- Is the software flexible?
- Can it be customized to your special ways of doing business?
- How easy is it to correct mistakes, issue refunds, and so on?
- How easy is it to call up a management report?
- Does it provide the type of information you need to run your business?
- Will it print mailing labels?
- How easily can you learn the product?
- Is it password protected?
- Do you decide who has access and which features must be protected?

Don't forget, one of the reasons for computerizing is to provide better services for your customers.

The second major consideration before you purchase is to learn whether the software is upgradable. It pays to look ahead to the not-too-distant future (software is upgraded frequently!) when new versions of your applications are released and to learn how much it will cost to "buy up."

Ask these questions of the software retailer or catalog vendor:

- If you decide to start up with only one computer, can you add additional computers if your business grows? Some software versions will only run on one computer at a time, so if you decide to add more computers (set up a multiuser network) you may have to purchase different software. Be sure the program you purchase is upgradable to a multiuser version or to a future release and find out how much the upgrade will cost.

- Is the software expandable? Many programs can *import* (read in) data accumulated in another program. Eventually you may find you would like to use the information that is being tracked by one program for use with another. For example, if you are using the computer for point-of-sale and inventory control, you may want to add a general ledger program. If the programs can be linked, the information gathered with the point-of-sale program can be used for the general ledger and so on. Check whether the software you purchase will link to other programs and whether the program is expandable.
- Can you (or a computer programmer) access the data from the program in case you would like to obtain additional information?

Don't buy a closed system! Some software programs store the data in a way that prevents you from looking at it except through the program itself. There is an endless amount of information in that computer and eventually you may want to be able to obtain information that the reports included with the program do not provide. Find out whether a local programmer can use the data from the program to create different reports. You can do this yourself if you want to try your hand at it.

Remember:

You probably will not find software that will do everything you want it to. In addition, as you gain more experience you will continually think of information that you would like to retrieve. If the software is upgradable, expandable, flexible, and if you can store more data, the system can grow along with your business.

Here's the third major consideration: Do you really want "accounting" software? Often, business owners say they want to computerize their accounting system. That statement makes software dealers happy, because accounting software can be very costly. To a typical computer dealer, accounting means keeping a ledger. Research indicates that over 90 percent of small businesses don't keep their own ledgers (accountants do it for them). Unfortunately, many business owners have purchased a full-blown accounting system only to find out that what they really wanted was to be able to control their inventory and find out their daily sales and profits—tasks that a standard spreadsheet package could handle easily. They were not doing "double-entry" accounting before they installed the computer and were certainly not prepared to do it after.

How many people or businesses are currently using the software you're thinking of purchasing? Talk to current users of the program you're considering. Most reputable software developers will be happy to provide references. Find out what they are and aren't happy with regarding their system. What do they know now that they didn't know when they bought the package? How do they rate the software developer on technical support? The advice you can get from those brave pioneers who blazed the trail before you is invaluable. Pick their brains. Again, users' groups can be helpful for this purpose.

Use the form in Figure 2-1 to help organize your thoughts regarding your computerization process.

Step 4. Selecting a Dealer

At this point you have gathered information and may have a good idea of what you would like a computer to do for you. The next step is to determine who to purchase it from. There are several different options: mail order, computer stores, independent resellers, or "your brother-in-law" who works for a major computer manufacturer.

Choosing the right dealer is as important a decision as selecting the hardware and software. You are making a rather large investment in both time and money. You need to feel confident that you are purchasing your system from a vendor that will give you the support and service you need. As a business owner you probably have very little spare time, but it is extremely important for you to take the time to carefully evaluate a vendor.

Ask the salesperson as many questions as you desire and keep asking until you get the answers you need. Don't feel intimidated by fast talking salespeople or computer wizards. If the sale is important to them, they will give you the attention you deserve.

Recommendation:

Purchase all hardware, software, peripherals, and service from the same vendor. This centralizes responsibility and circumvents the "pass-the-buck" excuses and explanations you may otherwise receive down the road. A stereo system may contain a CD, receiver, speakers, and tape player all from the same manufacturer. If the system doesn't work, it's up to the manufacturer to figure out the problem. Not so with computers! The hardware may include components from many different manufacturers, and the software will surely be written by yet another company. When your system isn't working properly, you want to deal with one company, not six. That company will be your vendor/dealer in computer system purchases.

ABOUT YOUR BUSINESS

Type of business: _____   Annual sales: $_____

Number of employees: _____

Number of regular customers: _____

Number of items in inventory: _____

Accounts receivable? Yes _____   No _____

Number of statements prepared monthly: _____

Number of letters prepared monthly: _____

Number of memos generated monthly: _____

Perceived Software Needs
(Check all areas you're considering for computerization and expand the list as necessary)

Sales Reports:

Daily sales reports _____	Weekly sales reports _____
Monthly sales reports _____	Sales tax reports _____
Sales by employee reports _____	Service breakdown reports _____
Product sales reports _____	Sales by department reports _____
Sales by vendor reports _____	Rental figures _____

Return on investment reports _____

Inventory Control:

Reorder reports _____	Store ordering information _____
Purchase orders _____	Backorders reports _____

Transactions/Invoices:

Store work orders _____	Store quotation _____
Variable sales tax %s _____	Multiple price levels _____
Multiple rental fees _____	Layaway sales _____
Split tender _____	House charge account _____
Packing list _____	Product discounts _____
Limited time promotions _____	Return merchandise _____

FIGURE 2-1 Precomputerization checklist for small-business owners

Accounting:

Invoice generation _____   Profit margin calculation _____

Sales tax calculation _____   Accounts receivable _____

Accounts payable _____   Check writing _____

Payroll _____   General ledger (double-entry bookkeeping) _____

Customer Information:

Customer history _____   Prior invoices _____

General:

Password protection _____   Track vendors _____

Mailing labels _____   Client letters _____   Post cards _____

Future Computer Uses
(Check all you're considering for computerization)

Invoicing _____   Word processing _____

Desktop publishing _____   Spreadsheet calculations _____

Bar code printing _____   Communications _____

Appointment scheduling _____   Check writing _____

Accounts payable _____   General ledger _____

Parcel shipping _____

Other _____

FIGURE 2-1 *Continued*

Qualities to look for in a dealer:

- How much initial training is the dealer willing to provide for you and your employees? Unless you or your staff have personal computer experience, arrange for the dealer to train everyone who will be using the system. It is difficult for an owner or manager alone to be trained and then try to find the time to train all of the employees. A lot of changes occur when the system is installed. Training should be done in at least two sessions. The first session should cover the initial procedures for entering information/data and running reports/printouts. The second session will review the first session material and then cover program maintenance, such as backing up, system updates, and so on. Also find out how much additional training will cost if you need it.

- Does the dealer offer extended software and hardware support? As discussed earlier, extended support for hardware and software is essential. As you use the system more, you will have additional questions. Support may be offered from the dealer or directly from the hardware manufacturer and software developer. Find out who is responsible, how much the contracts will cost, and how quickly your questions will get answered.

- If you purchase a system from a small firm, will the firm be there tomorrow? If not, are there other major service companies in your area that will be willing to support and service the system? Line up at least one other local dealer that can support the type of system you purchase. Ask for references from the dealer and be sure to follow up on them. Shop around for value, not just price. Mail-order companies may have the best prices but usually provide nothing in the way of the service and training you will eventually need. It is not realistic to expect your local dealer to match these prices. Also, the rate of attrition among resellers is dangerously high. Thus, a dealer or developer who doesn't charge a reasonable amount for services, training, or technical support may not be around to serve you as long as one who charges competitively. You may initially save a few hundred dollars but spend thousands more later to retrain employees or suffer "downtime" when the computer or software needs maintenance.

- Will the dealer put claims and promises in writing? If not, claims and promises aren't worth anything. Most sales literature promises tender, loving technical support "before, during, and after" the sale, but one company's view as to what this actually includes could be your nightmare. Get it in writing! Like any contract, this protects both parties. It gives you the security of a legally binding agreement to keep your system up and running and your staff sufficiently trained, and it gives the company or consultant an opportunity to provide additional levels of service in an economically feasible way.

What it comes down to is this: Most hardware will perform just fine, and many programs—aside from certain features and relative ease of use— can also capably handle your business needs, but if ever something isn't working right or if you have a question, you need prompt, dependable support. Not excuses. Not a runaround. Your business depends on it. Make sure you get it . . . in writing.

When you finally select the computer software and hardware you want to buy, you must decide how to pay for it. You can usually lease it through the vendor, buy it outright, or arrange your own financing. You should seek professional advice about the tax advantage that would be most beneficial to you.

Leasing is the customary way to purchase computer systems. A lease will typically run for three years on a $10,000 or smaller system and four to five years on a larger purchase. There is a *buyout* at the end of the lease. It can be a dollar, it can be 10 percent, or something called *fair market value*. As a rule, the better your lease rate, the more your buyout will be. The advantage of a lease is that it is tax deductible. Therefore a computer system purchased on a three-year lease can be written off in that time period, whereas an outright purchase must be deducted (depreciated) over five years.

It is usually best to lease, so that you match the expenditure of money to the additional income you will earn. In other words, let the computer pay for itself. Some companies will also rent you a system. When they rent, it may be a slightly higher price, but they will usually include support and maintenance. These will have to be paid on a yearly basis when buying outright or with a lease. No answer is right for everyone, and not every business will qualify for a lease.

When is it OK to purchase mail order?

Purchasing through mail order is okay when you have some experience under your belt. It is okay when you are purchasing a computer for home, when you don't have to rely on it 12 to 14 hours a day, or when it will only be used as a standby machine.

Summary:

Don't wait too long to take the leap into automation. The popularity of personal computers continues to grow. There are numerous programs available today that can effectively benefit your business—and they are easier than ever to master. For this reason, it is easy to go into "information overload" when you scout the market. Beware of making the "perfect" computer buying decision—it's not necessary and probably not possible. If you've done your homework and followed these recommendations, you'll do fine. Three to six months to reach a buying decision is usually an adequate timeframe. Don't wait too long before you discover, like thousands of other small business owners, that computerizing your business pays far more than it costs. According to a 1991 Price Waterhouse report given by David Burns ("Financial Systems: Enabling a Competitive Advantage for the '90s"), 13 percent of America's retail and service businesses will add computers for the first time this year. You deserve this competitive advantage too!

Step 5. Select the Hardware

If you think you have plenty of software to choose from, wait until you see your hardware options! There is an almost unlimited amount of hardware and manufacturers to explore. As you begin your hardware search you will hear terms such as *multiuser, single-user, hard disk size, 286, 386, 486, networks, modems, cash drawers, RAM,* and *megabytes.* It can become confusing to someone whose business is anything but computers. Don't let your head spin. Here are a few things to keep in mind when you look at hardware:

Don't concern yourself with bits, bytes, and nanoseconds. Shopping for a personal computer can be like strolling into a foreign street market with a fistful of dollars and no clue to either the local language or the quality of the merchandise.

You'll find yourself bombarded with claims and smothered by technobabble. Keep your eye on the ball. Two important factors in choosing a personal computer are how much memory is included and how much disk storage capacity it features. They can play a greater role in your satisfaction with your computer than the minor differences in processing speed that computer vendors love to play up.

A general knowledge of these terms, however, makes it easier to talk to computer people and understand specifications. During the course of this book (as you've experienced so far) you'll be slowly introduced to and familiarized with the terminology necessary for your purposes. The most technical information you need to know when you purchase hardware is how fast it will process the data and how much data it will enable you to save.

Many people spend a lot of time reading up on the latest technologies and try to become hardware experts. The truth is, many computer dealers can't keep up with the new technologies either. If you can buy a car without understanding how fuel injection works, you can also buy a computer without understanding bits, bytes, and nanoseconds. All you need to know is that the system will do what you need it to now and in the foreseeable future.

Tip:

Don't rush out to buy the very latest in hardware. Let someone else work out the "bugs."

A bargain may be very expensive. Many potential computer purchasers read the business section of the newspaper or the last page of a computer magazine and ask why they shouldn't order the XYZ computer system from Joe's Computer Warehouse. "It's only $2,000—what a deal!" Sometimes such ads offer even brand name computers at ridiculously low prices. On close examination you will very likely find that the store has purchased a stripped-down model and has inserted a cheaper hard drive or a no-name floppy drive in order to save money.

Bargains can turn out to be very expensive when the components are not compatible. Your time is too valuable to be spent chasing companies that go out of business overnight or figuring out which parts work with which. It's not necessary to purchase the most expensive brand of hardware; just be sure you purchase all of the components from the same dealer and make sure it is a reputable one. You can't get something for nothing.

Know your operating system. You will hear operating system names such as DOS, MS-DOS, PC DOS, OS/2, XENIX, and UNIX. There are also hundreds of "no-name" brand operating systems available. Some can be purchased for very little money and although some are excellent, you do not want to be a test site for the product. Don't purchase an operating system unless it has been selling for at least one year and you can easily find several dealers in your area that support it. It controls the entire computer and your system cannot function without it.

Tip:

If you're a first-time computer buyer, it is strongly suggested that you stick with either MS-DOS or PC DOS, which for your purposes are the same. (One is distributed by Microsoft and the other is distributed by IBM, but they are almost identical. Both were developed by Microsoft.)

Buy a larger hard disk than you think you will need. The hard disk is the portion of the computer that permanently stores all of the programs and the data. If you begin to run out of vital storage space down the road, it can adversely affect the operation of the system. Also, the more information you are able to store, the more history you can retrieve to produce reports. If you are looking to cut corners, please don't do it here.

Be sure you can expand the system. This is as important for hardware as for software. Ensure that your system can be expanded when you would like to add more memory or peripherals. This is normally a function of the number of "add-on" slots and memory slots in the computer. Check also whether you can add add-on devices such as bar code readers, cash drawers, additional printers, and modems. (These are commonly known as *peripherals.*)

Service is key. This can't be stressed enough. Eventually your entire business will depend on the system, and you will be surprised how quickly you forget how to run without the computer. It is not uncommon for business owners who have run their business for 30 years without a computer to find now they can't be without it for 30 minutes.

Tip: _____

As you purchase a computer you should purchase a service contract. When a computer breaks down few parts are repaired, most are replaced, and some can be very costly. The price for a service contract is usually recovered if your machine breaks down one time. If your dealer doesn't offer service contracts for the hardware, find a firm that does.

_____

When you discuss the service contract, find out the following information, in advance:

- How long does the original warranty last?
- What is the price of the service contract?
- What labor and parts does it cover?
- What is the guaranteed turnaround time?
- Is the machine repaired on or off site?
- If the computer has to leave your location, can the company provide a loaner?
- What will this cost?

An on-site maintenance contract is recommended. Another good idea is to have "remote operating software" and a modem installed for use of the service organization. This allows the use of "remote diagnostics." With these items, the service organization can dial into your machine(s)—on a moment's notice, wherever the firm is located—to look at your system status, software, and data. With remote diagnostics the service technician can even operate the computer from the service site.

Why is this important? Time is money. Suppose that you have just accidentally erased a file and you don't have a backup copy. You don't know how to retrieve the file. If the service provider drives over to your business, he or she will have to charge you for the half-hour it takes each way to get to your office, plus the 10 minutes it takes to correct your error and the 15 minutes it takes to lecture you about backing up. If the service technician can just dial your system up, he or she can get you fixed up in 10 minutes. Which would you prefer? It is easy to see that this minor extra, which normally costs around $200 per year, will pay for itself in short time.

As far as the on-site service contract goes, it is a convenience for both the customer and the computer store. A small computer store may have one or two technicians to service the hardware. These technicians can travel to the location where the equipment is. It is far easier for these technicians to come to you than it is for you to interrupt your day (your business is going to be disrupted as it is, with the computer not working) to disconnect all the cables in the back of the computer, drag it down to the computer center, wait there for the technician to get it fixed—if a one-day fix is possible—and then try to hook it all back up later.

Avoid the brother-in-law syndrome. Everyone has a brother-in-law who works for IBM or AT&T who can get 40 percent off on a computer. That's great, but that is the computer you should put in your home, not your business. Why?

Because:

- Your brother-in-law will not be available whenever you want to do something with the computer, and need help.
- You create extra aggravation and work for the computer consultant, and it may cost you more in the long run. Not all peripherals work with all computers. Not all "compatible computers" work the same. AT&T computers, for example, have some very significant differences in the way they are built. The differences are not apparent to you—and probably are not apparent to your brother-in-law either— but they exist and they can make life difficult. As an example, AT&T keyboards do not have a standard keyboard connector, despite the fact that they are "IBM compatibles" . . . they will run DOS software but replacement hardware must be AT&T pluggable.

The key point is this: Keeping your business running smoothly is the *most important benefit computers provide.* Buy the right tool for the job. Trying to save $500 now may cost you $5,000 later on.

3

Looking at Hardware Requirements

When you get ready to purchase computer equipment, you will need to decide whether you want a single or multiuser system. A *single-user system* is one computer and one or more printers. A *multiuser system* is two or more computers and printers linked together through *network* hardware and software to share the same information. A basic single-user computer system will be described here. Multiuser systems will be described briefly later. *Peripherals* like printers and modems can be used by either single- or multiuser systems and are best purchased along with the computer itself. Chapter 4 covers peripherals and supplies in detail.

This chapter attempts to provide you with as much information as necessary to make your hardware selections without getting overly complicated or technical.

There are basically two types of personal computer systems available for business use, IBM (and compatibles) and Apple. Both are fine machines, each with its own strengths and weaknesses. For graphic design and desktop publishing, the Apple Macintosh is probably the best option. For everything else, IBM and compatible computers (so-called clones or simply PCs) are recommended. Why? First, there are more business applications available for PCs than for Macintoshes. Next, there are more companies that manufacture peripherals (cash drawers, electronic scanners, laser printers) for the IBM environment, especially because Apple has prevented competitors from copying its system design. Last, it is much easier to get immediate service on IBM and compatible equipment. One

headache you don't want is to send your computer back to the manufacturer for two weeks or longer to get it repaired.

Single-User Systems

A basic single-user personal computer system, shown in Figure 3-1, consists of a central processing unit (CPU), keyboard, monitor, disk drives,
printer, and possibly a mouse.

Central Processing Unit (CPU)

Generally, the CPU refers to the housing that holds the main components
of the system:

- *The motherboard*—a circuit board containing random-access memory (RAM), read-only memory (ROM), and a microprocessor. Add-
  on cards, hard disk(s), floppy disk(s), and a power supply are also
  included in the CPU housing and their circuits are connected to
  the motherboard.
- *Microprocessor*—The integrated circuit chip that tracks, controls,
  and executes the machine language instructions. Popular micro-

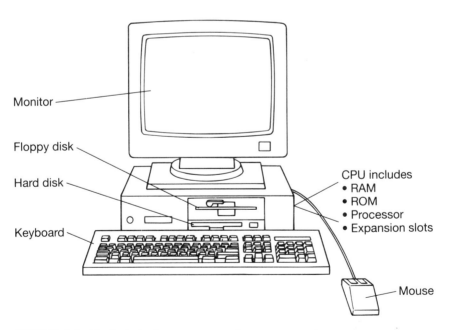

FIGURE 3-1   Typical single-user personal computer system

processors come in a 16-bit size (in the 286 microprocessor) or 32-bit size (in 386, 486, and 586 microprocessors). A 32-bit processor processes information faster than a 16-bit processor. Older units have 4-bit and 8-bit microprocessors. These are very slow in comparison to the newer 32-bit, 486 or 586 chip units.

- *Read-only memory (ROM)*—ROM is permanent memory used to store information needed by the microprocessor and is part of the computer's basic design. As the name implies, the computer reads from this memory but does not add to or in any way change its stored information. This information is used during the "boot" or power-on sequencing of the system.

Processors (short for microprocessors) also work at different speeds. A 25 MHz (for *megahertz,* or 1 million cycles per second) chip is faster than a 16 MHz chip. The minimum system that you should purchase to run a business is a 286, which is adequate if you will run one computer and use the MS-DOS operating system described earlier. The 386 chip, successor to the 286, has been around since the late 1980s and is slowly giving way in popularity to the 486 and 586 chips in computers that must work with large files, run multiple applications using a system like Microsoft Windows, or run in a network.

If price is not as important to you as speed of operation or the ability to run multiple programs simultaneously, the 486 or 586 (when available) processor is desirable and well worth the money. You probably won't recognize the difference between a 386 machine and a more recent generation of processor when you are just starting out with your system. However, after a year of running your computer system you will have more data to work with and more applications you want to use. With a 386, you'll begin to notice that reports take longer to run and spreadsheet calculations take longer to complete. The power of the faster chip will be appreciated. Additionally, you may want to add another computer someday, and the more recent chips have the power and capability needed to run in networks.

Data Storage Systems

For computer buyers, no issues are more confusing than memory and data storage. These are among the most important factors in choosing a personal computer, yet the computer industry seems determined to make distinguishing among them as opaque as possible.

Even distinguishing between memory and data storage isn't easy for novices. The two are quite different, but memory chips and hard disks hold the same kinds of information, and their capacities are measured in the same unfamiliar units, such as kilobytes and megabytes.

Then there are different types of disks. Some kinds of "floppy" disks are flexible, but others are rigid—yet they aren't "hard" disks, which are something else entirely. What's more, little floppy disks hold much more information than bigger ones.

It's no wonder that regular people get confused by all this, and computer junkies like to act superior because they understand the distinctions.

RAM: Your Computer's Temporary Storage System

Here's a brief primer on memory and disk storage.

Computers must have a way to store the information people enter so it can be called up again the next time users boot the system. Data is stored as users enter it in a set of special chips (circuits) called *memory chips,* or *RAM,* for random-access memory. As you type words that appear on your screen, they are stored only in the computer's memory chips.

RAM works well, but it has two huge limitations. First, its capacity is limited to the number of chips that can be stuffed into the computer. Second, and more important, it is strictly temporary. RAM remembers what's stored there only while the computer is turned on. Once the power is switched off, everything stored in RAM memory is wiped out.

The Challenges of Selecting Disk Drives

Because no one wants to lose all that data every time the system is turned off, computers also feature a second way to store data that offers both higher capacity and permanence: disks. *Disks* are spinning platters coated with a substance similar to that used on audio- or videotapes. They record the same kind of information held in memory chips, but they can hold more of it and they retain it when the power goes off.

Personal computers copy or move data often between these two kinds of storage. When you load a software program from a disk, you are copying the program's contents into the computer's memory chips. When you enter information (data), you should transfer that material often from temporary memory (storage) to permanent disk storage by saving your *file* (entered data) onto the disk.

Think of memory as being roughly analogous to the temporary assembly of documents on your desk for completing some project: They are usually cleaned off the desk when you're finished. Disk storage, in contrast, is more like a file cabinet in which you permanently store those documents.

The capacity of both memory chips and disks is measured in bytes. A *byte* is roughly equal to a single typed character. A *kilobyte,* abbreviated as "K bytes" or just "K," is roughly a thousand bytes, or about 150 words. A *megabyte,* abbreviated "M byte" or "M," is a million bytes—enough to store a good-sized book's text.

References to a computer's memory or RAM are describing the temporary memory in the chips. References to storage involve permanent disk storage capacity. Disk storage isn't normally called "memory."

So much for the difference between memory and disk storage. How about the differences among the various types of disks? Again, the computer industry seems to have done its best to make things confusing.

There are two basic kinds of disks:

1. *Floppy disks* are small, flexible round platters inside square outer shells. You store data on them and retrieve data from them by inserting them into *disk drives,* which are analogous to tape recorders.

2. *Hard disks* are rigid metal platters in sealed devices. The tape-recorder mechanism is built in, and the disk can't be removed from its drive. Hard disk drives are usually hidden inside the computer and hold many times more data than floppies.

But wait! There are two standard sizes of floppy disks. The larger, 5.25-inch size, that older IBM-compatible computers use, have flexible coverings and usually hold only 360 kilobytes of data. The smaller 3.5-inch size, used by Apple's Macintosh computers, most laptop and notebook computers, and many newer IBM-compatibles, have rigid plastic coverings. Although the 3.5-inch disks are physically smaller, they are engineered to pack more data on their surfaces than do 5.25-inch disks.

To cause more bewilderment, the industry sells floppy disks in two *capacities* known by helpful names. Today the low-capacity type is called "double sided/double density" or "DD" for short. The high-capacity type is called "high density" ("HD") and requires a higher-performing floppy disk drive. In the case of 5.25-inch disks, the high-density version holds 1.2 megabytes instead of the usual DD of 360K bytes. In the case of 3.5-inch disks, the lowest-capacity version holds 720K bytes (for IBM-compatible machines) or 800K bytes (for Macs), and high-density disks hold 1.44M bytes. The latter type of 3.5-inch disk usually has the letters "HD" stamped on its rigid plastic cover. Though these little disks are hard to the touch and say "HD," they aren't "hard disks."

Confused? Perhaps Table 3-1 can help.

Hard Disks

Remember, hard disks are those sealed-up, unremovable kinds of disks, distinguished chiefly by their much greater capacity. Today's popular computer configurations include hard disks that usually have more than

TABLE 3-1 PC Disk Sizes and Densities

Disk Size and Density	Amount of Data Stored
5.25-inch double density	360K bytes
5.25-inch high density	1.2M bytes
3.5-inch low density	720K bytes
3.5-inch high density	1.4M bytes

40 megabytes of capacity, and often have 100 megabytes or more. Got it? If not, reread this section, because this is computer jargon at its best and you'll certainly be hearing these references as you shop for your computer system. You'll have to understand the distinctions among disks to order the proper type for your floppy disk drives.

Tip:

Buy as much as you can afford at first, even if it means sacrificing other bells and whistles.

There's nothing more frustrating than spending thousands of dollars for a computer and then finding you can't run new programs or even load them on your hard disk because it's out of space. Some modern software will use up most of a megabyte (the equivalent of a million typed characters) of your memory just to load, and even some games take up 4M bytes on a hard disk. In general, software will run faster, and with fewer *crashes* (a term used to describe a software malfunction that halts the program and can delete your data), if you have plenty of memory and hard drive space. Cutting either to the bone invites headaches.

Moreover, extra memory and added hard disk space are relatively inexpensive parts of a PC's overall price. Once you're putting together a configuration, an added megabyte of memory can often be had for $50 or $60, and a 50 percent increase in hard disk capacity can cost less than $200.

So What Should Your System Contain?

Given today's hardware and software, 2M bytes of memory and an 80M-byte hard disk drive are a bare minimum on either a Macintosh or an IBM-compatible PC. At least 4M bytes of memory and a 100M-byte hard drive is advised, especially if you're planning to run Microsoft's Windows 3.1 software system on an IBM-compatible.

IBM-compatible buyers should also be sure to get two floppy drives (to handle both 5.25-inch and 3.5-inch disks), and a computer whose memory can be expanded using easily insertable modules called *SIMMs* and *SIPPs*. These modules can be bought by mail for under $50 per megabyte of capacity.

Even with extra memory installed, IBM-compatible owners will have to delve into product manuals to make sure their computers and software can use it properly. Incredibly, the standard operating system for these popular machines, Microsoft's MS-DOS, is still based on an old concept that limited usable memory to just 640K bytes. The latest version, 5.0, strives to overcome its roots with a special program called a *memory manager* to fool the system into using more memory. But it can be tricky to get every program to share memory smoothly.

One way around this is to rely on the Windows program and those application programs specifically designed to work with it. They automatically recognize and apportion added memory if the initializing files, CONFIG.SYS and AUTOEXEC.BAT, are set up to recognize and manage the added memory. (These files will be covered in detail in Chapter 8.)

Armed with your knowledge about memory, you'll find some of the computer ads you see a bit less confusing. Take the Zeos International ad in a current computer magazine. It offers for "only $1,195" a computer with "ultra high-speed" memory chips. Unfortunately, there aren't enough of them to do much useful work with modern software.

Indeed, this bargain Zeos comes with merely a half-megabyte of memory and a 42M-byte hard drive. The machine also lacks a 3.5-inch floppy disk drive. A call to the company reveals that Zeos charges $1,662.75 for the same unit with 4M bytes of memory, an 85M-byte hard drive, and the 3.5-inch floppy disk drive. (Adding a color monitor, mouse device, and Windows software brings it to over $2,000.)

The Zeos ad isn't unique, nor is its advertising deceptive; all the details are plainly spelled out. And the company, which has a reputation for both good quality and low prices, offers more complete configurations on other pages of the same magazine. But a novice buyer might never get past the alluring $1,195 price and could wind up with plenty of heartburn.

If you're absolutely certain you're going to run only text-based word processors or spreadsheets on an IBM-compatible, or simple word processors and spreadsheets on a Mac, you can settle for a basic box with 1M byte of memory and a 40M-byte hard drive. If not, go for as much capacity as possible. You won't regret it.

Expansion Slots

Connectors that accept add-on circuit cards and adapters in the CPU are called *expansion slots*. Some examples of these are slots to parallel port connectors (a *port* is a connection point to an external device such as a printer), serial port connectors, game ports, and monitor adapters. Although most systems include one slot each for a parallel and a serial port, you may need to add more pieces of equipment that connect through ports to slots. The number of ports you will need depends on the *peripherals* (equipment like printers and bar code readers) you add to the system. When you purchase a peripheral (such as a printer or cash drawer) the dealer should let you know if you will need additional ports installed within the system.

Keyboard

The *keyboard* is used to enter information (data and commands) into the computer.

Mouse

A *mouse* is an input device like the keyboard but is used for entering commands by a process called *clicking* and working with graphics information, such as drawing a line or circle by *dragging* the shapes to move them or change their size.

Monitor

Your *monitor* (display) is the box that houses the computer screen. Screens are available in *monochrome* (one color, such as green, white, or amber) and *color*. Color monitors are available in various degrees of resolution. *Resolution* refers to the sharpness of the picture—the higher the resolution, the clearer the image. *VGA* is the new standard, and *Super VGA* has the highest resolution.

The monitor you choose is really a matter of preference and the funds available. For many business applications, monochrome monitors are fine; however, it's easy to get used to the niceties of colors for your work.

Multiuser Systems/Multitasking Systems

What is a multiuser system?

In a *multiuser system,* two or more computers are hooked together to share data and peripherals. A server-based, multiuser system includes a central computer (known as a file server) and one or more attached computers called nodes, stations, workstations, or terminals. This type of system is also known as a *network* or *LAN (local area network)*. Figure 3-2 shows how a single LAN connects three computers.

All stations can share the same hard disk on the central computer or *file server* and may share other devices that are attached to the network, such as printers. The software is installed on the file server's hard disk and is used by each *workstation* (other computer in the network). In addition, information gathered at each workstation is saved on the file server to share with other network users, or it can be saved "locally" on the workstation's hard disk or a floppy.

A system for a retail or service business might include one or more workstations at the front counter and one in the back office. With this type of system, the counter personnel can ring up a sale while the back office is printing reports, creating spreadsheets or databases, or preparing mailing labels. The file server, which is the most critical of the machines in terms of security and dependability, can be located in the back office safely away from the hustle and bustle of the front counter.

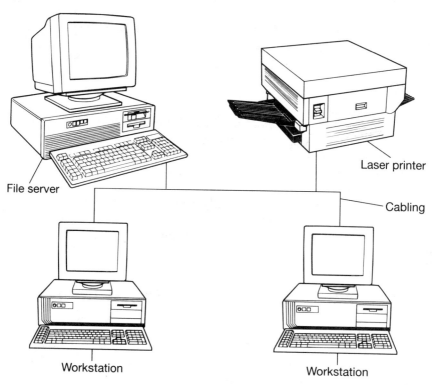

FIGURE 3-2   Typical multiuser network

A typical LAN would include:

- *File server*—The most powerful computer with the network's largest-capacity hard disk should be selected to be a file server, because programs and large amounts of data are stored on this system. The server is shared by two or more workstations. It is called a "server" because it responds to the requests (serves) of the other computers connected to it.
- *Workstations*—Other cable attached computers (also known as nodes or terminals). The stations use the file server for data storage. Stations may also have their own hard drives for data storage. On other networks, such as Lantastic, each station on the network may share its hard drive and printers with the other stations.
- *Cabling*—The wire connecting each of the workstations and the file server for communications purposes. The cabling can be simple telephone (twisted-pair) wiring or coaxial cable, depending on the system design.
- *Network operating system*—A set of operating instructions that keep track of each user and his or her priorities and access code assignment.
- *Network interface cards (NICs)*—Circuit boards installed in each of the workstations that provide a unique address and data conversion for proper communications protocol to the network.
- *Network versions of applications*—Many of the better word processing, spreadsheet, and database programs must be purchased in their network form in order to work reliably on a network. Be sure to specify the network version when you order products for a network system.

Considerations for Purchasing a Multiuser System or Network

Following are some questions about networking that are dependent on some business decisions you are making about how you do your work.

- How many users will be on this network now?

    Two, 3, or 33? It does make a difference. Some networks only support 4 or 5 users before you have to upgrade them.
- Are all the computer users in the business to be part of the network?

    There is a cost per user: Each computer is of course an expense. Plus, it must contain a network interface card (a NIC), which costs in the neighborhood of $200. Some networks will be far less expensive than others but their limitations are greater. Also, there can be substantial savings in LANs from sharing expensive equipment, such as laser printers.

- How many users could the network possibly grow to have? Over the next three years, will the network include more users?

    If the network will grow, by how many users? Try to buy a network that will cover your needs for the next three years. You will very likely recoup your entire investment many times over in those three years.

- How much can be spent on the network?

    Networks vary dramatically in price. It is very important to calculate the costs of the network before choosing the components listed earlier. For example, a network can start at $500 (which covers just the cost of the network administration software and a NIC or two) and can exceed $12,000 (for the software alone). Figure on a cost of about $250 per user initially for the NIC, operating system software, and cable connection. You can do it for less, but you may compromise reasonable performance.

Caution:

Be cautious of the lower cost networks. Some are advertised as *zero-card* or *zero-slot* LANs, meaning that the system doesn't require any network cards, just cables. Communication is done through the serial port. The performance of these LANs is not adequate for business uses.

- Who will administer and perform the necessary maintenance for the network?

    Some networks are simple and easy to maintain. The more sophisticated a network is, the more complicated it becomes to maintain. In fact, it may well be beyond the capability of anyone in your business to run the network *and* get his or her regular work done! If that happens, you will want to evaluate the hourly cost of contracting with a network consultant. Although he or she may only be needed a few hours a month, it is good to have an estimate of the costs in advance.

- What kind of programs will be on the network?

    Will you use word processing or database programs or industry-specific programs or accounting programs? Will several people be using them at the same time? What will be the costs for the multiuser or network versions of the software that you need?

Remember:

Software that enables several people to use it at the same time costs more than software that only supports one user at a time. Why? Because it is more complicated to develop "shared" software. For example, if two people are using an accounting program and both of them want to work on the same customer's file at the same time, what happens? Who gets to look at it? Can both employees make changes to the file at the same time? Software that supports one user at a time doesn't have to deal with the consequences of such a circumstance. But multiuser software must handle such cases. Consequently, these programs are significantly more difficult to develop and they cost more.

- Will your new multiuser software have to be purchased?

  The software you are using now (if any) is probably "single user." This means that only one person can use it at a time. If you expect to have two or more people using it simultaneously, will it work? When in doubt, ask your consultant. Get it in writing, but get it straight. The single-user program you have may cost $295. The multiuser version may cost $995.

- What will the overhead be?

  The *overhead* in this sense is how much memory (RAM) is required to run the software you want to use. Some programs that run fine on a stand-alone computer won't run once that computer is connected to a network. The network operating software may use up RAM. Be sure to ask your consultant whether your systems have adequate memory.

- Are there peripherals to share among network users?

  Will everyone be sharing a laser printer? Will the printer handle the workload adequately? Will the network you want to buy allow someone who is not on the network to print on it? Do you expect to share other devices?

LAN Setup Costs

The costs associated with a network setup are as follows:

- Installation of the network—this can mean paying a consultant for 30 minutes or 30 hours, depending on the sophistication of the network.
- Training personnel to use the network.
- Costs of the networking software itself.

- Costs of the networking hardware and accessories.
- The cost of the cabling—this can be even higher than the cost of the network hardware and software if cable has to be run through walls and concrete floors, or down elevator shafts.

Typical Starting Network Software Configurations

Following are software items and LAN startup packages that provide a basis for new networks:

- Operating system—MS-DOS or PC DOS.
- Lantastic Starter Kit (two-user network)—Includes two network cards, network software, and cable for connecting the two computers. To add additional users, purchase additional cards and cables. The software supports over 100 users.

Or for very busy locations, instead of the Lantastic Starter Kit, consider

- Novell ELS I (entry level system)—Supports up to five users. Add two or more network cards and cable. For more than five users, you must upgrade to Level II.

Multitasking Systems Versus Multiuser Networks

A *multitasking system* is one that enables you to do many tasks at one time. For example, in a multitasking system you could be printing an accounting report, recalculating a spreadsheet, and receiving a fax transmission with the fax board in your computer—all simultaneously. Does it sound a bit confusing? Most of us tend to do one thing at a time. Yet computer makers are determined to give us this multitasking capability—now available in UNIX-based systems and in Microsoft Windows applications. Doubtless we will eventually begin to use it, but at this time multitasking is of limited value.

In a business environment where you have one main focus, it is questionable whether multitasking is of benefit to you. Furthermore, to use a multitasking system efficiently requires more RAM and usually a 486 or 586 computer. The proper installation and setup of a multitasking system requires someone with several years of experience. This type of consultant is likely to charge more for his or her time. A multitasking system is not recommended as a starting system. This is something you can add on later, through a software and/or hardware upgrade as the true need presents itself.

4

Peripherals and Supplies

A *peripheral* is an additional device attached to a computer, such as a printer, modem, or cash drawer. There are thousands of different items on the market today. This chapter briefly covers the most widely used items.

Printers

It's hard to think of a business use for computers that doesn't include some type of printouts. Accounting, database, spreadsheet, and certainly word processing applications thrive on creating paper copies of file contents. Thus, a printer is a major consideration as you set up your computer system and is probably the peripheral that is replaced and upgraded most frequently.

Systems can be set up with one or more printers if necessary. The type of printer you select will depend on your needs and the software you require. Software developers/suppliers specify in their documentation which brands and models of printer they "support." Applications come with *printer driver* programs that help the software and printer work smoothly together.

Dot-Matrix

Dot-matrix printers are the least expensive of all printer types. They create characters (letters, numbers, and symbols) by using a series of dots. This is the type of printing you recognize on most computer-generated forms and mailing labels. The quality of dot-matrix printers (and their prices!) is measured by the number of "pins" they use: Older printers with 9 pins on the print head produce jagged-looking type; today's 24-pin printers can create typewriter-quality characters.

The printing quality of dot-matrix printers may be enhanced by using the "near letter-quality" printing mode. With a good dot-matrix printer, this quality is fine for most correspondence. Most software companies recommend a "push" tractor feed because it saves paper waste on continuous-feed paper and forms. A *tractor feed* is the set of sprockets found on either side of the *platen* (roller bar) that can push (or pull) the paper through the printer.

Be sure to ask for one of the printers that the software company recommends and supports. Many printers contain subtle differences in printing that may cause them not to line up properly with preprinted forms.

Daisy-Wheel

Letter-quality or daisy-wheel printers produce documents that look like they were created on a good typewriter. (Some typewriters can be modified to attach to a computer.) It works in the same way. Each letter is on the print wheel and when the computer sends the signal, the letter is printed by impact. Of course, all this quality costs you something valuable . . . time! Daisy-wheel printers are very slow. These printers are seldom used today; they are being replaced rapidly by laser printers for professional-looking documents that can include multiple typefaces.

Invoices are usually printed on 80-column impact type printers, such as dot-matrix or daisy-wheel printers. You might want two printers— one 80-column dot-matrix for receipts and other multicopy forms and a laser printer for everything else.

Laser

Laser printers can handle quality graphics as well as text. The output from most desktop laser printers today is excellent in both quality of print and speed. Laser printers are an invaluable tool for desktop publishing because of their flexibility of printed output (text and graphics mix) and print quality. However, laser printers can only print one-part forms. They cannot print on a two- or three-part paper form, because they are not "impact" printers.

Receipt Printers

Receipt printers provide 40-column customer tear receipts. Although some reports may be printed on this type of printer, most detail is lost on the printouts because it is less than half the width of other printers.

If you plan to use a 40-column printer for receipts, you should consider purchasing an 80-column printer for other printing needs. The advantage of a 40-column receipt printer is that the paper is only three to four inches wide and it is a less-expensive supply than continuous-form full-sized paper.

Bar Code Readers/Laser Scanners

A *bar code reader* (also called a *scanner*) is a handheld or counter device that can read manufacturers' bar code labels. The purposes of a reader/scanner are to save time for customers and improve accuracy of transactions as goods are sold and to enter new items to the inventory quickly and accurately. When the scanner comes in contact with the bar code label, the stock number of the item is entered into the computer just as if you had typed the number on a computer keyboard.

It is almost impossible for the scanner to read the bar code incorrectly. Individuals typing numbers all day will certainly make many more mistakes than a bar code reader. All too often business owners looking to cut corners decide not to purchase this component with the system. If you are a retailer with inventory, this is definitely not the item to cut from your shopping list. The payoff from this investment is phenomenal and, if you are adding a scanner, it will be five times as much work to add it on later, because of the counter modifications that become necessary.

A "wand" or "pen" style reader works well for small-ticket items. The light at the tip of the pen is run over the bar code label in a sweeping motion. Its advantage is that it is inexpensive. Its disadvantage is that it is only good in a business with clean, dry bar codes. It is not recommended for beverage centers where you might have frost on the bar codes or for any store where the bar codes are not flat.

A handheld scanner can read the label from a slight distance. This makes it an ideal solution for items that are packaged in odd sized containers. This is an excellent solution for liquor stores and other environments with bar codes that are not smooth, dry, and clean.

In-counter scanners are mounted in the sales counter. The item is simply dragged over the scanning device. This is the type of scanner usually found in grocery stores. It works well with heavy or cumbersome merchandise.

On-counter scanners are also suitable for large, odd shaped products. The scanner mounts on top of the sales counter and the bar code label is passed through the light beam.

Electronic Keypad

A *keypad* is a tabletop pad with buttons that correspond to products or services. Each product or service is programmed into the keypad. During a transaction, the operator presses a button instead of typing a stock or service number. This is appropriate for a business that handles fewer than 200 products and/or services, such as small retail stores. Some cash registers use these pads instead of numeric keypads—and some cash registers use a combination product and numeric keypad.

Cash Drawers

A *cash drawer* is simply the drawer portion of a cash register. The drawer may be installed under the front counter and linked to the computer. When a sale is rung, the drawer opens automatically as it would on a cash register. Most point-of-sale programs can operate cash drawers.

A combination cash drawer and receipt printer combines the drawer and printer units. The benefit of using this type of unit is that it plugs into one port of the computer instead of two. If your computer has a limited number of expansion slots, a combination unit is the better choice.

Modem

Once you have invested in a personal computer, you can vastly expand its ability to help you do productive work by installing a modem to help the computer exchange data with other computers using telephone lines. A *modem* is either an internal device on an integrated circuit card or a separate device that allows your computer to communicate with another system via a telephone line connection.

The uses for modems are many. For example, if you have a computer and modem at home, you can access the data in the computer at the office. You can send files to branch offices and off-site employees, and receive files of any size in just the time it takes to complete a phone call.

Modems are also needed to process on-line credit card authorizations and to link to on-line data services such as Prodigy or CompuServe.

Over regular phone wires, from any home or office, computers with modems can tap into a vast array of information and contacts, so you can send messages, memos, reports, and drawings to other computers worldwide, and communicate with your office from home or hotels.

Some computers may come with built-in modems. Laptops and notebook computers often include this feature. Alternatively, you can install a modem card in one of the expansion slots within the CPU, and the telephone line can plug directly into the back of the card. If your computer has few remaining expansion slots, you can purchase an external modem. External modems are small box type items that sit near the computer. The telephone line is plugged into it and a separate cable connects it to the computer. The type you choose will depend on the amount of expansion slots available in your computer and the amount of space on your desk top or counter.

Prices of modems are determined by their speed, which is measured in terms of baud rates (300, 1200, 2400, 9600, and so on). It is best to purchase the fastest modem you can afford that matches the fastest speed of the services you intend to use with it. This will save money in the time your computer and you are tied up in communications sessions and also will cut your telephone charges.

To use a modem in your system, you need a telephone jack installed nearby. It is not necessary to have a separate telephone line if you don't use the modem all the time.

Caution:

If you have the call waiting feature on your modem's telephone line, the signals will cause problems with your data transmissions.

Most modems are inexpensive; they're not particularly hard to install; and with the right software to control them, they can be pretty straightforward to operate. But learning about them is cloaked in dense communications jargon. Eyes glaze over when the experts start trying to define the word "modem" by plunging into a discussion of something called *modulation* (from which the "mo" of "modem" is derived) and *demodulation* (from which the "dem" of "modem" is derived).

That won't happen here. You don't need to know about modulation and protocol standards to buy or use a modem. Instead, think of a modem as a telephone for your computer, a specialized phone designed to send computerized data—such as text and graphics—instead of human voices, over phone lines. That's the essential job modems perform.

When you set out to buy a modem, there are two main issues to consider: style and speed. Modems come in three styles—the built-in style, separate circuit board style, and the external unit style. Built-in and internal modems need no cables to connect to the computer and draw their electrical power from the computer power supply.

External modems pack the same circuitry into a little box that sits on the desk and plugs into an electrical outlet. They connect to the computer through a cable that fits into a standard socket called a *serial port* on the back of the computer.

All modems include at least one modular phone jack. You can connect them to your regular phone line, but again be forewarned: Modem sessions can prevent callers from getting through, and data transmission or reception can be disrupted if someone picks up the phone while the modem is in use.

There are lots of advantages to internal modems: fewer cables, and no need to give up desk space, and no separate electrical outlets or serial port use. But some people prefer external modems because they don't require you to fool around inside the computer and often feature indicator lights that can tell you at a glance the status of a call.

Judge a Modem by Its Speed

The major issue is the speed with which a modem can transmit data over phone lines. This is measured in *bits*—the smallest unit of computer data—*per second,* or *bps.* The most commonly available modems today are rated at 1200, 2400, or 9600 bps. (These ratings are also expressed in terms of *baud* rather than bps, but the numbers are virtually the same.) Older modems were very slow at 300 bps.

Speed matters. The faster you can send or receive data, the less you'll pay in phone bills and connection fees to commercial services, which often charge by the minute. But the fastest modems carry a steep price premium.

For the vast majority of users, a 2400 bps modem is the best choice. A good one can be had for under $200. Most commercial and corporate databases now run at 2400 bps or slower. The 9600 bps models often cost $500 to $1,000 and only run at top speed when you call another 9600 bps modem. The extra cost may or may not be worth it, depending on your particular situation.

Some modems can also send documents from your computer screen to fax machines. They often cost only $50 or $100 more.

Modems are becoming mass-market items, but you should steer away from the very cheapest models and the most obscure brands. There are too many quality brands to list here, but some major ones with competitive prices are U.S. Robotics, Practical Peripherals, and Zoom Telephonics.

Hayes Compatibility

Make sure your modem is "Hayes-compatible," meaning it responds to a standard set of commands popularized by Hayes Microcomputer Products, a big modem maker. Most are. Make sure as well that the modem can automatically dial and answer phone calls. Most now can. But the average user can ignore most of the costly special features modem makers promote, such as circuitry to correct transmission errors or compress data.

Communications Software

What you can't ignore is software. The final value of your modem purchase depends on getting a communications program that's both sophisticated and easy to use. Many modems come bundled with simple software, but two popular commercial programs are ProComm Plus, by Datastorm, for IBM compatibles, which sells for about $65, and MicroPhone II (about $215), by Software Ventures, for Apple's Macintosh computers and IBM compatibles that use Microsoft's Windows. Both programs will hide the modem's complexity behind simple commands and screen displays that will help you roam the world by phone from your desk.

Fax Machine

To be competitive today, an office must have a facsimile (fax) machine. An office without a fax is almost like an office without a telephone, which is unimaginable. Despite electronic communications and records management of all kinds and levels, there's still a crucial need for the rapid transfer of paper. The success of fax is due in part to the effective application of digital technology to the functions of scanning, sending, receiving, and printing images on documents.

Although it's not the only option, fax has become the method of choice for quick, point-to-point message exchange.

Take a look at the statistics of its success. Although facsimile technology has been around since the late 1940s, it did not start to become widespread until the 1970s. From 1986 to 1989, approximately 4 million fax machines were purchased, another 1.6 million units are expected to be shipped in 1992, 3.2 million in 1993, and 5 million in 1995, according to BIS Strategic Decisions of Norwell, Massachusetts.

The number of companies manufacturing original equipment has doubled from 20 in 1986 to 40 today, and the number of brands also has doubled, from 40 to 80, over the same period. There are presently about 2 million U.S. offices equipped with fax technology, transmitting more than 30 billion pages of information each year.

Enhancements

Extended fax capabilities and enhancements have become almost over-whelming for the prospective buyer. Some of the choices involve the hardware itself, including the connection of fax boards to a computer, networking options, and a variety of adjunct devices that increase fax effectiveness and convenience.

Interactive Faxes

Among the alternatives is an innovation called *interactive facsimile,* which enables the user to access information by dialing a telephone number. There's a merging of voice response and fax, permitting a caller to access a database and retrieve or input information through a touch-tone telephone. A synthesized voice relays the requested information to the caller, who can then have the data faxed to him or entered directly into his database by fax.

This interaction is a combination of facsimile, computer, and image technology, allowing for data store-and-forward capabilities. It can include a fax mailbox with a security code, message-waiting notification on the phone, and the convenience of message acquisition, especially attractive to salespeople and others who travel frequently.

Telephone Fax Switches

A less costly alternative is a relatively simple device, a telephone/fax switch. This box-shaped device has connectors to accept telephone and fax lines or modems. Most units allow two devices to share one line—the telephone and the fax machine—but some can accept three.

As telephone calls come in, the switch determines the kind of call and then connects it to the appropriate device. The type of call is identified by a tone—the caller's voice by voice recognition circuitry or by a person who controls the direction of the call at the transmission or receiving points with touchtone codes. (For some directions, a voice recording tells the caller what to do via touchtone to direct the call.) If no one is available to take a call, switches can be programmed to transfer the call automatically to the appropriate device or extension.

Although a dedicated line is considered best for firms that get over 15 fax calls a day, the telephone/fax switch is best for organizations with a low volume of fax and telephone calls.

Adapters

There are other choices for the discriminating buyer. One major company is offering an "adapter" (a device that's a mixture of fax board and multifunctional peripheral, providing printing and scanning capabilities and fax transmission).

Interoperability
There are a number of modems available. As alternative devices to fax boards, some modems operate as external computer-to-fax connections, enabling users to transmit information from one computer to another or from a computer to a fax. One modem available, when equipped with special software, provides four levels of magnification of incoming faxes and offers many high-end fax features.

Fax Machines as Printers
A modem also assists in the use of the fax as a printer for word processing, spreadsheet, or other PC functions. The inexpensive methodology permits users to send computer-generated faxes. Some units send just as well as most computer fax boards but lose the screening, forwarding, and digitizing capabilities of a full-featured fax board.

Fax Boards and Fax Modems for Computers

The mixing of technologies is almost old hat. It didn't take long for people to realize that computers and fax machines make a good combination. A *fax board* is a circuit card that is mounted in an expansion slot within the CPU. This card enables your computer to act like a fax machine. Incoming faxes are received by the computer and may be printed on any printer attached to your system. Fax messages are typed at the keyboard and sent via the internal fax. An added document scanner enables you to fax original documents and illustrations.

Fax boards give fax capabilities to a PC. Although in some situations the stand-alone fax machine is faster than a PC/fax board, today's common fax board is a workhorse. With 65 manufacturers in the market, prices are coming down; the range is now less than $100 to $1,200.

Fax boards are often used in offices where telecommunications are a crucial part of daily business activities and much of the data to be communicated is already in a PC's database. PC/fax boards can communicate with other fax board-equipped PCs as well as with any fax machine.

With a fax board, you can receive faxes, print them, and then store the information on a hard disk. Outgoing faxes can be created from text and graphics files in addition to images that have been scanned. Many fax boards can function as *fax servers* for large networks of computers— sending, receiving, and routing faxes to meet the needs of an entire office.

Fax boards perform certain functions better than stand-alone fax machines. Text and graphics created on a PC often are clearer at the receiving end than documents fed through a fax machine's scanner. In addition, broadcasts are simply a matter of preparing a list of numbers and allowing the computer to do the calling. Some fax vendors offer their own products, and others are producing units that add PC capabilities to their fax-board models. One manufacturer has a fax-to-computer interface that allows mainframes, minis, and PCs to communicate with fax machines.

There are limitations to faxing with internal fax boards. The biggest drawback is that most setups can only send computerized documents, not paper ones. But on the receiving end, you have the pleasure of being free from greasy, curly fax paper. You can simply read faxes on the screen, or print them out on regular paper using your computer's laser printer.

The most popular faxing device for computers is a *fax modem*. These products combine, in one unit, a standard modem and the telephonic guts of a fax machine.

To transmit a fax with these devices, you use special software to send an electronic document through the fax modem to a regular fax machine elsewhere. When someone sends a fax to you from a fax machine, the fax modem answers the call and turns the transmission into a computer graphic image that can be displayed on your screen or printed on your laser printer (but would require massaging before it could be edited in your word processor).

I've tried two fax modems: the $179 Fax96 1-Liner by Frecom (Fremont, California) for the IBM-compatible PC, and the $269 DoveFax, by Dove Computer (Wilmington, North Carolina), for the Macintosh computer. Both work well, but there are many others.

Before choosing a fax modem, consider the software it includes. The software should be easy to use and install, and should let you maintain an automated phone list to enable you to quickly and simply send, view, and manipulate incoming faxes and create customized cover pages.

Dove's software and other Macintosh faxing programs enable you to fax documents directly from word processors or other programs by going through the same steps as to print the document by selecting the fax modem as your "printer." An impressive $75 program called Winfax, from Delrina Technology (Toronto), lets you do the same thing on IBM-compatible computers running the Microsoft Windows program.

Some fax programs have special features. The Fax96 modem's software automatically determines whether an incoming call is a regular voice phone call, a fax call, or a standard computer data transmission.

Calera Recognition Systems (Sunnyvale, California) offers a $99 Windows environment program called FaxGrabber that automatically turns faxes being received by a fax modem into text that can be edited in your word processor.

Note: _____

A key advantage of using your computer with a fax board as a fax machine is that you can simply look at faxes on the screen and delete the ones you don't want without wasting time or paper by printing them; plus, you get plain-paper faxes because you print out transmissions on your printer. But a disadvantage is that if you receive a lot of faxes, they can hog your computer's memory and disk space.

Fax Server

As the connection between fax machines and computers becomes stronger, so do the products that complement them. Fax servers—fax boards with network service software—expand facsimile capabilities to the users of a local area network (LAN).

The server, unlike a PC/fax board, goes to many PCs, not a single-user PC. Normally, 10 users require 10 fax boards, but a fax server eliminates this duplication by accommodating a group of PC users. The transmission speeds are about the same as most fax machines, but time is saved by eliminating the need to print a document, prepare a cover sheet, go to the fax machine, and load the document. Some fax servers use a dedicated printer and some use any printer on the network, but either way, these systems have an almost unlimited market potential.

Stand-Alone Fax Machines

Stand-alone fax machines remain both valuable and useful despite the many other options available. Costing $300 to $1,200 adds to their appeal, and the wide range of functions has also influenced their ever-increasing sales.

Their many options include the following:

- Sheet cutter (except for some low-end models)
- Automatically adjusted baud rates
- Multipage document feeder
- Ability to switch between voice and fax to communicate to another user
- Fax numbers for automatically sending a single transmission to many receivers
- Ability to track individual user and message location
- High-resolution laser printing
- Automatic redialing for busy telephone numbers
- Receipt of items into memory when the machine is out of paper, inoperable, or disconnected
- Security mailboxes to keep sensitive faxes private

Smallest Size

About a dozen portable fax units are on the market. One, heralded as the "world's smallest fax: 5.5 pounds," is a cellular machine. The unit works with a choice of three separate power sources—an adapter for a car cigarette lighter, a rechargeable battery pack, and an AC adapter for use in standard wall outlets. It can send or receive documents from any indoor or outdoor location, including a car, a golf cart, a pay phone, or an office.

Salespeople can send or receive faxes in their hotel rooms by using the telephone, or they can plug their machines into a car cigarette lighter and transmit documents over a cellular phone. Some of the units contain a headset and built-in answering capability.

Tied to cellular-phone growth, the portable fax market is expected to boom. Cellular-telephone sales are predicted to reach 10.4 million placements by 1993, up from the 3.5 million this year.

Similarly, some 100,000 portable faxes are expected to be in use by 1995, an explosive rise from the 14,000 units in use in 1990, according to BIS Strategic Decisions. Prices range from $950 to $1,700.

Largest Size

Not everything in communications is getting smaller. The *Guinness Book of Records* has recently acknowledged a Canadian facsimile machine as the "world's largest." It can transmit blueprints, engineering drawings, and other oversize documents up to 24 inches in width. It's also portable and can be taken to construction sites and other field locations.

If this machine is sending to a standard-size fax machine, it can either reduce the drawing or send it in three 8-inch-wide strips for pasteup at the receiving end. The unit has a versatile copier that prints onto a variety of materials, from erasable fax paper to thermal Mylar. The price is about $14,000.

How Fax Machines Work and How to Select One

Fax technology, like the telephone on which it depends, is a kind of miracle to most of us. Fax machines are now smaller, lighter, more mobile, and crucial to most businesses. Fortunately, as prices decline, technological features improve, such as autodial capability, transmission speed, memory capacity, and delayed-transmission choices, among others.

Many Group 3 fax machines are rated at a transmission speed of 20 seconds per page, with some units reaching speeds below 10 seconds. It seems the future is here.

Fax machines are, at heart, simple to understand. They are best thought of as long-distance versions of that familiar office device, the photocopier.

Like copiers, fax machines accept original documents with electronic sensors, then spit out copies (facsimiles). The difference, of course, is that the copy is sent to a distant fax machine, via special telephone circuitry built into both faxes.

But as fax machines have become ubiquitous, makers have offered so many features in so many combinations that shopping for a machine can be trying. Prices range from $300 or so to thousands of dollars. Ads are littered with terms such as *Group 3, broadcast,* and *fine mode.*

Recommendation:

Buy only the features you need and will need soon. The simplest little fax machine may be enough for home use or low-volume professions. So analyze your likely needs and shun superfluous bells and whistles.

To help, here's a guide to some important features of fax machines, especially stand-alone units.

First, let's clear away the underbrush. Fax ads are laden with certain buzzwords that you can ignore, because they apply to nearly every machine at every price. One is "Group 3 compatibility." This simply means the machine can send and receive according to the currently prevalent international standard. Another is the ability to handle both "normal" and "fine" output; this comes with Group 3 compatibility.

Then there is the claim that a stand-alone machine can double as a copier. Nearly every fax machine can, by "sending" a transmission to itself. But most make poor copiers, because they yield only one copy at a time and use waxy fax paper (unless you get a plain-paper fax machine, described in a moment).

The rest of the key features can be divided into three categories: those that affect how you feed documents into the machines, those that affect how you receive faxes sent by others, and those that affect the telephone functions of the machine.

Document Feeding

On the input end of the fax process, one feature is especially important: document feeding. The most basic machines require users to feed each page of a document by hand. That's fine for a college student faxing an occasional letter or research paper. But even for most small businesses, it's essential to get a machine with an automatic feeder that lets you stack up at least a few pages and walk away.

Thermal Versus Plain Paper

On the receiving end, the biggest decision is whether a machine produces faxes on the familiar special fax paper or on regular paper. Most machines use rolls of the old-style thermal fax paper, and they cost less initially than plain-paper faxes. But fax paper curls and turns dark and brittle. It often must be photocopied if you want to keep it permanently, adding time and cost.

Plain-paper faxes using the same printing mechanism as copiers and laser printers are dropping rapidly in price. Some can be had for $1,700 and include a strong array of other features. They also have lower per-page operating costs because they use standard office paper. But bear in mind that, like copiers and printers, plain-paper fax machines require the periodic purchase of supplies that thermal-paper fax machines don't need.

Other Handy Features

If you opt for thermal fax paper and receive more than a dozen faxed pages a day, you should get a machine with an *automatic paper cutter* to separate faxes into cut pages. Otherwise, somebody has to manually snip the pages apart. And be sure to get a machine that can accept paper rolls long enough to meet your needs. Another useful feature is built-in memory, which helps the machine to store pages electronically if your paper roll runs out as you receive a fax and then print it when you insert a new roll.

When you use the same phone line for regular calls and faxes, consider getting *voice/fax switching.* This feature enables the machine to recognize whether an incoming call is a voice or fax transmission. Otherwise, a human must answer the phone and decide. But to use such switching, you must make the fax machine's built-in phone your primary one for all incoming calls.

Finally, fax machines offer an array of dialing options to automate transmissions. Most offer some sort of *speed dialing,* where you can program frequently called numbers into the fax machine's memory and later dial them by pressing single buttons or entering two-digit codes. Some machines *redial* busy numbers automatically; others can be set for *delayed transmission* at a specified time (such as during the night with cheaper long-distance rates).

Pricier machines offer *broadcasting*—the ability to transmit a single outgoing fax to a group of recipients whose numbers have been programmed into the machine (this is the haven of "junk" faxers). Others can do *polling,* or calls to a group of fax machines to see whether they have material ready to send.

As with telephones, VCRs, and other high-tech gizmos, these programmable features may look nice on paper but can be difficult to operate using the fax machine's limited keypads and display screens. So if you choose a complex machine, be sure to try it before you buy it.

One solution is to buy an add-on device that turns a laser printer into a stand-alone fax machine, without requiring incoming faxes to go through your computer. The JetFax II by JetFax (Menlo Park, California) was an early entry in this market. A slender box, the JetFax II sits beside a Hewlett-Packard LaserJet or compatible printer and automatically routes incoming faxes to the printer. HP now offers its own competing fax add-on, a bigger unit called the LaserJet Fax. Both devices can send computer files as faxes, but the HP can also send paper documents.

These two products are relatively costly (around $700 for the JetFax II, nearly $1,000 for the LaserJet Fax). Tall Tree Systems (Palo Alto, California) offers a compact, $399 alternative called Fax-O-Matic. This little black box merely lets an HP or compatible laser printer receive faxes, without the involvement of the computer. Extended Systems (Boise, Idaho) makes a $599 device, the FaxConnection, that goes inside an HP laser printer to enable it to receive faxes.

The most elegant solution is the LaserScript Fax by Everex Systems (Fremont, California). This is a laser printer with built-in fax circuitry. It will automatically receive faxes and let you send faxes from the computer. LaserScript Fax sells for $2,500 to $3,000.

Note:

Eventually, most laser printer makers will offer built-in faxing like this, further eroding the need for separate fax machines and that awful fax paper.

Accessories and Supplies

This section mentions some of the accessories and office-supply items you'll need to purchase.

Customer Pole Display

A *customer pole display* displays the description, prices, taxes, and totals at the time of sale on point-of-sale systems. The display is mounted near the computer in an area where the customer can see it. Some states require this option in retail operations.

Credit Card Reader

A *credit card reader* is also known as a *magnetic strip reader.* This device may be built into a keyboard or sold as a separate unit. When a credit card is presented, the operator simply runs the card through the slot, reading its recorded data, instead of typing the card data.

Tape Backup Unit

A *tape backup unit* copies the contents of a hard disk to a tape cartridge. This eliminates the need to *back up* (duplicate for use in case of damage to the original) to floppy disks. To back up to disks, a new disk must be placed in the drive each time the previous one is full. The amount of disks you need for backups depends on the amount of data stored on the disk, but tape cartridges hold far more than even a high-density 3.5-inch disk. A tape backup makes the task faster and easier. (You'll learn later why it's so important to back up your system regularly.)

Uninterruptible Power Supply (UPS)

Although the supply of electrical power to computer systems has always been an issue, it's usually one of the things small companies—strapped for cash but eager to automate—put on the back burner. Along with other disaster-prevention steps such as conscientious backup procedures and virus scanning, people tend to think that power loss is possible but won't happen at a critical time to us. We don't need to spend the time or money for an *uninterruptible power supply (UPS)* right now.

Perilous weather is probably the most obvious hazard to normally continuous power sources, but it's only one of many. The important, sometimes irreplaceable, data stored on costly hardware is in constant danger.

Tip:

Learn to identify the potential risks you face by not protecting your investment of time and money, and explore the options available to safeguard them. It's crucial. Even a brief interruption in electrical power can cause considerable loss in a computerized office.

How serious is the problem? Disaster stories about computer data loss abound, though they tend to focus on the threat of viruses and the hazards of data files that aren't conscientiously backed up. You're not as likely to hear about an office site that suffered serious financial loss because of a power failure, but it happens. Studies indicate that power loss, due to any number of factors, happens more frequently than most people realize.

Short- or long-term interference with normal power sources can seriously damage computer hardware and delete unsaved data. These disturbances vary greatly in cause, duration, and the amount of damage they inflict.

Utility companies, for example, occasionally disrupt service to subscribers, such as when they restore power after a blackout or brownout. The vast majority of problems, however, are caused by the utility company's customers or by unavoidable occurrences. Homes or appliances are improperly wired. Lightning strikes a tree and it crashes into a power pole.

To further complicate the problems experienced by modern-office high-tech equipment, the newer electronic circuits can be more temperamental because they operate at higher speeds, though they have lower voltage needs than more common electrical appliances.

Some geographical areas seem to be experiencing more minor, short-term flickers and outages than ever before. We're using an inordinate amount of power in this country because of all the technology that requires electricity and also because of our desire for comfortable living.

Many levels of help are available. The process of choosing the right power-protection device for your office is similar to selecting any kind of electronic equipment. Don't buy a device that has more features than you currently need or will need in the foreseeable future. Buy more rather than less actual power protection, because inadequate protection can have devastating results.

First, define the most-likely electrical failure risks:

- Is the geographical area prone to hazardous weather conditions?
- Are there easily avoidable overloads anywhere? Map the layout of electrically powered equipment that shares circuits with computer-related equipment.
- What is the normal number of surges or complete outages that occur in the average year?
- Are there plans anytime in the near future to do a lot of construction in the area where your office is located? Construction projects themselves sometimes create occasional power losses, and the additional short-term drain on existing power sources may affect you.
- When is energy use at its peak? Try to get a general idea of what your average electrical needs are.

Using the previous list of questions and the assistance of your power company, prepare a power profile in a written format and be as specific as possible. You may actually have more information than necessary when it's time to start looking at ads and talking to salespeople, but you'll be better equipped to make the best possible choice if you have the information available.

Be aware that people sometimes use different terms to describe the same specification or piece of equipment, and salespeople occasionally try to cover up their lack of understanding by intimidating you with meaningless jargon. Know what you need and ask whether the product can do that. For whom is the product recommended? How much does it cost? What warranty is offered?

Electrical security equipment is built in a variety of configurations; each class is designed to guard against different potential problems.

The UPS offers backup power and helps to prevent unevenness in the power flow. A UPS will protect your data in the event of a power brownout or outage. Without a UPS, if you lose power, any information entered into the computer that hasn't been saved to disk will be lost. Also, you obviously cannot use the system at all. An uninterruptible power supply will keep the system running for a limited time with internal battery power even when there is no utility power. The length of time the power will last depends on the unit—usually about 3, 10, or 20 minutes. This period gives you enough time to properly save your work and shut the system down. If you have frequent power problems in your area, this is a necessity. A UPS is essential for businesses planning to install computers and that also have heavy equipment such as compressors, lathes, or any other power equipment. Stores with refrigerated display cases also fall into this category. Have you ever noticed that the lights dim when these refrigerator units start up? What do you think that might do to a sensitive piece of electronic equipment like your computer?

Surge Protectors/Suppressors

Surge protectors and *suppressors* do just what their names suggest: They stop power surges from damaging electrical equipment by preventing bursts of current from reaching the CPU. The bad news: If the surge is strong enough, power may be shut off to the equipment, causing data loss. Figure 4-1 illustrates a typical surge and line noise suppressor.

Power surges can cause any number of problems. A surge suppressor will protect the computer against electrical power surges that will destroy data. It is a strip of outlets (approximately six). If you don't have an uninterruptible power supply, you should at least have a surge suppressor.

FIGURE 4-1 Typical surge/noise suppressor

Caution:

Unchecked power surges can do more than just shut things down for a while; they can cause damage to semiconductor and microprocessor chips.

Surge protectors are sold in a broad range of prices and with varying features. You can spend anywhere from about $20 to $50,000 on electrical protection equipment and systems, and the actual physical configurations can range from an internal PC card to a small unit connected to the computer system, an AC wall outlet, or large boxes. Once you've determined the class of protection needed and compiled the names of vendors, shop around. Computer and electronics magazines are good sources for this kind of information. You might also consult members of a local computer-users' group; a consumer-relations representative at your local utility company; or employees at other businesses about the same size as yours, who have similar electronic equipment.

If you find that your risk is heavy during particular times of the year, you might consider leasing a system for those crucial time periods.

Thoughtful consideration about steady power supplies is important. The problems created by electrical disturbances involve more than just lost data. Anytime power is cut off for a period of time, especially to organizations that provide emergency services, such as a medical office, there can be no compromising when determining how to protect a constant electrical current.

But even in nonlife-threatening situations, there are many issues to consider in the decision to buy electrical protection. After all, you probably spent a lot of time and money on the purchase of the hardware itself; insuring that investment should be important, too.

What are the issues involved in selecting surge protection?

- The value of the data being protected.
- The costs of overtime.
- The repair or replacement costs for damaged hardware and software.

- Any applicable insurance requirements.
- The lifetime of the electrical protection product. (If the system is failing, is any warning system offered?)
- The quality of the product, and the reputation of the vendor, if possible.
- The product's features and how they fit your requirements.

One final consideration: Local area networks (LANs) have especially critical needs for safeguarding against data loss. Protection for networks is crucial, given the number of people that can be affected by a breakdown. At least one vendor offers a system that provides for an automatic, orderly shutdown and both remote and local notification in the event of a power failure.

Note:

Ensuring a steady supply of power is one more expense, but a crucial one. Putting together a hardware and software system for your office can seem like an endless procession of things you have to spend money on. Those appealingly low price tags on computers are sometimes just a fraction of the total financial output necessary to automate an office.

The hidden costs of setting up a computer system can seem like an irritating extra step, especially if you're on a tight budget. Companies have to separate the niceties from the necessities.

Insurance against electrical damage is a necessity for an office of any size. Consumers can skip a few days of playing "Windows Solitaire" while an electrical glitch is repaired, but businesses can face serious losses—some have been known to shut down—because of an electrically induced computer failure.

Line Regulator/Conditioner

Line regulators (also known as *voltage regulators*) and *conditioners* are generally most appropriate for use by large companies. These devices operate similarly to a surge suppressor but more effectively. If your utility power is subject to lightning strikes, startups and power-downs of heavy equipment, or any other constant source of power interruptions, line conditioning devices are a recommended addition. But they are expensive—in the range of $500 and more. So be sure one is absolutely needed prior to purchasing one. Consult your utility service group and/or an electrical contractor in your area. The device is designed to ensure the voltage to your computer system remains at a constant level regardless of the conditions of its input (utility-provided) power. Some UPS manufacturers have a product line that combines the line regulator with the UPS. Again, these combined units are expensive, so make sure your situation justifies their purchase.

Recommendation:

A hidden cost of printers is their operating supplies—ribbons and continuous-form paper for dot-matrix and daisy-wheel printers, and cartridges and toner for lasers. Before you purchase a printer, comparison shop among the supplies for each model you're considering; savings between one type of ribbon and another, for example, can be substantial. During the life of the printer you may spend several times the cost of the printer itself in the supplies it requires.

Floppy Disks

You learned about floppy disks and their capacities in Chapter 3. Recall that they are available in 3.5-inch or 5.25-inch sizes and in low and high densities. The type of disks you need—and you will need many if you exchange disks with other users or perform backups onto floppies—is determined by the type of floppy drive installed in your machine. To find out, consult your dealer or the computer manual and the previous discussion on data storage in this book. Figure 4-2 illustrates both sides of these standard disks.

Cables

Cables connect devices such as printers, modems, monitors, and keyboards to your computer's CPU. The cable runs from the device to the port (connecting point) located on the computer. There are many different types of cables available, and you can shop around for the best prices once you know which kind you require. Noncomputer electronics shops carry a broad range of cabling and connectors.

Tip:

Many peripheral devices such as printers do not come with the cable that attaches it to the computer. To find out the type of cables needed, consult the product manual and your dealer.

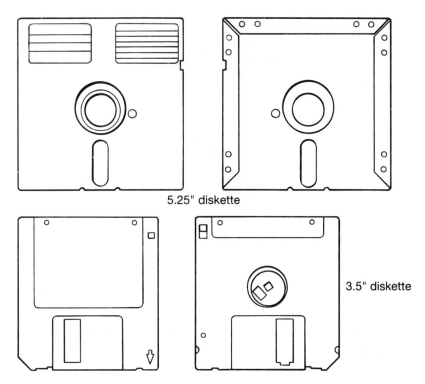

FIGURE 4-2   Typical disk configurations (front and back views)

Buying and Installing Your System

Should you consider leasing instead of buying? As the owner of a small business, you're well aware that it's best not to tie up your capital unnecessarily. One of the advantages of today's personal computers is that you don't need to spend all that much to get a nice system. A minimal system, such as the ones recommended, shouldn't cost more than $5,000, and probably less. Such a system includes the computer itself, a high-quality monitor, a laser printer, a modem, and a mouse. But there are some advantages to leasing, including tax advantages in some cases (you would be wise to discuss this matter with an accountant). In either case the selection and installation processes are the same.

Buying Your System

Before you buy your system, review the products you've compared with your Computer Purchasing Worksheet (refer to Appendix A), reconsider the features that are important to you, then think about some last-minute issues. If you've decided on DOS or Windows, do you want to buy a genuine IBM system, or will an IBM compatible suffice? What can you expect from warranties? Where is it best to buy your system? What should you ask the dealer? Should you buy a used computer?

Buying an IBM or Clone

If you've decided on a DOS or Windows system, you'll be faced with a choice between a genuine IBM computer (one of its PS/1 or PS/2 models) and an IBM compatible (a clone). You can find high-quality IBM compatibles; IBM's much-touted Micro Channel Bus Architecture does not offer decisive technical advantages for the applications discussed here. Consider IBM machines along with IBM compatibles as you shop, but make your decision on the basis of features, support, warranties, service, and cost/price.

Examining Warranties

Be sure to carefully investigate the dealer's guarantee and the equipment manufacturer's warranty before signing on the dotted line, regardless of where you buy your system. If your computer isn't working, who fixes it? This question takes on an extra significance if you're buying from a mailorder firm. If you order by mail, by all means investigate the warranty with special care.

Increasingly, you can find stores and especially mailorder firms that will refund the full price of a computer system if you return it in 30 days, no questions asked. If you can find a firm that will give you these terms, you're protected in the unlikely event you get stuck with a computer that doesn't run well and doesn't meet your needs.

Beware of 90-day warranties; they're all too common. Hold out, if possible, for a 1-year warranty, at the minimum, on all the equipment you buy. And 5-year CPU warranties are beginning to appear.

In some cases, you may be invited to purchase an extended warranty, and it isn't a bad idea. The average cost of a disk drive repair is $250. So a $100 to $200 expenditure for an extended 1-year warranty is worth considering.

Performing Setup Tasks

If you buy your computer locally, you're in luck—you probably can get the dealer to deliver it and set it up for you. This procedure should involve at least the following:

* Formatting the hard disk.

- Installing the operating system on the hard disk so that the computer starts automatically.
- Connecting all peripherals (including mouse, modem, and printer) to the computer and making sure all of them are working correctly.
- Making sure the printer prints all the fonts that you've purchased (if any) or that come with the system.
- Running diagnostic tests to make sure the computer is working correctly.

If you've purchased a mailorder computer, get some help from a local computer whiz, if at all possible; the manuals provided with mailorder systems vary considerably in quality.

5

Setting It All Up

This chapter explores some typical business systems and then walks you through how to design and set up a sample single-user system.

Sample Configurations for Typical Small Business Computers

The following system configurations will give you an idea of the type of systems that are needed for specific businesses. These are intended as guides only. Each business is different and the software you select may have different hardware requirements.

Auto Repair Shop: Single-user, Point-of-Sale/Business Management System

Hardware

Computer   AT (80286 or 80386) or compatible computer
                   640KB RAM
                   40MB hard disk
                   1.44MB floppy disk drive
                   Keyboard
                   Monitor (monochrome or color)

Peripherals   Bar code reader or keypad
                   Cash drawer

                    Tape backup (optional)
                    Dot matrix (180cps, 80 column) or laser printer
                    Printer cables (as needed)
Software
                    Disk Operating System version 5.0
                    Auto repair shop software compatible with DOS 5.0
Supplies
Accessories   Battery backup (UPS)
                    Power surge protector
Other   Hardware and software support contract
                    Installation and training

Retail Store: Single-user, Point-of-Sale/Business Management System

Hardware
Computer   AT (80286 or 80386) or compatible computer
                    640KB RAM
                    40MB hard disk
                    1.44MB floppy disk drive
                    Keyboard
                    Monitor (monochrome or color)
Peripherals   Bar code reader or keypad
                    Cash drawer
                    Tape backup (optional)
                    Dot matrix (180cps, 80 column) or laser printer
                    40-column receipt printer
                    Printer cables (as needed)
Software
                    Disk Operating System ver. 5.0
                    Retail store software compatible with DOS 5.0
Supplies
Accessories   Battery backup (UPS)
                    Power surge protector
Other   Hardware and software support contract
                    Installation and training

Liquor Store: Multiuser Point-of-Sale/Business Management System

Hardware
Computer   Three stations—2 at the front sales counter, 1 station
                    in the manager's office

Sales counter (2)
AT (80286, 80386, 80486) or compatible computer
4MB RAM
100MB hard disk
1.44MB floppy disk drive
Keyboard
Monitor (monochrome or color)

Manager's office (1)(file server)
AT (80286, 80386, 80486) or compatible computer
4MB RAM
100MB hard disk
1.44MB floppy disk drive
Keyboard
Monitor (monochrome or color)

Peripherals
In-counter/handheld bar code scanners (2)
Cash drawers (2)
Tape backup (1) (optional)
Dot-matrix (180cps, 80 column) or laser printer (re-
  ports) (1)
40-column receipt printers (2)
Printer cables (as needed)

Network
(Multiuser)
Equipment
Network hub (1)
Network cards (3)
Network cables (as needed)

Software

Disk Operating System version 5.0
Multiuser (network) liquor store software compatible
  with DOS 5.0

Supplies
Accessories
Battery backups (UPS) (3)
Power surge protectors (3)

Other
Hardware and software support contract
Installation and training

Your Hypothetical System

Now we are going to assume you are a typical small business owner
unfamiliar with computers but knowing they are here to stay and you
must begin to use them if you are to remain competitive. You have read
all the foregoing material, done your homework, and have decided your

needs to be word processing, spreadsheet analysis, accounting, and communications (telephone and fax data transfers).

Your hardware and software solutions are as follows:

Item	*Cost*
Hardware	
386 clone computer running at 33 MHz	$2,900
8MB RAM (included with system)	0
14-inch color monitor (.28 dot pitch, 1024 by 768 resolution) Super VGA controller (included with system)	0
210MB fixed disk (included with system)	0
Floppy disk drives	
A: 3.5-inch, 1.44MB (included with system)	0
B: 5.25-inch, 1.2MB (included with system)	0
Enhanced (101-key) keyboard (included with system)	0
Ports (included with system)	0
2 serial	
1 parallel	
Serial mouse	80
Printers	
Hewlett-Packard HP LaserJet IIIP	1,200
Okidata 321 dot-matrix	400
Hayes compatible 1200/2400 baud (internal) modem	100
Frecom FAX96 with FAX96 1-Liner (internal)	260
Cables	
DB25, male-to-male, 6-foot (comp. to switch) (1)	25
DB25 to Centronix, male-to-male, 6-foot (switch to printers)	20
TOTAL HARDWARE	$4,985
Software	
DOS version 5.0 (included with system)	0
WordPerfect version 5.1 word processor	$270
Lotus 1-2-3 version 2.3 spreadsheet	350
dBASE IV revision 1.1 database management system	450
Quicken version 5.0 accounting system	50
Norton Utilities version 6.1 (utility system)	90

PCTools version 7.1 utility package	120
BitCom communications system (included with system)	0
Mouse software (included with mouse)	0
FAX96 fax software with 1-Liner (included with system)	0
TOTAL SOFTWARE	$1,330
TOTAL SYSTEM COST	$6,315

Preparing Your Staff

The change from a manual to a computerized system can be strenuous and stressful, but it can also be a very exciting time for you and your staff. Hopefully everyone will be anxious to get their hands on the new "toy." It is suggested that you let any interested employees use the system (with supervision, of course). The time to allow experimenting is before all the data has been entered and you start using the system to collect current business information or before "going live," to use computer jargon.

To implement your system and make the conversion and implementation process as smooth and as painless as possible, some of the following suggestions will help you get in the right "frame of mind." The balance will explain procedures that should be followed. Keep in mind that all computers and programs are different. It would be impossible to cover every step, so use the following as a guideline.

- Read your product user and installation manuals carefully—especially the "getting started" and installation sections.
- Recognize that computers are sturdier than you think. They will not blow up if you look at them the wrong way or press the wrong key, even though "blow up" and "crash" are common terms used to express that something unexpected happened when using the computer. Computers normally withstand heavy daily use. Nothing you are likely to do will damage or ruin the system short of hitting it with a mallet out of frustration. (Hey! We've all had those times with a computer.)
- Develop a positive attitude. Your staff will certainly pick up on your cues (especially negative ones), so make sure you're sending the right signals. You need patience, the desire to learn new skills, and the determination to learn new methods. In learning about com-

puters, you are going to be exposed to new vocabulary, new methods, and new ideas. Millions of businesses have already done it. You can too. Take pride in the fact that you're demonstrating a solid, progressive commitment toward your financial success. Don't expect to know how to do everything at once, even if you are the boss. Keep your goal in mind: a more efficient, more controllable, and more profitable business.

- Expect that some things will evolve differently than you planned. Unless you have already computerized another business, you probably only have a vague idea of what to expect. Computers can and do make your life easier over the long term. Getting computerized may, however, cause a few gray hairs. (I've been working with computers since 1965, and I'm mostly bald!)

- You will learn how well you have been running your business: what kinds of manual "systems" you have in place and how various people on your staff do things differently. Surprise! The computer wants things done more consistently. What kind of inconsistencies will you find? Different people on your staff may be giving discounts differently, they may be charging the wrong prices and/or giving incorrect information to customers. These differences will show up as you automate your business.

- Get the entire staff on board. This has been mentioned before, but it bears repeating. The first and most important thing to do is to prepare your staff. Be sure they understand and support the changes that will occur.

You will find that you are not alone in your computer fears. To your employees, it can represent a new way of doing things that they may find difficult to understand. Reassure them by communicating that your real objectives are to:

- Provide better service to customers.
- Obtain more productivity, allowing the business to compete more effectively.

Also stress that computerization is a long-term, gradual process. It is not something you are going to impose on staff and expect them to instantly understand. Set realistic expectations—nobody needs to become a computer whiz overnight; they should just give it their best shot.

- Designate someone as the computer "expert" besides yourself. It is important that you do not become a slave to the new computer system. Even if you spend 12 hours a day at your business, you still have other matters to attend to. The computer expert can attend training classes or read up on the system. That person should know it as well as you. Don't worry about selecting an expert. Someone will very likely want to learn all about the computer. Every business has at least one computer enthusiast. The new expert will probably enjoy the assignment. His or her responsibilities could include:

o Entering data or supervising its entry

o Answering questions when you're unavailable

o Backing up the system regularly

o Training other employees to use the system

- Attend training sessions. If your dealer offers training, take advantage of it. At the very least, you and your expert should attend. Your dealer may also offer additional free training sessions. You should have as many employees as possible trained by the dealer. This will ensure accurate and consistent training and free up some of your time.

Prepare Your Work Space

Following are some more tips, these geared toward ensuring that your place of business is ready for the computer installation:

- Read the manual(s) and follow instructions. If the program calls for specific information, make sure you enter it. Don't think you can avoid following the rules. You may soon find yourself redoing work. If there is a question, call the support line to your dealer or the manufacturer of the item you're having trouble with, be it hardware or software.

- Organize work areas. Check the counters, desks, and any other areas to see that the systems will fit comfortably. If you have purchased printers, external modems, cash drawers, bar code readers, or scanners, be sure you have made room for them. Plan exactly where each part of the system will be placed. Keep in mind you probably will want the cash drawer to be mounted somewhere under the counter. Never place a cash drawer or printer directly above or below the hard disk. The hard disk is the most fragile part of the system. The vibrations of a printer or the slamming of the cash drawer can have a damaging effect.

- If any components need to be installed in countertops, check with the dealer to see who is responsible for the cutting, drilling, running cables, and so on. If you are installing a multiuser system (local area network), the dealer will be running cable between the machines; plan where and how you would like the cable to be placed.

- Have a clean electric power line available to dedicate to the system. Make sure you do not have appliances that draw a lot of electricity on the same line as the computer, causing brownouts (refrigerators, air conditioners, compactors, diagnostic machines, copiers, and so on). If there are other machines on the same circuit, you must install electrical lines that are on separate circuits. These are known as "dedicated" power lines.

- Organize your work. Each item you intend to enter will be added to the system for later use. Try to line up the entry of data so that it will be keyed in an organized, trackable manner. This care will avoid double entry of data and other mistakes. Refer to your system software documentation to see how your work should be organized. If you do this beforehand it will save time later.

- Enter your data for test and training purposes. Once the system is installed, begin entering your data. Don't start relying on the system for productive output. Until a few months have gone by, and everyone can accurately operate the computer, it is futile to attempt to maintain reliable, current data. Employees will make mistakes. Be sure to save (record on disk) your data at regular intervals throughout the day while you are entering it. If anything should happen to the system, your work will be saved. Keep multiple sets of full backups (at least three) in case one gets damaged.

- Start using the system for your initial or primary purpose. Once you are entering "live data," you will be gathering the data you need. Learning to enter data is the hardest part of the process; from this, everything else will follow. When you start entering data, your system or at least the newly entered data should be backed up after each day (depending on your operation and the quantity and importance of the data). This is the best time to start good habits. Backups should be done on three separate sets of diskettes (or tapes, if you have a tape backup system installed); use a different set each day. This is an extra precaution but it is well worth the effort. One set should be kept in a remote location, such as your home, in case of damage to the facility (water, fire, and so on).

  Also review any program-generated reports. Do they look accurate? Spot-checking these reports is a good way to decide whether everyone is using the system correctly.

- Don't throw away any of your manual systems. This is a very common mistake. Once the computer arrives, commonly all manual records fall by the wayside. It will take a while for the system to produce accurate, complete records. One way to be sure the system is operating properly is to run the manual and computer systems in parallel for a while and compare the records from both.

- Relax, don't worry, and enjoy! Don't expect the entire business to be computerized overnight. You should expect to computerize aspects of your company in small doses. It normally takes 60 to 90 days to fully implement the first application of a new computer system. Hopefully you are approaching this with a good grasp of what you have to do. There is no magic wand that any one can wave and magically computerize your business. Experiencing frustration during the first few months is normal. Gradually everything will speed up.

As you feel more and more comfortable, try all the features of the application. Once you have them mastered, no doubt you will be ready to start adding to your system.

The Installation

Now, with all the foregoing information to guide you and your staff's approach to this computerization task, you are ready to install the hardware.

Starting the Installation: Having What You Need

You have opened all the boxes and taken out all the various parts and cables and everything seems to be there.

But wait! Remember, you were told earlier that printers normally did not come with data cables for connection to the computer. Better check. Sure enough, they're not there. So now here's another trip back to the dealer to purchase the proper cable—and remember, you have two printers, so you must purchase two cables. Because you're going to install them both on parallel ports, the cables will have the same connectors on their comparable ends but each end is different. One end is a DB-25 male (pins showing) connector. The other is a Centronix parallel connector—also male (see Figure 5-1).

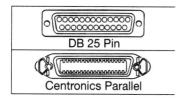

FIGURE 5-1 Parallel printer cable connectors

These cables come in lengths of 3, 6, 10, 12, 15, and 25 feet. It is not recommended that you make the cable longer than 15 feet for a parallel connection, because it takes power to send a signal down a length of wire and 15 feet is the practical maximum driving distance of most parallel printer driver circuits. Sure, sometimes with all conditions just right the printer can work well with longer distances, but why risk it? To go greater distances you will have to purchase and install a different cabling scheme along with circuit assemblies called *parallel line amplifiers*.

Continuing to Install Your Hardware

Recall that before your side trip to purchase more cables, you had taken all the items from their boxes and checked each box's contents with its packing list—all items are there. So, armed with the cables as well, you're prepared for the setup.

First, place the computer, monitor, and keyboard on a desk or countertop that is clear of all papers and other items you do not want damaged.

The system you purchased may or may not look like the one illustrated in Figure 5-2, but we're going to assume it does and work accordingly—all computers have power switches and cable connectors and that's what you're really interested in.

As you can see, your system consists of a monitor, central processing unit (CPU), keyboard (Enhanced type, with 101 keys), mouse, and printers (laser and dot-matrix).

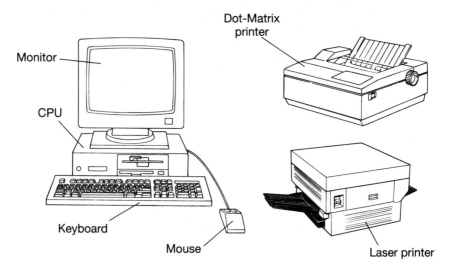

FIGURE 5-2   Your system—Monitor, CPU, keyboard, mouse, and printers

Let's continue the installation process by giving the CPU a good lookover. The front of the CPU (Figure 5-3) has a turbo switch (press button); a reset switch that, when pressed, causes the computer to restart as though you had turned the power off and back on (don't press it unless you have no data to save and you have exited your program properly or your computer is "locked-up" and you have no choice); and a keylock (to lock the power on or off—your choice).

Also, there are openings for 3.5-inch and 5.25-inch floppy diskettes. These drives are known, from left to right or top to bottom, as drives A and B. They have appropriate indicator lights and a diskette release button (3.5-inch drive) or lever (5.25-inch drive). It is recommended the 3.5-inch drive be installed as drive A. The hard disk (drive C) is not visible. Remember, it is mounted internally in the CPU. However, there are three indicator lights at the upper left of the front panel. One of these lights indicates when the hard disk is active (erratic blinking when the program is running and the disk is being accessed); the others indicate power on/off and whether the computer is operating at its highest (turbo) speed (which can be hardware [switch] or software selectable).

The back of the CPU, shown in Figure 5-4, has the power switch, a universal AC input power connector (male), a monitor power daisy-chain connector (female), a line voltage selection switch (110 volts or 220 volts), a fan opening with protective grill, a keyboard connector, and the appropriate peripheral connectors: the monitor connector, printer connectors (you ordered 2 printers, so you should have two connectors labeled LPT1 and LPT2), and serial connectors labeled COM1 and COM2 and a game connector. (Remember, these connectors are referred to as "ports.")

The back of this computer also has five cover mounting screws. These are important because if your computer should begin to act up,

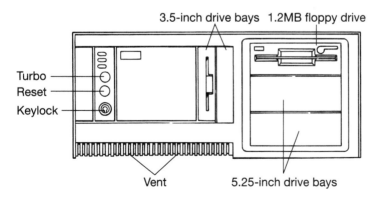

FIGURE 5-3   Front panel of a typical CPU

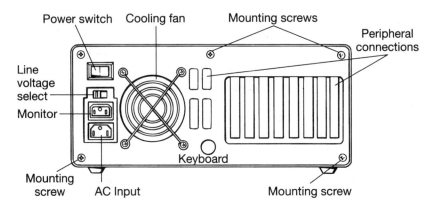

FIGURE 5-4   Back panel of a typical CPU

there is a good possibility that it is merely an internal cable or circuit card connection problem and that simply turning off the power, removing the cover, and securely reseating the cables and cards in their appropriate connectors will cure the problem. So be sure to locate these cover mounting screws on your computer.

Connecting the Monitor

Now locate the power switch on the monitor. Normally it is located at the front of the unit and is a press button. But it can be located practically anywhere on the unit. In our case we'll locate it at the front lower right corner of the screen. Other controls for brightness and contrast (similar to a TV) are located on the monitor. In some cases other display controls are located at the back of the unit or in a covered compartment at the top or back of the unit. Locate these controls with the use of the manufacturer's manual that should accompany the unit (if you didn't get a manual, go back to the dealer and get one). At the back of the monitor, shown in Figure 5-5, is a universal power connector and a signal cable with a 15-pin D-sub male (pins showing) plug.

Place the monitor close to (usually on top of) the CPU and connect its signal cable to the appropriate connector at the back of the CPU. This should not be difficult, because there is normally only one 15-pin jack (female connector) that will mate with the plug. Secure it with the mounting screws of the plug.

Connecting the Keyboard

Now let's look at the keyboard, which is shown in Figure 5-6. This Enhanced model has 101 keys, substantially more than the 84-key type that came with early PCs. The function ("F" keys) keys are located in a hor-

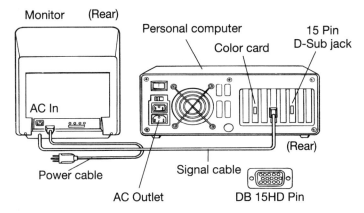

FIGURE 5-5 Connection between the monitor and CPU that takes a DB 15HD pin connector

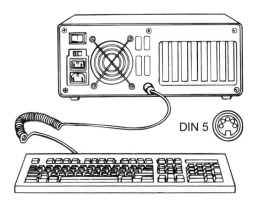

FIGURE 5-6 Connection between the keyboard and CPU that takes a DIN 5 connector

izontal row across the top of the keyboard, and the numeric keypad, cursor control (arrow) keys, and other control keys are located to the right of the main (alphabetic) keyboard. We will go into the special function and control keys in depth later. For now, locate the cable at the back of the keyboard and its connector (5-pin DIN male) plug and connect it to its mating connection at the back of the CPU.

Powering On the System
You are now ready to apply power to the system for its initial checkout. But first you must locate the power cords for the monitor and CPU. Also,

if you have purchased a surge suppressor, connect it to a convenient electrical wall outlet and connect the power cords to it. Then locate the universal power connector on the back of the CPU and make sure the line voltage select switch is proper for your input power (110/115 volts or 220 volts). Figure 5-7 illustrates this switch. (The normal U.S. setting is 110/115.) Now you can connect the power cords (jack) to the power receptacle (plug) at the back of the monitor and CPU. Be sure these are pressed in firmly as they have a tendency to be stiff.

At this time be sure there are no diskettes in the floppy drives.

Now is the moment of truth! If the dealer has done the "dealer prep" right, when you turn on the power to your system it should come up with the C> DOS prompt. If the prep was not performed properly, an error message of some sort will be displayed, and you will have to take appropriate action—probably calling the dealer support line.

Turn on the power of the monitor first and wait a few seconds. This gives the monitor a chance to warm up the display so you can see what's happening from the very first actions of the CPU.

Now, turn on the CPU power and watch the screen. Things will probably happen at a fairly rapid pace on the screen, but notice what you can and write it down so if anything seems wrong you can discuss it intelligently with the dealer support people. But, nothing went wrong! The system went through its "boot routine" (remember ROM) and came up beautifully, finally displaying the C> prompt as it should.

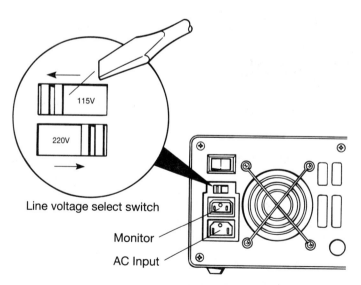

FIGURE 5-7 Universal power connector and line voltage select switch

Understanding the Keyboard

Before you start installing software and organizing files on your hard disk, you should understand a bit more about the function and control keys on your keyboard. So let's learn about your keyboard first.

Generally, the typewriter area of all keyboards conforms to the industry-standard, 101-key layout shown in Figure 5-8. In the United States, this is what's known as the "QWERTY" layout (from the first six letter keys in the upper left area of the keyboard). All the white keys in the typewriter area are "typematic," repeating as long as you hold them down.

Note: If you are used to typing on a typewriter, you may have used a lowercase letter *L* or uppercase *I* for the number one. Similarly, you may have used an uppercase letter *O* for the number zero. Because the keyboard sends unique scan codes for each key on the keyboard, the above substitutions can create unpredictable results. *Always use numeric keys for one and zero.*

The noncharacter keys located in the typewriter area are described here.

Backspace   The Backspace key is used to delete characters. Pressing Backspace moves the cursor one position to the left, removing that character. The function of the Backspace key may vary slightly, depending on the software you're using.

Enter   The Enter key, either in the typewriter area or the numeric keypad area, normally works like a carriage return, moving the cursor to the start of a new line. It ends a line of text and positions the cursor at the beginning of the following line. The key also performs "Enter" functions, instructing the computer to perform a specific command or start a job. When working

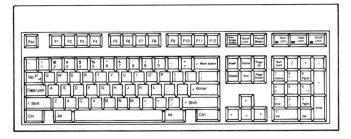

FIGURE 5-8 Typical Enhanced Keyboard layout

with a word processor program and typing text, Enter is normally pressed only at the end of a paragraph to terminate the paragraph and insert a blank line.

Shift
Use either of the two Shift keys to enter uppercase letters or to enter the symbol or character shown in the upper position of the keycap. In most application programs, a Shift key may be used together with the numeric keys to enter numbers when the numeric keypad is in cursor control mode.

Ctrl
The Ctrl (control) key is used with another key or key combination to perform a command or function. Instructions may be passed to WordStar files, for example, through Ctrl + *key* combinations.

Note: To activate a Ctrl + *key* command, press and hold down the Ctrl key first and then press the second key.

Function
There are 12 multipurpose function keys on an Enhanced keyboard, labeled F1 through F12, located across the top of the keyboard for easy access. (Some older keyboards only have F1 through F10 function keys.) The function keys are defined by the application program you are using.

Escape
The function of the Esc (escape) key varies among applications. It is often used to display menus (lists of available commands), to exit a function, or to cancel a command.

Print Scrn
The Print Scrn (print screen) key is a dual-function key. When this key is pressed alone, the data displayed on your monitor is sent to the printer via LPT1 (first parallel port) and printed (if the printer is turned on). Sometimes it is required that this key be pressed along with the Shift key to cause the screen display to be sent to the printer and printed.

An Alt + Print Scrn combination performs the System Request (Sys Rq) function. This function is defined in your operating system or application program manual.

Scroll Lock
The function of the Scroll Lock key varies among applications. Typically, when Scroll Lock is enabled, cursor key movement causes the text on the screen to move (scroll) behind the cursor while the cursor remains stationary. When Scroll Lock is disabled, the

cursor moves over the text while the text remains stationary.

When Scroll Lock is enabled, the Scroll Lock LED in the LED control panel is ON.

Pause   The Pause key is a dual-function key. Pressing the Pause key stops screen listings so that you can read the screen. Pressing any key will resume the listing.

A Ctrl+Pause combination performs the Break function. Break typically is used to cancel the current operation and terminate the program.

Alt   The Alt (alternate) key can be used in combination with other keys to obtain different characters or key functions. For example, you can use Alt with certain letter keys to enter BASIC statement keywords quickly. Some application programs use Alt-key combinations. Lotus 1-2-3 uses the Alt key to trigger macro commands. (Refer to the Lotus 1-2-3 manual for an explanation of macro commands.)

Caps Lock   The Caps Lock key enables and disables the capital letters function. The Caps Lock LED in the LED control panel indicates whether the Caps Lock function is active or inactive.

The Caps Lock function only affects the alphabetic keys. Use a Shift key to type a symbol shown on the upper portion of other keys.

Tab   The Tab key moves the cursor to the right, to the next tab stop. In some applications, such as DOS, a Shift+Tab moves the cursor left, to the previous tab setting. Some programs also use this Shift+Tab combination to move from one field to another and to reverse the cursor movement back through fields.

Num Lock   The Num Lock key changes the operational mode of the numerical keypad from numerical mode to cursor control mode. The Num Lock LED indicates whether the keypad is in numbers mode (LED is ON) or in cursor control mode (LED is OFF).

Keypad Keys The /, *, -, +, and Enter keys of the keypad are active in numerical mode. In most programs, they remain active even when Num Lock is OFF (keypad in cursor control mode).

Note: When the Num Lock LED is OFF and the numeric keypad is in cursor control mode, numbers can still be entered by pressing the Shift key with the desired number.

Also, most programs enable you to use the cursor keys while the numeric keypad is in numbers mode, by pressing Shift with the desired key.

When the numeric keypad is in cursor control mode, it performs the cursor movement, document control, and editing functions marked on the keycaps.

Connecting the Peripherals

We now have the computer powered up and we know a little about the keyboard key functions, so we're ready to set up our peripherals.

Printers

Let's connect the two printers—the dot-matrix and the laser printers we purchased. This will require switching the computer power off, locating and installing the printer cables you had to go back to the dealer to purchase, connecting the power cables to the printers, and loading the printers with appropriate paper.

The printer signal connectors at the back of the computer are 25-pin DB type female connectors, shown in Figure 5-9. One should be labeled LPT1, the other, LPT2. Let's install the laser printer on LPT1 and the dot-matrix on LPT2. This choice is purely arbitrary.

With the connections made and the printers' power turned on, switch the computer power on.

While the computer is "booting" up you will probably see the indicator lights on the printers blink and the dot-matrix printer will "hiccough." These are all good signs that the computer's printer circuitry is working.

Once the monitor is displaying the C> prompt, locate the Print Scrn key on the keyboard and press it. The laser printer's "form feed" light should come on and stay on. Press the "on-line" and form feed buttons on the laser printer in that sequence, then the on-line button

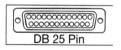

FIGURE 5-9   Computer/printer parallel connector

once more. The printer should print a page showing all that is displayed on the screen of the monitor. If not, recheck all your printer connections and try again. If this still doesn't work, call your dealer support line for assistance.

But let's say that everything works like it should. You now have your system's hardware completely installed and you are ready to install the software.

The Mouse

Oops! Forgot one more item—the mouse. A computer mouse is what is known as a "pointing device." With proper software installed and an application program that can use it, such as WordPerfect 5.1, Windows 3.0 and above, and most of the computer-aided design (CAD) programs, you can easily move from one function to another within a program. That increases the productivity of your system. Windows 3.1 makes very effective use of the mouse.

To do the hardware installation for the mouse, you merely locate the COM1 connector on the back of your computer and connect the mouse's connector with the appropriate mating connector. The mouse comes with a 9-pin DB female connector attached to its cable (molded plug) and a 9-pin DB to 25-pin DB connector adapter.

The mating connector on the computer is usually a 9-pin DB male connector but can be a 25-pin DB male connector. Figure 5-10 shows both types.

For your information, the COM2 connector is usually a 25-pin DB male connector but can be a 9-pin DB male connector. No industry standard has been established for this port.

Installing the "Add-ons"

Normally, when you receive your system from the dealers and you have ordered all the items you need, the dealer will install them for you before

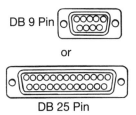

DB 9 Pin

or

DB 25 Pin

FIGURE 5-10   Computer COM1 Mouse Connector

delivery. But in this case let's say the add-ons were an afterthought and it is your responsibility to install these circuit boards.

When you install "add-on" circuit boards such as the extra printer and modem ports and the fax board, it will be necessary to remove the CPU cover to gain access to the expansion slots (connectors) of the motherboard (primary circuit board). To do this you must turn off the power to the CPU and remove the five cover retaining screws at the back of the CPU housing. Ensure that the keylock is in the unlocked position. Remove the key. Then, in some cases, slide the cover forward a few inches and lift straight up, as shown in Figure 5-11. For some other cases, you slide the cover forward or lift it straight up. Check that the cover does not catch on any ribbon cables or wires in the chassis. Also, sometimes these covers are a little stubborn when they're new, so be persistent.

The motherboard contains eight expansion slots, described here and shown in Figure 5-12.

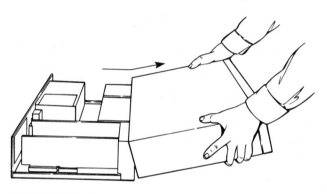

FIGURE 5-11   Removing the CPU cover

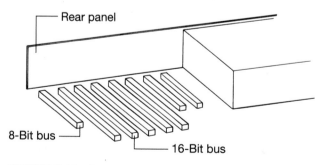

FIGURE 5-12   Expansion slots (add-on circuit board connectors)

- Three 8-bit slots for use exclusively by PC/XT-compatible boards.
- Five 16-bit slots for use by both AT-compatible and PC-compatible boards.

The 8-bit slots can accept any expansion board that works in a PC or AT, including drop cards. *Drop cards* are circuit boards that gain extra surface area by dropping down immediately after the 8-bit connector. The drop cards are not compatible with the 16-bit slots, because the longer 16-bit slots allow the dropped portion of the drop card to be inserted, thus causing potential shorting of the circuitry on the dropped portion of the card.

In addition to the 16-bit PC/AT board, the 16-bit slots will also accept 8-bit PC/AT-compatible boards.

Any expansion board is sensitive to electrostatic discharge (ESD) and always requires careful handling. The precautions included in the following instructions will help ensure that the boards are installed without being damaged. The following general procedures can be used to install any board.

1. Once the CPU cover is removed, select the slot in which to install the circuit board. (Refer to the board's documentation to determine whether it requires an 8-bit or 16-bit slot.
2. Remove the rear slot cover from the expansion slot by unfastening the retaining screw at its top. Figure 5-13 shows how the cover is lifted off.

Caution: ————————————————————————

Before you remove the board from its protective wrapper, it is strongly recommended that you maintain body contact with the frame of the CPU chassis to avoid generating an electrostatic discharge through the integrated circuits of the board. This can be done by merely touching an unpainted portion of the chassis.

3. Remove the board from its wrapper, holding the board by the edges only. Avoid touching the board elements and the gold connectors, shown in Figure 5-14. Do not lay the board on any ungrounded surface. The flat surface of the top of the CPU power supply is a good surface on which to temporarily lay the board.
4. Record the board's serial number in an equipment log, which can be merely a notebook that contains the definition of the system as purchased and room for notes of any changes made to the system as well as any peculiar operation of the hardware and/or software.

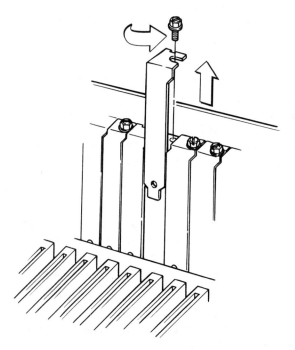

FIGURE 5-13   Removing the rear slot cover

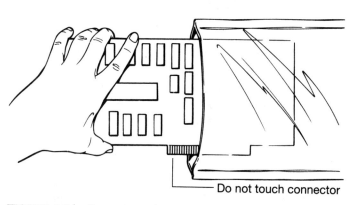

Do not touch connector

FIGURE 5-14   Removing a board from its wrapper

5. Make any necessary jumper or switch settings indicated by the documentation of the board. The modem board and the fax board are both communications boards and will use COM2 and COM3 ports, respectively, because the mouse is using COM1. Set the port (COM)

and interrupt (IRQ) jumpers accordingly and continue with the installation. (It is recommended you get the assistance of your dealer's support people to do these settings.)

6. Insert the board's connectors into the motherboard expansion slot by firmly pressing the board into the slot while holding the board by its top edge or upper corners. Figure 5-15 shows this seating process.

7. The card's retaining bracket fits into the space that was previously occupied by the expansion slot cover. Align the screw slot in the board's retaining bracket with the screw hole in the expansion slot frame.

8. Insert the screw as shown in Figure 5-16, making certain that the bracket screw slot is pushed all the way against the screw before tightening. If this is not done, the expansion (add-on) board bracket may interfere with an adjacent bracket.

9. Repeat the procedure for each add-on board to be installed in the system.

10. When you have finished installing add-on boards, check that no tools or loose parts have been inadvertently left in the interior of the chassis and that all interior cables are properly connected and secure. Ensure that all expansion boards are firmly seated in their respective slots.

11. Carefully fold or coil the ribbon cables and press them down into the area between the power supply and the peripheral device bays. The cables should not project above the level of the power supply.

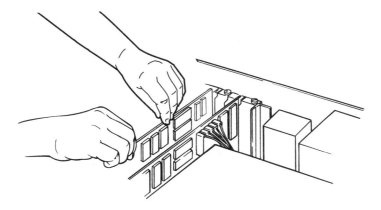

FIGURE 5-15   Seating the board

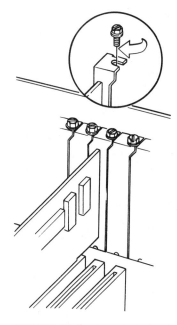

FIGURE 5-16 Securing the add-on board bracket

12. Position the cover even with the front of the chassis. Carefully slide the cover a short distance under the rail on the frame, then lift it up against the rail and slide it onto the chassis to approximately midpoint.

13. Check that the ribbon cables are clear as you continue sliding the cover over the chassis. As the rear of the cover approaches the rear of the chassis vertical plate, it may be necessary to slightly lift up the cover at the rear to easily clear the plate and EMI gasket.

14. With the cover all the way on, check that the cover screw holes line up with the mating holes in the chassis.

15. Replace the five cover retaining screws.

Installing the Applications Software

Now, with all the circuit boards installed, let's continue with the installation of the software. Remember, your dealer installed the operating system (MS-DOS version 5.0). That's why your system "booted" up and you got the C> prompt when you first powered on the machine. But the operating system only consists of three files in the "root" directory—two hidden files and the COMMAND.COM file. There are a lot more files to be stored in your computer before it becomes the "system" you want.

Let's continue the learning process to the concept of DOS (your computer's disk operating system) and "files," "directories," "subdirectories," and the "root directory."

The Backup Routine
The following is a backup routine that has proven successful.

1. Start with a full backup. This first backup may take 1, 2, or more diskettes. Label each of these diskettes backup "A." The first diskette will be "A-1," the next will be "A-2," and so on.
2. The next day when you back up, use a new set of diskettes. This will be set "B."
3. The day after, you will use set "C."
4. On the fourth day, you will use set "A" again.
5. At the end of the month you take set "A" home, put them in the closet, and forget about them. Do not throw them out! Buy a new set of diskettes and label them "D." At the end of the next month you take home set "B" and start set "E," and so on.

Month 1

Day of Week	Monday	Tuesday	Wednesday	Thursday	Friday	Monday
Backup Set	A	B	C	·	Reuse A	Reuse B Reuse C

Month 2—Permanently store set A

Day of Week	Monday	Tuesday	Wednesday	Thursday	Friday	Monday
Backup Set	D (new)	B	C		Reuse D	Reuse B Reuse C

Month 3—Permanently store set B
(Continue process starting with new set E)

Why Are Backups So Important?
How does the data really get damaged? Data can get damaged many ways. Here are just a few:

- The power goes off in the middle of the day and any data in temporary storage (RAM) is lost.
- Someone is moving past the computer carrying a big box and bumps the computer. The hard disk "head" (like the needle on a record player) bounces and damages the disk, and a hundred customers' names are deleted.
- You are out on business for the morning. There is low power in the area because lines are down. You thought your staff would know enough to shut the computer down, but they are busy with other

activities, perhaps negotiating vacation days with each other. The new clerk who is taking care of the 12 customers on-line isn't familiar enough with the computer system to know that it's malfunctioning, and she or he is so busy that the power brownout is unnoticed until it's too late. Damage!

- You are out of the office and the assistant managers decide to see whether they can figure out your password. So they attempt to get into the option to delete old customer records. After 350 attempts they hit on your password (you used your spouse's birthday) and they wind up deleting all customers' records since 1945. No one has the courage to own up to this for a week, until you try to look up something that you know you entered and find it missing.

- You come in to the store one fine morning to see that you had a nocturnal visitor. He (or she) has absconded with your computer AND the nearby box of diskettes (containing backups A, B, and C).

- One day your computer breaks down, only six months after you bought it. "We'll have to replace your hard drive," the repairperson says, "but don't worry, it's under warranty! It won't cost you a dime." And it doesn't, but it takes you two months of evenings to reenter all the data.

- You have a power blackout—sudden and unexpected. You never bought that battery backup (UPS), because you just couldn't justify spending $400 on a box with blinking lights. When the power comes back on, you're panicked! Is the data okay? You bring up your list of customers and breath a sigh of relief. The relief lasts until the end of the month, as you start sending out your past due notices, when you suddenly find that all the customer records between M and P are missing! Of course you've been backing up every day, so that you've already overwritten your good backups with your bad data! If only you had made that extra set and taken it home. . . .

It is said that the average hard disk has over $50,000 worth of data on it. Believe it and protect it.

Possible Problems with Installed Software

Two common problems testify to the wisdom of backing up your hard disk: computer viruses and full hard disks.

Viruses

Yes, you read right! Just like humans, computers catch viruses from one another. *Viruses* are programs written (by questionable individuals) to destroy programs or create problems with data stored on a hard disk and, in some cases, the hard disk itself. They cause a computer to do strange, illogical things, and may eventually cause the system to completely shut down.

Viruses are spread from computer to computer via floppy diskettes and communication lines to bulletin boards. That means if your friend's computer has a virus and he or she copies a program to give to you, your machine will become infected. Viruses are also found in public domain software and on rare occasions, you may receive an infected diskette direct from the manufacturer. The main cause, however, is pirated software. This is one more good reason not to share software with your friends and colleagues.

The major problem with viruses is that they can go undetected for a very long time and then simply shut down the system. (Many times viruses have delayed activation on significant dates like April 1 or Friday the 13th.) When this happens, your backups may not even be helpful if some of the information you've backed up is destroyed. There are several good virus detection software programs available. *Before* you suspect your system has a virus, purchase such a program and run it occasionally.

Full Hard Disk
All good things must come to an end. Sooner or later you will have accumulated so much information on your hard disk that it will be full. This may happen in one year, two years, six months, or the day after your neighbor's kid puts his games on your computer. Sometimes, when you fill up a hard disk to its full capacity, you will damage a file. When that happens, if you have backed up you have nothing to worry about. Just call your local computer store and have a larger hard disk installed.

6

Your Disk Operating System

If your dealer performed the dealer prep properly, the disk operating system (DOS) has already been installed on your system. You can tell whether DOS is present when you apply power; the system should go through its "self-test" and ultimately the DOS prompt, C:\>, as the last characters displayed if the system was properly installed. The screen also shows the cursor blinking, waiting for you to type in a command.

But what is DOS? How can you make it work for you? To understand the workings and benefits of DOS, you must first understand files and file naming rules; and directories, subdirectories, and commands and how to use them. These are not difficult if you merely want to use the basics. Basic operations are all that are needed at this point, because you're not interested in becoming a programmer, you merely want to get your applications to run so you can be more productive. So let's learn a little about DOS before we start installing the application software for your system.

How DOS Operates

DOS controls the movement of information within the computer. You can think of DOS as the police officer who directs traffic at a busy intersection. In much the same way, DOS controls the way the computer uses applications programs.

DOS makes it easy for you to use applications and create and manage directories, subdirectories, and files (a memo or letter is a file to DOS) on your computer. DOS also enables you to use devices such as printers, disk drives, and hard disks with the computer.

DOS Files and How They Are Stored

Files

A *file* is any stored document or program. A memo, or a letter, or a chapter in a book can be a file. Usually, you'll want to group your data meaningfully in each file, that is, storing a single report as a file, or a month's transactions in your spreadsheet as one file.

Directories

A *directory* is a reference on disk of where a group of related files are stored. This group of files can be a specific program (like dBASE IV) and its related data (sales databases, expense records, or customer histories). Or a directory can reference a group of letters or memos. Normally, a directory consists of *related* information (data) you store on a diskette or a fixed disk. You can make this comparison to help understand the concept of files and directories:

- A file is like a manila folder of individual sheets of paper.
- A directory is like a file cabinet drawer that holds many folders.
- A hard disk or diskette is like an entire file cabinet that contains several file cabinet drawers.

Subdirectories

A *subdirectory* is yet another level of organization for your information. To carry on our file cabinet example,

- A subdirectory is like a divider in the file cabinet drawer (directory).

The subdirectory, too, is a recorded reference to a group of stored files usually directly related to (linked to) a directory.

Each file, subdirectory, and directory must have a unique name, just like the name on the tab of a file folder. When you want DOS to find a file, you give DOS the drive designation (A, B, C, and so on), the directory name, the subdirectory name, and the filename. These "names" are used so that DOS can find the specific information that you need when you request it. In other words, they provide a "path" for DOS to follow to the requested file. And, in fact, this process of giving DOS the directions to a particular file is referred to as "the path."

File Structure in DOS

You can store any combination of files on a diskette or a hard disk. Each file within a directory must have a unique name from all others in that directory, but you can use the same filename in different diskettes or different directories. Each directory must have a unique or different name. Subdirectories of different directories can have the same names.

DOS looks at directories, subdirectories, and files as though they all are merely files and applies the same rules of construction and order to them all.

Filenames

A file's name is made up of a filename and an optional extension (suffix) separated with a period (.). For example:

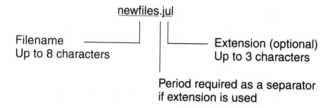

In DOS, filenames contain from one to eight characters. When you type a filename, DOS checks for invalid characters. The following characters are invalid in filenames:

$$. \; " \; / \; \backslash \; [\;] \; : \; | \; (\text{space}) \; < \; > \; + \; = \; ; \; ,$$

Filename Extensions

A filename can be followed by an optional short name called an extension. An extension starts with a period and has 1, 2, or 3 characters. The extension follows immediately after the filename and period. The same characters that are invalid for filenames are also invalid for filename extensions.

Important:

If a filename is followed by an extension, you must use both parts to tell DOS about that file.

A good name for a file is a meaningful one that will help you remember what kind of information is in the file, and perhaps whether it's a file that contains a program or data. For example, ADDRLIST.BAS is a good name for a BASIC (a computer programming language) program file that prints an address list.

In a business environment it is good to establish a filenaming protocol that all people of the business use. This makes it easier for all employees to find a file, whether it is on their own diskette or someone else's.

File Specifications

To locate a file, in addition to the filename and extension, DOS must know which drive, directory, and subdirectory (if any) to search. The things that DOS must know—the drive letter, the directory name, the subdirectory name, filename, and the extension—are called a *file specification* and/or *path*. For example,

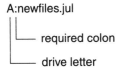

A:newfiles.jul

└── required colon

└── drive letter

The drive letter and the colon are called the *drive specifier*. The drive letter tells DOS on which disk drive the file is located. You always need to type the colon (:) after the drive letter as a separator. If the drive, directory, or subdirectory is not given, DOS assumes the current drive, directory, or subdirectory. In other words, DOS assumes where you currently are in the system is where all desired files are.

The filename and extension immediately follow the drive specifier. Do not put any spaces between the three parts.

In this example, the file newfiles.jul would be located in the "root," or first directory, because no other directory is indicated.

Root Directory

The root directory is the first directory on a disk and is unnamed. From the root directory all other directories are formed. You cannot have more than 112 files and/or subdirectories in the root directory of a floppy diskette, or 512 in the root directory of a hard disk. If these amounts are approached, the system will display an error condition telling you the disk is full, even though there is still lots of room on the disk. Also, you may experience system "lockup" or file damage.

So be careful to keep the root directories clean of unnecessary data/program files and only keep needed DOS command files and subdirectory names in it. Again, DOS looks at directory/subdirectory names as though they are filenames.

When You First Need DOS

DOS must be available when you first load or start the system—in other words, when you turn on the power. Loading DOS means that a copy of internal DOS commands (the two hidden files and the COMMAND.COM file) are read from the DOS directory on your hard disk or a DOS diskette and placed in the computer's memory. This is also called "booting the system." DOS can only be "booted" from the A (diskette) or C (fixed/hard) drives.

Certain DOS commands are called *internal* commands because they are loaded in and stay in the computer's memory until you switch it off. Then you must reload DOS. Because internal commands are loaded in memory when the system is "booted," you do not need to keep DOS available on disk or diskette to use them.

The rest of the DOS commands are called *external* commands, because they are not read into the computer's memory when you load DOS. Because the commands are not loaded in memory, you need DOS in an accessible disk drive to use the external commands. Again, this drive can be either the A drive or the C (hard) drive. (In today's systems it is normally the C drive.)

Important DOS Commands

The following shows the internal and external commands that are covered in this section:

Internal Commands	*External Commands*
COPY	CHKDSK
DIR	COMP
CD	DISKCOPY
MD	DISKCOMP
RD	FORMAT
ERASE	
MEM	
RENAME	
TYPE	

DOS can be a bit scary when you first see the C> prompt. And when you look in the DOS manual and find more than 60 different DOS commands, it's enough to make you want to turn off your computer.

Don't worry. You can take care of nearly all your DOS needs with just the 14 commands we'll discuss in this chapter and a dozen or so optional *switches* (command modifiers).

With these DOS commands under your belt, you're about to become a DOS expert. (Now that's really scary!) The following is a full description of each of these commands and how you use them.

To give DOS a command:

1. Wait until you see the DOS prompt, C>.
2. Type the command and any other parts (modifiers) the command requires (for example, a drive specifier or a file specification).

   You can type commands in uppercase or lowercase letters (or a combination). For example, dir C: requests DOS to display all file names in the current directory of drive C.

Note:

The term *current directory* means the directory last entered. When the system is turned on it normally comes to rest in the root directory. So the root directory files will normally be shown when you enter the dir C: command.

Use a blank space (press the Spacebar) to separate the various parts of the command.

3. Press Enter when you have finished constructing the command.

If you use the DIR command, a file name or group of filenames would normally appear on your display screen such as

NEWFILES   JUL   1024   07-29-92   7:25 p

if data has been stored on the disk. Or an error message of no files found will be displayed if no data has been stored on the disk. (The numbers to the right of the filename indicate the size of the file and when it was last changed.)

Notice that the period (.) between the filename and extension does not appear on the screen, but you must use the period when you enter a filename and its extension.

Let's start the explanation and use of these 14 key commands, starting with the internal commands.

These explanations merely give examples of the use of these commands and may not include all possible uses and variations. The explanations given normally assume the hard disk system configuration that has been previously defined, with some side comments to alert you that other system configurations exist and require you to use the commands in a slightly different way. Many DOS commands can do several jobs. This is accomplished through the use of modifiers called *switches*. For complete explanations of each command and its switches, refer to your *DOS Reference Manual.*

COPY

Purpose
The COPY command duplicates one or more files between one disk or directory and another. If the path or filename is omitted for the target drive, COPY will default to the same path or filename that was designated on the source drive. If only the drive letter is specified on the target drive, COPY will default to the current directory. (If you try to copy a file to the same drive and directory using the same filename and extension, you get an error message that a file cannot be copied to itself.)

DOS helps you by giving you two wildcard characters, * and ?, that you can substitute for actual characters in a filename. Like wildcards in a poker game, the wildcard characters can represent any other character. They differ only in that ? can substitute for one character, whereas * can substitute for any number of characters.

Switch
/V verifies copied files.

Examples
COPY C:\WORD*.TXT A:

Requests all the files in the WORD directory of drive C with names that end in .TXT to be copied to the root directory of drive A.

COPY A:*.* B:

Requests all files on drive A be copied to drive B.

COPY C:MYFILE.DOC A:YOURFILE.DOC

Requests a single file on the hard drive, MYFILE.DOC, to be copied to the diskette in drive A under the new filename YOURFILE.DOC.

Description
You can use COPY to make a duplicate of one file instead of a whole diskette or directory.

You need:

- The hard disk or diskette that contains the file you want to copy—called the *source* disk or diskette.
- The hard disk or diskette that will contain the copy of the file when you are done—called the *target* disk or diskette.

If DOS has already been loaded, you do not need your DOS diskette for this procedure; COPY is an internal command. Also decide on the name for the copied file on the target diskette.

Finally, you can also use COPY to duplicate a file or group of files from one diskette to another even if you only have one floppy drive. To accomplish this process, your single floppy drive doubles as drives A and B. It's easier to remember which diskette to insert if you think "B is for backup." Insert the target (backup) diskette when the drive B message appears.

1. Make sure DOS is ready and C> is displayed.
2. Insert the source diskette in drive A.
3. Type the following: copy a:filename.ext b:
   Substitute the name of the file you want to copy for filename.ext.
4. Press Enter. This message is displayed:
   ```
   Insert diskette for drive B:
   and strike any key when ready
   ```
5. Remove the source diskette from drive A.
6. Insert the target diskette in drive A.
7. Press any key.
   Note: Depending on the amount of memory in your computer, you may have to switch the diskettes. You will be prompted which diskette to insert (source or target). Keep switching diskettes until this message is displayed:
   ```
   n File(s) copied
   A>
   n = number of files copied
   ```
8. Remove the copied diskette from drive A. Label and date it using a felt-tip pen. Using a soft-tipped pen to label or otherwise mark diskettes is good practice; 5.25-inch diskettes have soft covers, and ball-point pens can damage their recording surface. Also, *never* use a pencil. The graphite can flake off, get on the recording surface, and destroy data.

DIR (Directory)

Purpose
Displays a directory listing of files. If a filename isn't specified, DIR lists all files in the current directory. Like the COPY command, the DIR command recognizes wildcards designated with an asterisk (*).

Switches
/W provides wide display
/P pauses between screens—approximately every 24 lines
/S includes subdirectories of current directory
/ON sorts by name

/OD sorts by date

/O-S sorts by size, largest files first

Examples

DIR *.TXT

Displays all files in the current directory with .TXT extensions.

DIR C:\DOS*.*/W /P

Displays all files in DOS directory, in wide screen format, and pauses at each full screen.

DIR /ON

Displays files in the current directory sorted alphabetically by filename.

DIR MYFILE?.DOC

Displays all the files in the current directory or on the diskette that begin with the characters MYFILE and have one other character before the period, then the extension DOC. The command would tell DOS to list MYFILE1.DOC, MYFILE2.DOC, MYFILEN.DOC, and so on.

DIR C:\WORD\DOC*.* /O-S

Displays all files in the DOC subdirectory and sorts the list by size of the file, largest file first.

Description

Use the DIR command to find out what files are on a diskette or in a hard disk directory—perhaps because you need to find out how a particular filename is spelled, or because you cannot recall what's on a seldom-used diskette.

You need the diskette whose file directory you want to see.

1. Make sure the DOS prompt is displayed.

2. Insert the diskette that has the directory you want to list in drive A.

3. Type in any of the following commands to simply list an entire diskette's contents or the current directory:
   dir a: (for a listing of files on the first floppy drive).
   dir b: (to list the directory of drive B).
   dir c: (to list the current directory of your hard drive).

4. Press Enter. Remember: If the screen listing is moving too fast for you to read, you can use the Ctrl+S (control and S keys pressed simultaneously) function to stop and start the screen. Or use the /P switch with the command, right after the drive designation. You can also use the Print Scrn key to print what appears on the screen.

5. Watch the screen. The first message to appear shows the volume label of the diskette (if it has one), followed by the name of the directory being listed. Then the names of the files in that directory are listed.

The screen displays the filename, the extension, the size of the file (in bytes), and the date and time that information was last written in the file. One line is displayed for each file on the diskette.

After the files have been listed, DIR displays the total number of files and the space they use, plus a final line that tells you the amount of free space left on the diskette (in bytes).

After all the files are displayed, the DOS prompt is displayed.

CD (Change Directory)

Switches the current directory to another directory.

Example
```
CD C:\DOS\UTIL
```

Makes the UTIL subdirectory under the DOS directory the current directory.

```
CD\
```

Makes the root directory the current directory. If the drive is not designated, the current drive is used.

MD (Make Directory)

Creates a new directory or subdirectory. If the backslash is omitted before the path (the route DOS takes to find the file or directory), the subdirectory is placed in the current directory.

Examples
```
MD C:\WORD\MEMOS
```

Creates the MEMOS subdirectory under the WORD directory, which is a subdirectory of the ROOT directory.

```
MD MEMOS
```

Creates the MEMOS subdirectory to the current directory.

Remember:

The current directory is the directory or subdirectory DOS is currently operating in.

RD (Remove Directory)

Deletes a subdirectory. This command can't remove the root directory, the current subdirectory, or any subdirectory that contains files—the files must first be erased.

Examples
RD C:\WORD\MEMOS

Deletes the MEMOS subdirectory from the WORD directory.

RD MEMOS

Deletes the MEMOS subdirectory from the current directory.

ERASE

Erases one or more files. Like the COPY command, ERASE recognizes wildcards designated with an asterisk (*) or question mark (?).

Switch
/P Requests DOS to prompt before erasing.

Examples
ERASE C:\WORD\MEMO.TXT

Causes the MEMO.TXT file of the WORD directory to be erased. Because the full path is listed, you need not be using the WORD directory to erase this file—the current directory can be anywhere.

ERASE *.* /P

Causes all files in the current directory to be erased after pausing for your permission. This means that DOS asks you to confirm that you do want to erase each file before the file is actually erased.

Description
Use the ERASE command to remove files that you no longer need. You can use the wildcards ? and * to erase all files in a directory or subdirectory before you remove it with the RD command.

Erasing old files makes room for new information on a hard disk or diskette. It can eliminate a potential source of confusion, too—you are less likely to use an old version of a program or an old data file for processing.

Important:

Plan ahead and check your typing when you use ERASE. Once a file has been erased, it is difficult to get it back.

___

You need:

- The diskette containing the file that you want to erase.
- The exact path, filename(s), and extension of the file(s) (you can use DIR to get this information).

1. Make sure the DOS prompt is displayed.
2. Insert the diskette that has the file you want to erase in drive A or use CD command to switch to the directory that contains the file (this is not required, but it's easier to type the commands if your current directory contains the files you want to erase).
3. Type any of the following:
   erase a:*filename.ext*, substituting the name of the file you want to erase for *filename.ext*.
   erase b:*filename.ext* to erase a file in drive B, current directory.
   erase c:*filename.ext* to erase a file in drive C, current directory.
4. Press Enter.
   After the file is erased, the DOS prompt is displayed.

MEM (Memory)

Displays the amount of memory installed and available for programs. Our sample system includes 8M bytes of RAM, but most programs can run only in the first 640K bytes of RAM. The remaining memory is used as storage and a workspace area. When you are running some types of programs, such as Windows, the first 640K bytes of RAM can be very limiting. Also, remember that memory is RAM—a temporary storage area where programs operate. Permanent storage is provided by the disk system and is much larger than RAM (memory).

Switch
/PROGRAM Includes each program's name, location, size, and type.

Examples
MEM

Requests the amount of available memory be displayed.

MEM /PROGRAM

Requests the amount of available memory be displayed along with each program's name, location, size, and type.

RENAME

Changes the name of a file. The RENAME command enables you to alter any part or all of a file's name—its primary filename, its extension, or both. A file can be renamed within the same directory or diskette, or it can be copied to another diskette or subdirectory as it is renamed.

Examples

rename c:\docs\memos letters

Gives the file named MEMOS the new title LETTERS within the DOCS directory.

rename c:\docs\memos a:\letters

Gives the file MEMOS in the DOCS directory the name LETTERS on the A drive.

Description

You need:

- The diskette with the file that you want to rename.
- You also need to know its exact path, filename, and extension, if it has one. (Remember, you can use the DIR command to find out the filename and extension.)

1. Make sure the DOS prompt is displayed.
2. Insert the diskette that has the file you want to rename in drive A.
3. Type any of the following:
   rename a:*filename.ext filename.ext*, substituting the name of the file you want to rename for the first *filename.ext* and the new file name for the second *filename.ext*.
   rename b:*filename.ext filename.ext* to rename a file within drive B, current directory.
   rename c:*filename.ext newdir\filename.ext* to rename a file in drive C, current directory and place it in the new directory (substitute the actual name for *newdir*).
4. Press Enter.
   After the file is renamed, the DOS prompt is displayed.

TYPE

Displays what's in a file without loading the program you used to create it. The TYPE command enables you to "look into" a file from the DOS level; that is, TYPE displays the contents of a file whether it was created with spreadsheet, database, accounting, or word processing software—even if you don't have the program that was used to create the file. Text files are displayed in a legible format. Nontext files, such as program files, may not be legible, because characters that are neither alphabetic nor numeric are present.

Example
type c:word

Displays the contents of the file WORD.

Description
You need:

- The diskette that contains the file you want to display.
- You also need to know the exact path and name of the file you want to type (use DIR again).

1. Make sure the DOS prompt is displayed.
2. Insert the diskette that has the directory you want to list in drive A.
3. Type any of the following:
   type a:*filename.ext*, substituting the name of your file for *filename.ext*.
   type b:*filename.ext* to type a file in drive B, current directory.
   type c:*filename.ext* to type a file in drive C, current directory.
4. Press Enter.
   The contents of the file you specified are displayed on the screen.

Remember: _____

If the screen is moving too fast for you to read, you can use the Ctrl+S (Control and S keys pressed simultaneously) function to stop and start the screen. You can also use the "print screen" key to print what appears on the screen.

_____

5. After the file's contents are displayed, the DOS prompt is displayed.

Now that we've covered the "internal" commands of DOS, let's look at some of the "external" commands that help you use your computer effectively.

CHKDSK (Check Disk)

Checks the status of a disk.

Switches

/V Displays path and filename of each checked file and directory.
/F Corrects allocation errors if found.

Examples

CHKDSK C:\/F

Requests the root directory of the C drive be checked and allocation errors corrected.

CHKDSK C:\DOS/F

Requests the DOS directory of the C drive be checked and allocation errors corrected.

DISKCOPY

Makes an identical copy of a disk, automatically formatting your target disk, if necessary.

At first glance, COPYing all files on a diskette may appear to have the same purpose as DISKCOPY. It does, but only when copying to a diskette with no files on it.

With COPY, if files already exist on the target diskette, they will either be replaced (if files being copied have the same name) or left alone. This is because COPY goes through the original diskette, copying each file, one at a time. COPY does not disturb old files on the target diskette as long as their names aren't the same as files being copied.

DISKCOPY, however, makes an exact copy of the original diskette, wiping out all old files on the target diskette during the copying process.

Example

DISKCOPY A: A:

Causes the directories, subdirectories, and files on a source diskette in drive A to be copied to a target diskette in drive A.

Description

Use the DISKCOPY command to make a complete copy of an entire diskette on another diskette. Use the copy made for your day-to-day operations. Store the original in a safe place.

Note: The DISKCOPY command is used to make a duplicate of an entire diskette. The COPY command is used to copy one or more discrete files.

You need:

- The DOS diskette, or you should ensure that the current directory is the DOS directory with the DISKCOPY.COM file in it. (Use DIR for this.)
- The original diskette you want to copy—called the source diskette.
- The diskette that will become the copy—called the target diskette.

Warning:

If the *target* diskette contains information, the DISKCOPY command erases the information and replaces it with the information from the *source* diskette.

For a single floppy drive system:

You can remember which diskette to insert, if you remember "source = original" and "target = copy."

1. Make sure the current directory is the DOS directory and the DISK-COPY.COM file is in it. (Use the DIR and CD commands to check and ensure this.)
2. Type diskcopy a: a:.
3. Press Enter.
   This message is displayed:
   `Insert SOURCE diskette in drive A:`
   `Press any key when ready . . .`
4. Insert the source diskette in drive A.
5. Press any key.
   The A drive's in-use light comes on while the source diskette is read. Then this message is displayed:
   `Insert TARGET diskette in drive A:`
   `Press any key when ready . . .`
6. Remove the source diskette from drive A.
7. Insert the target diskette in drive A.
8. Press any key.
   Note: Depending on the amount of memory in your computer, you may have to switch the diskettes. You are prompted for which diskette to insert (source or target). Keep switching diskettes until this message is displayed:
   `Copy another diskette (Y/N)?`
9. Type either of the following:
   N to end the DISKCOPY command. Either the DOS prompt will be displayed or you will be asked to insert the diskette with

COMMAND.COM in drive A. Remove the copy. Label and date it using a felt-tip pen. Store the original diskette in a safe place. Insert the DOS diskette in drive A (unless DOS is on your hard drive) and press any key when ready. Note the DOS prompt A> is displayed, and the source diskette is copied.

Y to copy another diskette. Repeat the DISKCOPY procedure starting with step 6.

COMP (Compare)

Compares files to ensure that they are identical. Use the COMP command to compare two files to see whether they are identical. Usually you would use the COMP command after you use the COPY command to make sure the copy is identical to the original.

Example
```
comp c:memos a:memos
```

Compares the file MEMOS on drive C, current directory, with the file MEMOS on drive A, root directory.

You need:

- The DOS diskette or ensure that the current directory is the DOS directory with the COMP.COM file in it. (Use DIR for this.)
- The diskettes containing the files you want to compare.

For a single floppy drive system:

The source diskette is the first diskette and the target diskette is the second diskette.

1. Make sure the current directory is the DOS directory and the COMP.COM file is in it. (Use the DIR and CD commands to check and ensure this.)
2. Type comp.
3. Press Enter.
   This message is displayed:
   ```
   Enter primary file name
   ```
4. Insert the source diskette in drive A.
5. Type: a:*filename.ext*, substituting your filename with extension, if any, for *filename.ext*.
6. Press Enter.
   This message is displayed:
   ```
   Enter 2nd file name or drive identification
   ```

7. Type b:*filename.ext*, substituting your second filename with extension for *filename.ext*.

8. Press Enter.
   This message is displayed:
   ```
   Insert diskette for drive B: and strike
   any key when ready
   ```

9. Remove the source diskette from drive A.

10. Insert the target diskette in drive A.

11. Press Enter.
    Note: Depending on the amount of memory in your computer, you may have to switch the diskettes. You will be prompted which diskette to insert (source or target). Keep switching diskettes until this message is displayed:
    ```
    Files compare OK
    Compare more files (Y/N)?
    ```
    Note: If the diskettes do not compare, repeat the COPY and COMP procedures.

12. Type:
    o N to end the COMP command. The DOS A> prompt is displayed, and the source file has been compared to the target file.
    o Y to compare more files. Repeat the COMP procedure starting with step 6.
       Note: If you get the message:
       ```
       Insert COMMAND.COM diskette in drive x: and strike any key
       when ready
       ```
       before the DOS prompt is displayed, insert the DOS diskette in drive A and press any key. The DOS prompt will be displayed.

DISKCOMP

Compares all information on one diskette with another to ensure that they are identical.

Usually you use DISKCOMP after you use the DISKCOPY command to make sure the copied diskette is identical to the original diskette.

Description
You need:

• The DOS diskette, or you need to ensure that the current directory is the DOS directory with the DISKCOMP.COM file in it. (Use DIR for this.)

- The original diskette you want to compare—the source diskette.

- The diskette you want to compare the original with—the target diskette.

For a single floppy drive system:
For this procedure, the source diskette is the first diskette and the target diskette is the second diskette.

1. Make sure the current directory is the DOS directory and the DISK-COMP.COM file is in it. (Use the DIR and CD commands to check and ensure this.)

2. Type diskcomp a: a:

3. Press Enter.
   This message is displayed:
   Insert FIRST diskette in drive A:
   Press any key when ready . . .

4. Insert the source diskette in drive A.

5. Press any key.
   The drive A in-use light comes on while the source diskette is read. Then this message is displayed:
   Insert SECOND diskette in drive A:
   Press any key when ready . . .

6. Remove the source diskette from drive A.

7. Insert the target diskette in drive A.

8. Press any key.
   Note: Depending on the amount of memory in your computer, you may have to switch the diskettes. You are prompted for either the first or second (source or target) diskette. Keep switching diskettes until this message is displayed:
   Compare OK
   Compare more diskettes (Y/N)?
   Note: If the diskettes do not compare, repeat the DISKCOPY and DISKCOMP procedures.

9. Type:
   o N to end the DISKCOMP command. Now the DOS prompt is displayed, and the source diskette has been compared to the target diskette.
   o Y to compare more diskettes. Repeat the DISKCOMP procedure starting with step 6.

Note: If you get the message:
`Insert COMMAND.COM diskette in drive x: and strike any key when ready`
before the DOS prompt is displayed, insert the DOS diskette in drive A, and press any key. Then the DOS prompt A> will be displayed.

FORMAT

Prepares a disk for system use. Use the FORMAT command to prepare a diskette for use. FORMAT checks the diskette for bad spots and builds the "root" directory to hold information about the files and subdirectories that will eventually be written on it.

Warning:

If you format a disk or diskette that contains information, the information is erased.

Switches
/S Creates a DOS system diskette—a bootable diskette
/V:name Prompts you to assign a volume name to the diskette
/B Reserves space for DOS system files

Example
`FORMAT A: /V:MEMOS /S`

Formats drive A, gives it a volume name of MEMOS, and transfers the system files to make the disk bootable.

Description
You need:

- The DOS diskette or ensure that the current directory is the DOS directory with the FORMAT.COM file in it. (Use DIR for this.)
- The diskette you want to format.

When a *diskette* is new, it must be formatted before you can use it unless you purchase "preformatted" diskettes (this is noted on the diskette box, and these diskettes are more expensive). Unless your system comes with preinstalled software (many systems now are sold with DOS and Windows preinstalled, and sometimes applications as well), you must format the new or blank hard disk before DOS can use it. Do *not* use the FORMAT command on a program diskette or every time you want to put information on a diskette—only the first time you use a blank diskette or when you want to *erase all data* from a diskette so you can reuse it.

What if you format a diskette or write information on a diskette unintentionally? Important data could be lost in certain situations. For this reason, diskettes have a "write-protect" feature, but *hard disks do not have this feature.* You can read data from write-protected diskettes, but you cannot write data on them. Diskettes can be write-protected in the following way:

Some diskettes have a notch called a write-protect notch (see Figure 6-1). If the notch is covered, the diskette is write-protected. To write-protect a 5.25-inch diskette, cover the notch with the tab that came with the diskette (usually black or silver).

Some diskettes do not have a notch. This means that the diskette is already write-protected and information cannot be written on it. (These are normally program diskettes.)

On the 3.5-inch diskette, in the upper left corner, there is a write-protect window, as shown in Figure 6-2. When you slide the plastic tab (reverse side) so that the window is open, the diskette is write-protected. When the window is closed, data can be written on the diskette.

FORMAT procedure for a 3.5-inch single floppy drive system:

1. Make sure the current directory is the DOS directory and the FOR-MAT.COM file is in it. (Use the DIR and CD commands to ensure this.)

Caution:

Double-check that you type the command in step 2 correctly. If you omit the drive designation (A:), DOS will assume the current drive, C:, and format it, destroying all the system and application files you have stored on your hard disk! If this happens, do *not* take any further action with the system. Immediately call your dealer for the proper corrective action.

2. Type format a:. This will format a high-density diskette in drive A. Remember—the diskette must be labeled high density or HD or an "error reading track 0" will occur. For low-density diskette format refer to your DOS manual.
3. Press Enter.
    This message is displayed:
    ```
    Insert new diskette for drive A:
    Press Enter when ready . . .
    ```

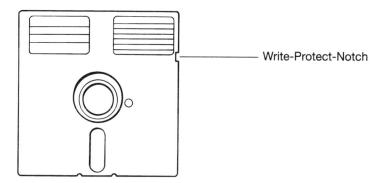

FIGURE 6-1   Write-protect notch for a 5.25-inch diskette

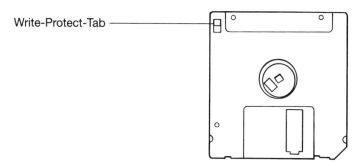

FIGURE 6-2   Write-protect tab for a 3.5-inch diskette

4. Insert the diskette to be formatted in drive A. (Be sure the write-protect window is closed.)

5. Press the Enter key.
   The drive A in-use light comes on. Then these messages are displayed:
   Checking existing disk format.
   Saving FORMAT information.
   Verifying 1.44M
   The percent of format completed is displayed as the diskette is formatted. Then you see
   Format complete.
   Volume label (11 characters, Enter for none)?

6. Type the label you desire. This is optional—you don't have to assign one.

7. Press Enter. The diskette's statistics are displayed along with the following message:
   Format another (Y/N)?

8. Type one of the following:
   o N to end the FORMAT command. Now the DOS prompt is displayed, and the diskette has been formatted and is ready for use.
   o Y to format more diskettes. Repeat the FORMAT procedure starting with step 4.

Helpful Hints for Working with DOS

Here are a few hints—they may save you some time or help you as you use your computer.

- Make copies of your diskettes regularly.
- When a command doesn't seem to work, you should:
  o Check your typing. Be sure the command format is correct.
  o Be sure you have the correct diskette in the drive.
  o Check the directory of the diskette with the DIR command.
  o Specify the correct diskette drive. If it is being assumed, be sure it is the correct one.
  o Include the colon. (Remember a colon is :, and a semicolon is ;.)
  o Spell the filename(s) correctly.
  o Use the extension. (In the case of BASIC program files, for example, it is easy to forget the .BAS the BASIC program uses for an extension.)
- Refer to your *DOS Reference Manual* for additional information if a command still doesn't seem to work. Be sure your manual reflects the version of DOS you're using.
- Print a directory of the disk frequently and store the listing with the diskette. Turn on the printer. From the current directory's system prompt, press Ctrl+P to activate a print mode that prints out all characters you type. Then type DIR. The directory listing will print out on your printer. Press Ctrl+P again to turn off the print mode.
- Commands (except DISKCOPY and DISKCOMP) that use files will work on both diskettes and fixed disks.
- The date and time references shown with each directory entry are the date and time of the last addition or change to that file. The date and time references are not changed during a COPY or a DISK-COPY.

Now you're prepared for organizing your information (programs and data) in your computer, putting some of these basic DOS commands to work.

7

Organizing Files on Your Hard Disk

When you learned about computer files in Chapter 6, we compared them to files in a standard filing cabinet. Each file folder and drawer in a filing cabinet contains information on a specific subject or group of subjects. Several of your files may be memos that pertain to a particular project. You may also have a number of files related to reports that you need to update regularly. Most likely, the files in your filing cabinet are subdivided into various categories or groups, which correspond to subdirectories in the file structure.

In the same way that you group files together in a filing cabinet, you can group files on your hard disk in subdirectories. (Sometimes they are simply called directories. There is only one true directory in any system—the "root" directory. All other directories are subdirectories of this root directory. The terms directory and subdirectory are used interchangeably.)

When your hard disk was prepared for use, the dealer installed DOS on it for you and copied the DOS boot files from your DOS diskettes to your hard disk. Those DOS boot files (two hidden files and the COMMAND.COM file) were copied to the root directory—the directory that you're in when DOS starts.

The root directory can be pictured in your imagination as a long hallway with rooms opening off from it. The root directory is represented by a backslash (\). Each room along the hallway represents a subdirectory for containing groups of related files.

Picture the nameplates above the doors to the rooms being blank. And the rooms are empty. That's to show that you haven't created any subdirectories yet. So far you have only the root directory on your hard disk. The root directory of a hard disk can have only a limited number of files and/or subdirectories (rooms) opening from it. That number is 512. The subdirectories are not subject to this limit.

Now you'll see how to create some subdirectories in which you can group related files and application programs.

Making Subdirectories

Let's assume that you have the two general groups of data files—memos and reports. You want to make two subdirectories branching off the root directory—one named MEMOS and one named REPORTS. MEMOS will contain the memos that you create with a word processing application. REPORTS will contain all your report files and your report application program.

Note: We're using MEMOS and REPORTS as examples. You can call your subdirectories by any valid DOS filenames that conform to the rules for filenames described in Chapter 6.

To create MEMOS:

1. Start DOS from your hard disk.
2. Using the DOS MD command, make a subdirectory called MEMOS. Type md \memos.
3. Press Enter.
   When the DOS prompt appears, the MEMOS subdirectory has been created on your hard disk.
4. Use the same command to make a subdirectory named REPORTS. Type md \reports.
5. Press Enter.
   When the DOS prompt reappears, the REPORTS subdirectory has been created.

You now have two subdirectories opening directly off the root directory. In your imagination, the name MEMOS appears above the first room. The name REPORTS appears above the second room. Remember, DOS is in the root directory (the hallway).

It is possible to have subdirectories organized one "behind" the other. For example, you could make a subdirectory called LETTERS behind MEMOS. The command that you would use for making this subdirectory is md \memos\letters.

Press Enter.

If you were to make the LETTERS subdirectory, a picture representing your hard disk organization would look like this (remember the backslash [\] represents the root directory):

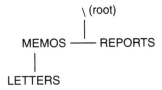

You will probably not need to make subdirectories like the ones shown here. But if you are interested in learning more about this concept, refer to your *DOS Reference Manual* for a detailed explanation.

Copying Files to Your Subdirectories

Program Files

Virtually all commercial software—spreadsheets, word processors, databases, accounting packages, and specialty software—you will purchase for your business provides an installation procedure that takes much of the pain out of setting up subdirectories for your program files. Follow the instructions for the software's INSTALL procedures—it's far more user friendly than copying hundreds of files to numerous subdirectories on your own.

Do *not* use the DOS commands for copying files and making directories to install your software unless the software's INSTALL procedures give you specific DOS installation instructions as the software's INSTALL procedure.

Data Files

Let's say you want to store some word processing files created by a data processing service for you before you bought your new system. You want to copy the files into a new word processing subdirectory. We'll call it WP (for all your WordPerfect data). To copy the data diskette to the subdirectory:

1. Put the data diskette in drive A.
2. To copy all the files from the diskette to the subdirectory on your hard disk, type copy a:*.* c:\wp.

3. Press Enter.
   The *.* in this command means that you want to copy all the files, not just a single file. (Remember wildcards—the * and ?.) Because you specified the destination directory, WP, that directory need not be the current directory as you copy the files.
4. When the DOS prompt reappears, remove the data diskette from drive A.

Now your WP subdirectory contains all your word processing data files. It's usually organizationally better to store your data outside the program's directory. That way you can back up just your data or delete just the obsolete data files without accidentally erasing necessary program files.

Copying a Single File to a Subdirectory

Suppose that you have just one file that needs to be copied to a subdirectory from your diskette. Use the same procedure described in the previous section, but in place of *.*, type the name of the file.

1. For example, to copy a file named NEWFILE to the \DATA\MEMOS subdirectory, type copy a:newfile c:\data\memos.
2. Press Enter.
   You have just copied NEWFILE from the diskette in drive A to the MEMOS subdirectory of the DATA directory on drive C.

(Remember, the DATA directory and MEMOS subdirectory must be created first by using the MD command.)

Erasing a File from a Subdirectory

Sometimes you want to erase files that are no longer needed. Let's say you want to erase NEWFILE from the REPORTS subdirectory.

1. Type erase c: \reports\newfile.
2. Press Enter.

You must type the name of the subdirectory first, then a backslash, then the complete name of the file, including its extension.

Moving Around in Your Directory Structure

As already mentioned, when you start DOS, you're at the root directory. In other words, the root directory is the current directory. The current directory is the one you are presently working in or the one you were working in on a different drive. DOS remembers the directory you were working in even if you're not presently accessing that drive.

Even though you made two subdirectories, you have not changed the current directory yet. The hallway doors on MEMOS and REPORTS are closed, indicating that your current directory is still the root directory.

But now you need to know how to move in and out of subdirectories on your hard disk to locate files and run applications. You'll use the change directory command (CD for short) to change the current directory to one you want to work in.

Viewing the Contents of a Directory

Suppose you want to look at the files in REPORTS. To make REPORTS the current directory:

1. Use the CD command. Type cd \reports.
2. Press Enter.
   The door is open on REPORTS now, indicating that the current directory is REPORTS.
3. To see the files that you have in REPORTS, type dir.
4. Press Enter. A list of files appears on your screen.

To change the directory to MEMOS (make MEMOS the current directory), type cd \memos.
Press Enter.
Now the door is open on MEMOS, indicating that MEMOS is the current directory.

Displaying the Current Directory's Name

If you're not sure which subdirectory you are in, you can display the directory name. Do not use a backslash with this command. Type cd. Press Enter.
If you're in MEMOS currently, the following appears on your screen:

C:\MEMOS

Returning to the Root Directory

To return to the root directory from any subdirectory, type cd \. Press Enter.
Now the root directory is current, so the doors on both subdirectories are closed.

Displaying the Contents of a Subdirectory

To display the entire contents of a subdirectory, use one of the following two methods:

- Use the CD (change directory) command followed by the DIR command.
- Tell DOS how to locate and display the files you want.

Here's an example of the first method. If the current directory is the root directory and you want to display the files in REPORTS,

1. Change directory to REPORTS. Type cd \reports.
2. Press Enter.
3. Use the DIR command to list the files on the screen. Type dir.
4. Press Enter.
   All the files in REPORTS are listed on the screen.

Using the second method, you can display all files in REPORTS while you are using the root directory, without changing to the REPORTS subdirectory.

1. First change to the root directory by typing cd \.
2. Press Enter.
3. Now enter the DIR command and the subdirectory name: dir \reports.
4. Press Enter.

The REPORTS files appear on the screen (and you didn't have to leave the root directory to display them).

Displaying One File in a Subdirectory

To display only one file in a subdirectory, if you know the name of the file you're looking for, use the DIR command. DOS must know the subdirectory where the file is located as well as the name of the file. Suppose the name of the file is MYFILE and it is stored in REPORTS. To display the name of the file, type dir \reports\myfile.
    Press Enter.

Removing a Subdirectory

Use the RD command to remove a subdirectory. Keep the following in mind:

- A subdirectory can be removed only if it is empty. That is, the subdirectory can contain only the special entries (.) and (..). When you display the contents of a subdirectory, using the DIR command, you see only those special entries listed.
- Only one subdirectory can be removed at a time.
- The root directory and the current directory cannot be removed.

Let's assume you want to remove the REPORTS subdirectory from your hard disk. Follow these steps:

1. Change directory to REPORTS. Type cd \reports.
2. Press Enter.
3. Erase all the files in REPORTS by entering erase *.*.

Important:

Do not type this command unless you are sure you're in the subdirectory in which you want to erase files. Otherwise, you may erase the wrong files unintentionally.

4. Press Enter. Answer Y to the question, Are you sure?
5. Change to the root directory. (You cannot remove a directory while you're working in that directory.) Type cd \.
6. Press Enter.
7. To remove the REPORTS subdirectory, use the RMDIR (RD) command. Type rd \reports.
8. Press Enter.
   The DOS prompt appears and REPORTS is removed from your hard disk.
   If you try to change directory to REPORTS, you get the message Invalid directory.

Displaying the Subdirectory Names on Your Hard Disk

You can display the names of all your subdirectories using the DOS TREE command. You can also see all the filenames in each subdirectory, if you use the /f option. Type tree /f. Press Enter.

To see just the subdirectory names without the filenames, simply type tree. Press Enter.

For more information, see the TREE command in your *DOS Reference Manual.*

Here we've covered the basics of how data is organized in your computer. The next chapter covers two special DOS files that reside in the root directory of your hard disk. These files help DOS to operate smoothly and efficiently with your particular system and must be created (written) for each system.

8

Two Special DOS Files

Now that you've been introduced to the initial set of DOS commands and know what they do and how to use them, you're ready to learn the benefits of creating two special DOS files: CONFIG.SYS and AUTO-EXEC.BAT. It is necessary for you to construct them because they differ with each system. They make the system uniquely yours.

Unlike the other DOS commands, which tell DOS what to do, these files act as commands that tell DOS how to do something, such as use a device or communicate with a disk drive. You will construct, or re-construct, these files normally when you add a device to your computer system (thereby changing its configuration). However, some application programs require you to add certain commands to the CONFIG.SYS file and/or the AUTOEXEC.BAT file so that the application can run properly. For example, an application might require that DOS be able to work with more files than the eight it is allowed by default.

These commands must be in the root directory of the DOS disk you use to boot the system. In our case they will be in the root directory of the C drive.

CONFIG.SYS

CONFIG.SYS is a file that contains configuration commands that define the hardware and software that make up your system. The file must be in the root directory—the topmost level—of the system disk. Each time

DOS starts, it carries out the commands in CONFIG.SYS. If there is no file named CONFIG.SYS in the root directory of the system disk, DOS assumes certain configuration values.

The DOS commands you can use in CONFIG.SYS include:

- BREAK, which controls how often DOS checks for Ctrl+C
- BUFFERS, which specifies how many disk buffers DOS sets aside
- COUNTRY, which specifies the country whose date and time format is to be used
- DEVICE, which identifies a file that contains a program to control a device (such a program is called a device driver)
- DEVICEHIGH, which enables DOS to load device drivers into the upper memory area (the portion of memory between 640K bytes and 1M byte) on computers with an 80386 or 80486 microprocessor and *extended* memory
- DOS, which serves two functions: telling DOS whether to load itself into conventional or extended memory, and maintaining access to the upper memory area so that programs can be loaded into it
- DRIVPARM, which defines the operating characteristics of a disk or a tape drive
- FCBS, which specifies the number of files controlled by File Control Blocks (FCBs) that can be open at the same time
- FILES, which specifies how many files can be open at the same time
- INSTALL, which loads a command file from CONFIG.SYS.
- LASTDRIV, which sets the highest drive letter that DOS recognizes
- SHELL, which specifies the name of a command processor to be used instead of COMMAND.COM
- STACKS, which tells DOS how much memory (RAM) to reserve for its temporary use
- SWITCHES, which blocks enhanced keyboard functions

Don't be alarmed by all these commands; you'll walk through a simple construction example to create a typical CONFIG.SYS file in this chapter. Then, when you add applications, the documentation for the application will instruct you on any change necessary for that application.

CONFIG.SYS is a text file; you can create it or modify an existing version with a text editor, such as EDIT or EDLIN, or with a word processor that can store a file in ASCII format (without formatting codes, a type of file also known as a text file).

AUTOEXEC.BAT

AUTOEXEC.BAT is a file that can contain from a few to many commands. However, two commands that are usually included are a PATH command, which tells DOS where to find command files, and a PROMPT command, which sets the system prompt to display the current directory.

Each time you start or restart the system, DOS goes through a startup procedure that includes searching the root directory of the system disk for this special batch file. DOS then carries out whatever commands you've listed here. This enables you to avoid having to manually enter these commands each time you start or restart the system.

Although DOS gives special treatment to AUTOEXEC.BAT, that doesn't mean the file is untouchable. You can add commands to it at any time, but you should always be careful not to change or delete any existing commands, especially those you don't understand. (You can encounter such commands in AUTOEXEC.BAT, particularly on systems that connect to a network and those that have been set up by someone else for maximum performance.)

When you install applications that ask whether they can make changes to your CONFIG.SYS and/or AUTOEXEC.BAT files, it is wise to say no. Make the necessary changes yourself, because the applications will, in some cases, delete some necessary commands you previously set for the operation of other programs.

Constructing These Special Files

Now that you know a little about these two special files, let's construct them for your system. We'll start with the CONFIG.SYS file.

CONFIG.SYS

Remember, CONFIG.SYS is the file containing the configuration commands that define the system hardware and software to your system when you apply power, reset, or otherwise "boot" DOS. So you should begin by writing the following command sequence on a sheet of paper for your system:

```
DEVICE=C:\DOS\SETVER.EXE
DEVICE=C:\DOS\HIMEM.SYS
DEVICE=C:\DOS\EMM386.EXE NOEMS
DOS=HIGH,UMB
DEVICEHIGH=C:\DOS\ANSI.SYS
DEVICE=C:\DOS\SMARTDRV.SYS 512
FILES=40
BUFFERS=20
FCBS=40,20
```

```
COUNTRY=001,437
STACKS=30,128
SHELL=COMMAND.COM /P
```

Now let's see what we've told DOS about the system. In the CON-FIG.SYS file the commands and their meanings are as follows:

SETVER.EXE   An executable file that sets the version number of DOS seen and used by some executable application files (files with the .EXE, .COM, and .BAT extensions).

HIMEM.SYS   A system file that enables DOS to use the RAM above the 640K bytes conventional memory area.

EMM386.EXE   An extended memory manager file that is used with the Intel 80386 and 80486 microprocessors to make use of memory above the conventional 640K bytes. The RAM specification is the address area of the extended memory.

DOS=HIGH,UMB   A command that causes DOS to load part of itself into the first 64K bytes of extended memory and causes DOS to maintain a link with upper memory blocks (UMBs). This allows DOS to make use of the memory area above the conventional 640K bytes memory allowing as much conventional memory as possible to remain free for application program use.

ANSI.SYS   A device driver (a program that controls an attached device--printer, keyboard, and so on) that permits advanced control of the display and keyboard.

SMARTDRV.SYS 512   A system file that creates a disk cache (high-speed program transfer area), which here contains 512K bytes (512,000 bytes) in extended or expanded (upper areas of) memory.

FILES=40   A command that tells DOS it can have up to 40 files open at one time. Some application programs require multiple open files to operate. (WordPerfect 5.1, for example, requires 30.)

BUFFERS=20   A command that tells DOS the number of work areas it can use in its transfers of data to and from the disk.

FCBS=40,20   A command that tells DOS the maximum number of files that can be open at the same time (here, 40) using file control blocks (FCBs). This also keeps DOS from automatically closing a certain minimum number of files (here, 20).

COUNTRY=001,437   A command that tells DOS to follow local conventions for a given country (001=U.S.) in such matters as date format, currency symbols, and decimal separators. It also specifies the internal codepage (here, 437) DOS is to use. Codepage references can be found in the appropriate section of your *DOS Reference Manual*. Note there is no path (C:\DOS\ ...) designation here. This requires the COUNTRY.COM file to be in the root directory.

STACKS=30,128   A command that reserves areas of memory for temporary use during hardware interrupts. It is required by some application programs. Here, 30 is the number of memory stacks to be allocated and 128 is the size of each stack in bytes.

SHELL=COMMAND.COM /P   A command that tells DOS the name and location of the file that contains the command processor, which is your interface to the operating system. /P disables the EXIT command and causes the newly loaded command processor to be held resident in memory until the computer is turned off.

AUTOEXEC.BAT

Now we'll look at and construct the AUTOEXEC.BAT file for your system. Remember, by storing this file in the root directory, you tell DOS to go through an initial set of commands, each time you power up the computer, that set the system to your particular needs. Because of this, the system must be able to find the different commands you specify. This is done by giving the PATH command. However, I recommend that you set the ECHO feature off first, preventing spurious displays from flashing on the screen when AUTOEXEC.BAT runs, making it confusing to look at. We'll write the following command sequence for your system.

```
ECHO OFF
PATH=C:\;C:\DOS;C:\MOUSE;C:\WP51;
   \C:\123R23;C:\BITCOM;C:\FRECOM;C:PCTOOLS;
MODE CO80,25
MOUSE 2
FRECOMRF /ON
PROMPT $P$G
```

In the AUTOEXEC.BAT file the commands and their meanings are as follows:

ECHO OFF   A command that tells DOS not to display the batch file commands as they are carried out.

PATH   A command that tells DOS the drive and location of each directory and gives DOS the route for an orderly search of your files when looking for a given command. (If two files have the same name in two different directories DOS will always use the first one it comes to in its search of this path.)

MODE CO80,25   A command that tells DOS that the system uses a color monitor with an 80-character (column) by 25-line (row) display field.

MOUSE 2   A command that tells DOS to execute the MOUSE command activating the mouse as an input device. DOS searches the PATH and executes the MOUSE command from the MOUSE directory.

FRECOMRF /ON   A command that tells DOS to execute the FRECOMRF (fax) command making the fax receive function active in the background. So if you're working in some program and a fax call comes in, DOS suspends your program, receives the fax, and then returns to executing your program where it left off.

PROMPT PG   A command that tells DOS to display the DOS prompt along with the current drive and directory. This makes it easier for you to determine your current directory (the directory you're operating from).

Now you have the structure of these important files. Any time you change the CONFIG.SYS file you must reboot the system in order for the change to be executed. When you change the AUTOEXEC.BAT file, you merely type autoexec and press Enter, and the change takes effect.

Storing CONFIG.SYS and AUTOEXEC.BAT

Now, how do you get these files into the root directory of your computer?
    First, locate the DOS system diskettes that came with your system and follow these steps:

1. Turn your system on. At the C> prompt, insert the first DOS system diskette in the A drive.

2. Type COPY A:EDLIN.COM C: and press Enter. The EDLIN file will be copied to the root directory on drive C. (If EDLIN is not on this first diskette, an error message will be displayed and you merely repeat the procedure using the second diskette, and so on, until the file is copied.)

3. Repeat step 2 for COUNTRY.SYS, ANSI.SYS, SMARTDRV.SYS, EMM386.SYS, SETVER.EXE, HIMEM.SYS, and MODE.COM.

4. Type MD \DOS and press Enter.

5. Type CD \DOS and press Enter.

6. Type DIR/W and press Enter. The display should indicate that you are in the DOS directory and only the . and .. files exist in it.

7. Type COPY A:*.* C:\DOS and press Enter. All the files on the diskette in drive A will be copied into the DOS directory on drive C.

8. Type CD\ and press Enter. This switches you back to the root directory.

9. Type EDLIN CONFIG.SYS and press Enter. EDLIN will respond with an asterisk (*).

10. At the asterisk type 1i and press Enter. EDLIN will respond with 1 . .

11. Type in the first command of the CONFIG.SYS file. Be very careful you type it exactly as shown, including spaces. The computer will only do *exactly* what it is told, and it must be told in a way that it comprehends. The slightest deviation and your CONFIG.SYS file may not do what you intended.

12. Repeat step 11 for the remainder of the CONFIG.SYS commands.

13. When you are finished entering the commands, type Ctrl+Z (Ctrl and Z keys pressed at the same time). The display will show ^Z. Then press Enter. The asterisk will appear.

14. At the asterisk type L and press Enter. Your CONFIG.SYS file will then be listed. Check each line for accuracy. If there are corrections to be made, merely type the line number and press Enter, retype the line properly, and press Enter when finished.

15. At the asterisk, when you're finished and satisfied each line is correct, type E and press Enter. You have now exited EDLIN, and your CONFIG.SYS file is constructed.

16. To check that the new file is in the directory merely type DIR/W and press Enter and the files of the root directory will be displayed. CONFIG.SYS should appear among them.

Now to construct the AUTOEXEC.BAT file in the root directory, repeat the same steps you just performed for the CONFIG.SYS file, starting with step 9.

When you have finished constructing the CONFIG.SYS file and the AUTOEXEC.BAT file, reboot the system. This will execute both files. Now you are ready to install your applications software, a process that is covered in the next chapter.

As a last step and check of the ROOT directory, at the C:\> prompt type DIR/W and press Enter. All the files and directories of the ROOT directory will be displayed. Check to see that the following files are listed:

```
ANSI.SYS
AUTOEXEC.BAT
COMMAND.COM
```

```
CONFIG.SYS
COUNTRY.SYS
EDLIN.COM
EMM386.SYS
HIMEM.SYS
MODE.COM
SETVER.EXE
SMARTDRV.SYS
```

Other files may also be listed but should not be of concern at the moment. As long as these files are listed, your system should be able to function as you have directed it in the CONFIG.SYS and AUTOEXEC.BAT files.

With these important files now constructed and in your root directory, you can begin installing your application programs. This you'll do in the next chapter.

9

Installing Your Applications

Now that you are acquainted with the computer basics, you can install your primary application program(s). You install a program by transferring the software from the distribution diskettes to your hard disk, as well as preparing the program for operation with your system components. But before that, it is wise to prepare your system to put the programs in directories of your choice. To do that, construct your directories as follows.

First, make directories for each of the applications including the mouse—just as they are listed in the PATH of your AUTOEXEC.BAT file using the MD command. Also, make two extra directories for data storage in the following manner: MD \WP51 \DATA and MD \123R23 \DATA. This makes the data storage subdirectories for your WordPerfect (word processor) and Lotus 1-2-3 (spreadsheet) programs.

Then, move to each directory in turn, using the CD command, and perform the program's installation as described in its operations manual. Using the INSTALL utility provided by the software is preferable to copying all the files into your directory using DOS commands. INSTALL copies just the files you need to run the program on your system, avoiding copying unnecessary files that would just consume your disk space.

Another reason to use the INSTALL utility is that some programs, such as WordPerfect, use "compressed" files for shipping and provide an INSTALL file that loads (copies) the program files, in decompressed form, onto the hard disk, making their own appropriate directories and/

or subdirectories. Simply copying the files with DISKCOPY or COPY won't decompress them.

Before you start installing any software, complete as much as you can of the following checklist. You will need this information to respond to some of your application program installation utility's on-screen questions. Information you're not sure of can probably be obtained from your dealer support group.

SOFTWARE INSTALLATION REFERENCE CHECKLIST

Computer:

_____ XT(8088 or 8086) _____ AT(80286) _____ 80386 _____ 80486

_____ 80586

Memory Capacity:

_____ K bytes RAM basic memory

_____ (K bytes or M bytes) expanded memory

_____ (K bytes or M bytes) extended memory

Monitor:

Color: _____ Yes _____ No

Type: _____ Monochrome/Text only _____ EGA

_____ Monochrome/Graphics _____ VGA (Monochrome or Gray Scale)

_____ SuperVGA _____ CGA _____ Multisync

Ports:

Number of serial ports: _____
Connected to:

_____ COM1 _____ COM3

_____ COM2 _____ COM4

Number of Parallel Ports: _____
Connected to:

_____ LPT1 _____ LPT3

_____ LPT2 _____ LPT4

Printer(s):

Manufacturer(s): _____

Model(s): _____

Type(s): _____ 9-pin dot-matrix _____ Laser printer

_____ 24-pin dot matrix _____ Daisy wheel

Connected to communications port(s): _____
(COM1, 2, 3, or 4 for serial printer, LPT1, 2, 3, or 4 for parallel printer)
Emulates the following printers:

1. _____   3. _____

2. _____   4. _____

Disk Drives:
Hard Disk(s):

Manufacturer(s): _____

Model(s): _____

Capacity: _____ Megabytes

Floppy Drive(s):

Number of floppy drives: _____
Capacity of drive(s) (enter number of drives at each capacity):

_____ 360K bytes _____ 1.2M bytes

_____ 720K bytes _____ 1.44M bytes
(Note: 360K-byte and 1.2M-byte drives use 5.25-inch diskettes; 720K-byte and 1.44M-byte drives use 3.5-inch diskettes.)

Mouse:

Manufacturer: _____

Type: _____ Bus _____ Serial Port
If Serial Mouse:

Connected to Serial Port _____ (COM1, 2, 3, or 4)
Emulates the following model(s):

_____ Mouse Systems _____ Microsoft Mouse

Modem:

Manufacturer: _____

Model: _____

Maximum baud rate _____ (9600/4800/2400/1200/300)

Connected to communications (serial) port COM _____
(1, 2, 3, or 4)

Fax Board:

Manufacturer: _____

Model: _____

Maximum baud rate _____ (9600/4800)

Connected to communications (serial) port COM _____
(1, 2, 3, or 4)

Keep an extra blank copy of this form at all times. Make changes on the form as you update or change your system.

Now, open the application software (program) package and read the installation instructions carefully. Almost all of today's programs include an installation utility, which guides you through the installation process step by step and makes any necessary modifications to your computer's system files. (Again, try to avoid letting the installation utility change the CONFIG.SYS and/or the AUTOEXEC.BAT files. And always check these files, using EDLIN, for changes after you have performed a program installation.)

Find out how to start the installation utility and follow the on-screen instructions to install the program on your computer's hard disk.

Learning Your Primary Application

After you install your primary application, you need some time to learn the program. Trying to learn it yourself may not be the best option. Your local community college or computer store may offer a class on the program. But to learn the program yourself, follow these steps:

1. Read through the computer's manuals to find out whether the program comes with an on-line tutorial. If so, use it.

2. If there's no on-line tutorial, check the manuals to see whether there's a keystroke-by-keystroke "getting started" tutorial. If all you find is a reference manual, look for a book at your local bookstore that includes a keystroke-by-keystroke tutorial.

3. Create a test application using fictitious data that resembles the real data you'll be entering, then try all the operations that you're planning to perform once the system becomes part of your business. Continue working with the test application until you're confident you understand what you're doing and how the program works.

If your employees will use the system, the time is right to train them, too. Use the test application and give your employees plenty of time to become comfortable with the system. Be open to their suggestions; they may have some very good ideas for improving your application design. You may want to hire someone to provide in-house training aimed at the business's specific needs.

Once you've learned your computer's operating system and thoroughly explored your primary application, you're ready to install and learn additional programs. You'll be amazed at how much easier it is the second time around—especially if you took the time to learn the first program well before proceeding.

Maintaining Your System

The following is a summary of the procedures to follow in maintaining your system:

- Backing up regularly is required for serious business use of the computer. Purchase a backup utility (PCTools is a good one!) and develop regular backup procedures.
- You can avoid most viruses by refusing to copy pirated and bulletin board software, but a virus utility will ensure that your system is free from virus codes. (Norton Utilities and PCTools provide such utilities.)
- Purchase a good utility package such as PCTools version 7.1 or Norton Utilities. Although some system utilities are included in the new DOS and Macintosh operating systems, these other packages give you more utilities and a higher level of protection.

Utility Software Suggestions

Here are some helpful system utilities for DOS computing environment.

DOS Utility Programs

- Central Point Anti-Virus (Central Point Software): Detects and "cures" most currently known/common viruses. Free updates are available from an Oregon bulletin board noted on the product package.
- Central Point Backup (Central Point Software): The backup utility from PCTools; works with a variety of tape drives.

- Disk Optimizer (SoftLogic Solutions): A file defragmentation program.
- Fast! (Future Soft Engineering Inc.): A disk-caching utility that can noticeably increase your computer's apparent speed.
- Fastback Plus (Fifth Generation Systems, Inc.): A backup program that's noted for speed and ease of use; not compatible with tape drives.
- PCTools (Central Point Software, Inc.): An amazing variety of system utilities and desktop accessories, including a DOS file manager; DOS and Windows backup; DOS and Windows undelete utilities; disk defragmentation; disk surface analysis, virus detection; telecommunications; a mini-word processor; an appointment scheduler with to-do list; fax support software; remote computer operation; laptop file transfer; and system-level security, including file encryption, disk caching, and much more. The backup utility works with a variety of tape drives.
- QEMM-386 (Quarterdeck Office Systems): A memory manager that takes full advantage of memory that DOS and Windows may not fully utilize, such as the upper area between 640K bytes and 1M bytes. Note, however, that MS-DOS 5.0 includes HIMEM.SYS (for 286-based systems) and EMM386.EXE (for 386-based systems), which provide the same capabilities.
- Stacker (Stac Electronics): A disk expansion program that automatically compresses files and applications when you're not using them and decompresses files when you want to use them.
- SuperStor (AddStor): A disk expansion program that automatically compresses files and applications when you're not using them, and decompresses files when you want to use them. Includes disk defragmentation.
- The Norton Anti-Virus (Symantec Corporation): A respected anti-virus package with frequent updates.
- The Norton Utilities (Symantec Corporation): An outstanding backup utility that's fast, capable, and tolerant of errors. Works with a variety of tape drives. The package also includes many other utilities, such as disk defragmentation and undelete.

Installing and Customizing
Your Word Processor Software

We selected WordPerfect version 5.1 as our word processing program to discuss in this book. There are many other word processing programs.

And many of them are probably just as good for your purposes as WordPerfect. But WordPerfect is the most popular word processing program of the moment and offers excellent on-line support, so it's a good choice for installation explanation purposes.

WordPerfect 5.1 comes on seven 3.5-inch diskettes labeled:

1. Install/Learn/Utilities
2. Program 1
3. Speller/Thesaurus
4. PTR Program/Graphics
5. Printer 1
6. Printer 2
7. Graphics Drivers

To start the installation process, the computer must be turned on and the C:\> prompt must be displayed at the cursor. When you see the DOS prompt, you are ready to start the installation. If not, reboot the computer with no diskette in the A drive. And at the C:\> prompt make the following directories using the MD command:

WP51 (for the program files)
WP51\DATA (for your data files)

Installing WordPerfect

1. Insert the Install/Learn/Utilities diskette in drive A.
2. Type a: and press Enter. The prompt will change to A:\>.
3. Type Install and press Enter. The installation process will proceed. Now all you have to do is answer the questions that appear on your screen and insert the proper diskettes when asked to.
4. When you get to the printer selection section, you have to press the Page Down key to select your printers (remember, in our sample installation you have an HP LaserJet IIIP and an Okidata 321). Next, type in the identification number of your printer when requested and exchange diskettes between the Printer 1 and Printer 2 diskettes when asked to. In this way the proper printer driver (control program) can be installed with the word processor program.

When you've completed this installation process, the program automatically returns you to the first screen of WordPerfect, which is a facsimile of a blank sheet of paper with the cursor in the upper left corner of the screen and the page identification and statistics information displayed in the lower right area of the screen. From here you are required to set up the program to your particular needs.

Setting Up WordPerfect

To set up the word processor, proceed as follows:

1. Activate the Setup feature by pressing the Shift and F1 keys at the same time.
2. Type 6 and make sure that all bold references indicate C:\WP51 or are blank. The blank ones should be items 1, 7, and 8. We'll change these later.
3. Now press F7 to exit back to the document screen.
4. Again press the Shift and F1 keys for the setup screen. Then press keys as follows:
   2 Display
   5 View
   1
   N
   2
   N
   3
   Y
   This action locks in your screen presentations to color mode instead of black and white.
5. Press F7 to exit Setup.

Now you're going to set up your printer(s) for proper use.

1. Press Shift and F7 keys at the same time to get to the print screen.
2. Press the S key to get to the printer select screen. From here you can select either the HP printer or the Okidata printer. For the moment, select the HP printer by placing the cursor (highlight) on it using the arrow keys and pressing the Enter key. This returns you to the print screen, and the HP printer is shown as the one selected. You must go through these steps each time you determine you need to select a different printer. (Remember, the HP is for single page high print quality output, Okidata for multipart forms output.)
3. Now press the Enter key to get back to the document screen.

You can now type some information on the screen and print it out by pressing the Shift+F7 keys and the 1 key to print the complete document or the 2 key to print the page that the cursor is currently positioned at.

Your word processor (WordPerfect) is now installed and initially set up. There's a lot more to learn to fine tune the program for your needs. If you intend to give the program heavy use, search around for classes and/or training aids for using this program. A whole training industry has been created to teach the use of all the various popular programs. These are expensive and vary in quality, but they are an option. I recommend a good audiocassette- or videocassette-based training program because they can be worked on at your convenience, are cost effective, and can be referred to at any time. However, you must contribute the self-discipline to use them, and some people find this difficult if not impossible because there's always something more important to do than train themselves how to use computer programs.

Installing and Customizing Your Spreadsheet Software

As noted before, we selected Lotus 1-2-3 Release 2.3 as your spreadsheet. There are other spreadsheets on the market, but Lotus is the most popular. However, Quattro Pro by Borland is making inroads in the market. But we'll stick with Lotus for the purposes of this book.

Lotus Release 2.3 comes on four 3.5-inch diskettes and has an INSTALL program file on the diskette labeled "Disk One (Install). This program sets up 1-2-3 on the system by prompting you with specific questions regarding your system as it "automatically" installs the program. When you use INSTALL for the first time, it starts by recording your name and organization name on your original copy of the diskettes. This is done for security reasons—to ensure that this copy is registered to you or your business. It then transfers the program files to your computer's hard disk. Finally, the INSTALL program enables you to select equipment specific to your system. If you plan to use Wysiwyg (what you see is what you get—a more representative but slower screen mode), the INSTALL program also lets you generate a set of font sizes to use with the graphics display and printer drivers (program routines that control the transfer of printer control codes and data) you select during the installation process.

To reduce the number of diskettes you receive in the package, the program files have been compressed. This is a mathematical process that reduces the program information to its smallest possible configuration. Compressed files cannot be directly used by a computer. They must be decompressed first. (Because the INSTALL program decompresses these files as it copies them to your hard disk, you cannot use the operating system COPY command to transfer the files.) You must use the INSTALL program to transfer the program files to your hard disk before you can use the program.

Release 2.3 includes several companion programs (called add-ins) that extend its features. The basic program along with these extended features requires at least 5M bytes of hard disk space. Because your system is configured with a 100M-byte hard disk, you have ample room to install (load) the basic program and all extended features.

The first time you use the INSTALL program, you must use the original Diskette 1 (Install) diskette and you must start the program from a floppy drive.

Starting the INSTALL Program

First, you want to make the following directories (at the C:\> prompt) to ensure that Lotus will configure to your system and work-style preferences:

> 123R23 (for the program files)
>
> 123R23\DATA (for your data files)

The following instructions assume you are starting INSTALL from floppy drive A.

1. Insert Diskette 1 (Install) in drive A.
2. At the operating system prompt (C:\>), type a: and press Enter.
3. Type install and press Enter.
4. Read the introductory screen and then press Enter.

Using the INSTALL Program

The first time you use INSTALL, you must complete the following steps:

1. Record your name and organization name (they both may be the same).
2. Transfer the program files to your hard disk.
3. Select your display adapter (VGA 80 X 25) and printer(s) (HP LaserJet IIIP and Okidata 321) so the program can work correctly with them.

The INSTALL screens guide you through the program. Follow the instructions on each screen to complete the INSTALL program. In most cases, the information you need to complete a step in INSTALL will be on the screen you are viewing. You merely make your selection and press Enter.

Use the following guidelines to make your selections:

- Select an item from the INSTALL Main menu by using the Up-arrow and Down-arrow keys to move the menu pointer (the rectangular highlight) until it covers the item you want, then press Enter. In most cases, a box appears on the right side of the screen to describe the menu item that is highlighted. As you move the menu pointer, the description in the box changes.

- If you need more information, press function key F1 (HELP) to see a Help screen. The Help screen provides information for the specific procedure you are trying to perform.

- The keys you can use during each step in the INSTALL program are listed at the bottom of the screen.

Lotus recommends you complete the entire INSTALL program (process) in one work session. If you need to end INSTALL before you complete all the steps, you can press Esc (escape) to back out through the various screens until INSTALL displays the Main menu and lets you select End Install. A message will appear that tells you what procedures you have not completed. If you end the INSTALL program without completing all the procedures, you will not be able to use 1-2-3 until you come back and complete the INSTALL procedures.

To use Lotus 1-2-3 after you've completed the INSTALL procedures, merely follow these steps:

1. At the C:> prompt, type cd \123r23 and press Enter.
2. At the C:\123R23> prompt, type lotus and press Enter.
   The Lotus screen will appear with 1-2-3 highlighted with the cursor.
3. Press Enter again.

The screen will go blank for an instant, then the spreadsheet will appear with the A1 cell highlighted. You may enter data at this point or press the forward slash (/) key to have the menu appear for your selection.

Now you must refer to the Lotus documentation to proceed to make use of the program. I wish you Happy Spreadsheeting! But remember, the spreadsheet will give you information based on the calculations you specify. If you've made an error in setting up a formula or referencing a cell or series of cells in your calculations, the spreadsheet will make that same error and your information will not be what you want. So always question a computer's calculated responses. And use the rule of "common sense"—does the answer look reasonable compared to your past experience? If not, review its calculation(s) thoroughly. As a spreadsheet is used more and more, any errors—"bugs"—will be found in this manner and can be corrected, so your work will become more and more reliable. But newly created spreadsheets (or programs for that matter) are always subject to the possibility of subtle (and sometimes not so subtle) errors.

Installing Your Fax Board, Modem, and Communications Software

There are numerous fax boards and fax software packages available on the market. Most all are good and would serve your purposes (sending and receiving faxes). But you have to select one, so in this book we'll install the FAX96 board and 1-Liner software.

The software should be installed first. But before we start, you should check your shipment. It should contain the following:

FAX96 software diskette

Fax add-in circuit board

Long telephone wire

Short telephone wire

Operator's manual

Quick reference guide

FAX96 1-Liner software diskette

1-Liner Option operator's manual

FAX96 and 1-Liner require 1.5M bytes and 360K bytes of hard disk space, respectively. By running the DOS command CHKDSK C: you can determine how much space you have on the hard disk. However, in our example you've purchased a 100M-byte hard disk drive so there should be plenty of room. Also, because you have both 5.25-inch and 3.5-inch floppy drives installed, you don't have to be concerned about the type of floppies the programs are distributed on.

Installing the Fax Software

You will need tools necessary to remove the cover of your computer and the add-in slot cover, because you're going to have to install the add-in circuit board. Merely follow the instructions given previously for installing add-in boards and make the board jumper settings detailed later in this text.

First, to be safe when you install any software package, be sure the write-protect tab is set to write protect the original diskette. Then make a copy of the original diskette by using the DOS DISKCOPY command. When that's done, you can use the copied diskette as a working diskette to do the installation, and store the original in a safe place in case something should happen to the copy.

Caution:

Always keep all diskettes away from telephones or any other electrical appliances containing motors or bells. These items create and radiate strong electromagnetic fields when the bell rings or the motor is turned on, which will erase the data on a diskette.

Now let's start the installation:

1. Place the diskette in the A drive. (If the diskette will only fit in the B drive because it is a 5.25-inch type then put it in the B drive and modify the following instructions accordingly.)
2. Type A: INSTALL A: C: and press the Enter key.
   This loads the program from floppy drive A to hard drive C. This takes a minute or two.
3. Read the instructions that appear on the screen. Press G.
4. Answer the questions on each screen as follows:

First Screen
1. Your Name—Your name as you want it to appear on the cover letter— the first page of a fax transmission that identifies the sender and receiver and may have an information note. Type your name and press Enter.
2. Your Company Name (if any)—Which also appears on the cover letter. Type your company's name and press Enter.
3. Your Address—Again as you want it to appear on the cover letter. Type your street address and press Enter.
4. Your Voice Telephone Number—Appears on the cover letter. Type your complete phone number and press Enter.
5. Your Fax Number—Appears on the cover letter. Also appears on the LCD of the fax you are sending to (in fax jargon, the TSI—Transmitting Subscriber Identification) or receiving from (CSI—Called Subscriber Identification). Type the complete phone number and press Enter.
6. G—Type G to go to the next screen.

Second Screen

1. Fax Storage Directory—Don't change this unless you have a good reason. FAX96 stores all incoming fax and a fax formatted copy of your last fax sent (as LASTSENT) in this directory. The recommended directory is \FRECOM\FAX96\, because it's going to make any tech support calls easier. Press Enter.

2. Your Telephone Type—Rotary (R) or Touch Tone (T). This tells FAX96 how to dial. Type R or T and press Enter.

3. I/O Port—the software I/O port address has to match the FAX96 board jumper configuration. This needs to be set to avoid conflict with other add-in boards and functions in your PC.

   Address 280 is recommended unless you are aware of another device in your PC that uses 280. The board is usually shipped with 280 set, but check it. Other choices are 288, 380, and 388. (Refer to the manufacturer's operator's manual for a more complete explanation of this item.)

   Type your choice and press Enter.

4. Interrupt Level—The software interrupt level to match the board jumper configuration. This needs to be set to avoid conflict with other boards in your PC. The board is shipped with IRQ3 set, but check it. Here you choose an IRQ (interrupt request query) by process of elimination.

If you have	Do not use
PC/AT or compatible	IRQ2
COM1 attached modem, mouse, and so on	IRQ4
COM2 attached modem, mouse, and so on	IRQ3
LPT2 attached printer	IRQ5

   Type 2 for IRQ2, 3 for IRQ3, 4 for IRQ4, or 5 for IRQ5. Press Enter. Here we will type a 5 for IRQ5, which is normally assigned to the printer. We do this because we will normally not be using the printer at the same time we are using the fax. (See! There is some logic and reasoning you must apply for your specific operation.)

   Now you take the fax board in hand and set the jumpers according to your above selections.

5. Printer Port—The port that your printer is attached to. In almost all cases this is LPT1. Change this only if you know your port is something other than LPT1.

   Type your choice and press Enter.

6. Number of Rings—The number of times (0 through 9) that the telephone will ring before the fax answers. If you have a dedicated

telephone line for the fax, 1 ring is recommended before answering. If you are sharing a line between your fax and voice calls, a higher number of 6 or 8 is recommended, so you have time to answer and see whether it's a person or a fax machine calling. Press Enter.

7. G—Type G to go to the next screen to choose your printer type.

Third Screen

1. Printer Type—The make and the model of your printer. Here you can use the arrow keys to see a complete list of printers the program recognizes. The HP LaserJets are listed here. Type in the corresponding identification number and press Enter.

2. G—Type G to go to the next screen to choose your scanner type.

Fourth Screen

1. Scanner Type—Here you would select the scanner make and model and the port it's attached to and enter this information. Since your system does not have a scanner attached, this is not necessary.

2. Type G to go to the next and last installation screen.

Congratulations! The software is now installed, the jumpers are set, and you are ready to install the board in the PC.

Installing the Fax Board

Now install the board as you would any add-in board, connect the telephone lines as shown in the operator's manual, and run the demonstration mode test and the on-line test with the manufacturer's office (product registration). If all of this checks out properly—and we will assume it does—proceed to install the 1-Liner software, which enables you to use the same telephone line for voice, answering machine, and fax, avoiding the need to purchase a separate telephone line for fax communication. However, if it doesn't check out properly, feel free to call the manufacturer's support line for help.

Installing the 1-Liner Software

Again, you make a copy of the original 1-Liner diskette using the DOS DISKCOPY command.

1. Using the copied diskette, insert it in drive A and type A:INSTALL A: C: and press Enter.
   This loads the program from the floppy drive A to the hard drive C and takes a minute or two.

2. First Screen: Read the instructions. Note that as you proceed you will see the same screens you saw during the above FAX96 installation. Press G.

3. Merely pass through this screen. It can be handled later if you experience any problems.

4. Third Screen: Reset the number of rings that you want the fax board to wait before answering. The recommended setting here is six rings, which is two rings greater than the normal four-ring setting of an answering machine. But, just a note of information—telephone ringing takes 6 seconds per ring—2 seconds of ring and 4 seconds of silence. At nine rings you and your answering machine have almost a minute to answer the call before the fax answers and blasts your caller with the 2100 Hz CED (Called Tone).

5. Fourth and subsequent screens: Check the information here. It's the same as you entered when you installed the fax board. Any changes here will automatically update your original settings. If you are happy with the information that you entered before, press G.

6. The software is now installed. Now proceed hooking up your answering machine and telephone. Refer to the manufacturer's operator's manual for details of this hookup.

7. Press G. The installation is complete.

Remember:

Always refer to the owner's manual (manufacturer's documentation) that comes with your purchase to make these installations. The instructions and procedures set down in this book are merely to give you an idea of how these procedures are described and accomplished. But they may be—and probably are—out of date. More up-to-date instructions are available in the current owner's manuals.

Installing Your Modem Board

We're going to install the hardware (internal modem board) first, then proceed to install the modem communications software (BitCom). Most installations of communications equipment of this nature are similar but, again, the following information is illustrative only. Always refer to your equipment and software manufacturer's documentation for the specific details for your equipment.

Before we start, check your shipment. The box should contain the following:

One diskette

Modem add-in circuit board

Telephone wire

Manufacturer's documentation, including installation and operating instructions

Again, because you have both 5.25-inch and 3.5-inch floppy drives installed, you don't have to be concerned about the type of floppies you've received with the programs on them.

You will need tools necessary to remove the cover of your computer and the add-in slot cover because you're going to have to install the add-in circuit board. Again, follow the instructions given previously for installing add-in boards and make the board jumper settings detailed later in this text.

Setting the Communications Port

Remove the modem board from its static protection envelope. The modem is normally factory set to COM2, because today's systems probably have a mouse attached, as yours indeed does, and the mouse uses COM1. This setting can be changed to COM 1, 3, or 4 by changing a jumper setting on the board. Because your system has a mouse using COM1, we'll use this "default" setting—but check it to be sure the factory didn't make a mistake in your case (it happens!). The fax board is not using a COM port so we don't have to be concerned about it here. But the fax board also uses an IRQ setting (we selected IRQ5), so you need to check to see that the IRQ setting on the modem board is the proper one for COM2, which is IRQ4. Once this is done and verified, you are ready to install the modem in the computer.

Installing the Modem

Turn off the power to your computer. Remove the power cord from both the computer and the AC wall outlet. Then follow these steps:

1. Remove the retaining screws that hold the cover on your system.

2. Slide the cover forward. When it stops sliding, tilt the cover up and lift it away.

3. Select an open expansion slot and remove the slot cover retaining screw.

4. Hold the modem by its top edge, and gently slide the modem into the expansion slot. Do not force the modem into place.

5. Make sure that the modem is seated securely in the slot and that the mounting bracket on the board aligns with the bracket slot on the back of the chassis.

6. Using the slot cover retaining screw you removed earlier, secure the modem in the system.

7. Replace the computer's cover.

The modem hardware installation is complete. Now, we move on to the software installation.

Installing the Communications Software

Make a directory for the BitCom disk files using the DOS MD command. We'll call the directory COMM for communications. So at the C:\> prompt, type md\comm and press Enter. Then change to that directory by typing cd\comm and pressing Enter. The C:\ prompt should now show C:\COMM>.

Copy all the files from the original BitCom program diskette into this directory using the DOS COPY command. After copying the files, store the original program diskette in a safe place.

In some cases the files are in compressed format and must be "extracted." If this is the case, follow the manufacturer's directions for accomplishing this. These instructions are normally not difficult, they just add a few extra steps to the installation process. Their advantage is that they allow a lot of program information to be stored and shipped on a minimum number of diskettes.

The BitCom communications software is now ready for operation.

Connecting the Telephone Cables

Because we are installing the modem along with the fax board, and both are to be connected to the same telephone line, the connection is a little different than the manufacturer would expect.

Connect the short cable from the fax telephone jack to the modem wall jack. (The modem jack labeled PHONE will remain empty.)

The long telephone cable supplied with the fax or modem plugs into the wall jack on the fax board. Plug the other end of this cable into your empty telephone wall outlet.

Testing the Modem

Use the manufacturer's documentation for tests to verify that the telephone line can be accessed through the modem and that the computer is communicating with the modem. If the modem fails to respond to these tests, consult the manufacturer's manual for more detailed troubleshooting instructions or call the tech support hot line.

Testing the Telephone Line to Modem Connection
To test the cabling and telephone connection, lift the telephone handset and listen for the dial tone. If you hear nothing, recheck that the cables are properly connected and completely inserted in their respective jacks. If there is a dial tone, the cabling and telephone connections are intact and proper.

Note: The modem phone jack can also be used to daisy chain an optional telephone device.

Testing the Software to Modem Connection
Follow the directions from your communication program and configure the software for a direct connection to the modem. Make sure to set the correct COM port, speed, and so on.

This completes the loading of your application programs. By following the manufacturer's instructions you should be able to access and use the programs. The tips provided in Chapter 10 will help make your applications easier to use.

This completes the installation of your applications. The next chapter will give you some help in making your system easier to use—as the manufacturers of software put it, "more user friendly."

10

Making Applications
Programs Easy to Access

Constructing the following BAT directory and batch files make it easy
to use the application programs you've just loaded into your system. This
is because you can construct a menu of your programs that will appear
on your screen when you power up your system. Then you can press a
single key and the Enter key and your selected program will be activated.
So here we go—you're now going to be an applications programmer.

Remember, the BAT directory is where you keep the batch files.
Batch files are time- and effort-saving executable files you construct to
do complex or repetitive tasks that involve more than one DOS command
or a DOS command with modifying switches.

Making the Menu Batch File

First, make a directory called BAT.

1. After you've powered up your computer, make sure you're in the
   root directory by typing CD\ and pressing Enter.
2. Type MD\BAT and press Enter. This, as you recall, will make your
   BAT directory.
3. Type CD\BAT and press Enter. This makes the BAT directory your
   current directory.
4. Now copy the EDLIN.COM or EDIT file into the BAT directory from
   your DOS system diskette. Remember—COPY A:EDLIN.COM and
   press Enter with the DOS system diskette in drive A.

5. Type EDLIN 1.BAT and press Enter. The EDLIN asterisk will appear.

6. Type 1i and press Enter. *1.* will appear and you're ready to start entering the instructions for your first batch file.

7. Let's say you've installed WordPerfect 5.1 as your word processor and you want this program to be the first listed in your menu. Now type CD\WP51 and press Enter. *2.* will appear and you're ready to type the next command.

8. Type wp.exe and press Enter. *3.* will appear.

9. Type CD\ and press Enter. *4.* will appear.

10. Type TYPE \BAT\MENU and press Enter. *5.* will appear.

11. Press the Ctrl and Z keys at the same time and ^Z will appear. Then press Enter. The EDLIN asterisk will again appear and the cursor will be next to it.

12. Type L and press Enter, and your batch file will be listed. Check the file to be sure there are no typographical errors. Correct any errors by typing the line number and pressing Enter, then typing the correction and pressing Enter.

13. When you're satisfied the file is correct, type E at the EDLIN asterisk and press Enter. You have just completed your first programming effort.

Now let's analyze what we've actually done, starting at step 5 and going through step 10:

Step 5 initiates a batch file program called 1.BAT. (Remember a batch file is an executable file, so DOS will perform each of the commands listed in this file.)

Step 6 initiates the first command line.

Step 7 is the first command, which causes DOS to go to (change directory) the WP51 directory and make it the current directory.

Step 8 tells DOS to execute the WP.EXE (executable) program file.

Step 9 makes the current directory the ROOT (\) directory.

Step 10 tells DOS to display the MENU file from the BAT directory and stop.

Repeat the process starting with step 5 for each of your other applications programs. Make sure you use the proper directory designation in step 7 and the proper executable filename in step 8 for each application. And write down the number you assign to each application program for reference when you construct the menu files, a process described next.

Making the Menu Display

When you're finished creating the batch file, perform the following procedure using WordPerfect to design the menu display:

1. Activate WordPerfect by typing 1 and pressing Enter. The Word-Perfect logo will appear, the program will load, and page 1 will appear and be ready for you to type the menu display, as follows.

2. Press Ctrl + F3 (screen function) and 2 (line draw) and then 2 (double-line) again. This sequence enables you to make a double-line border for your menu.

3. Using the arrow keys, make a border that goes from the upper left corner of the screen to about 3/4 the height of the screen down the left edge, then across the screen to as far right as the cursor will go, then up the right edge to the upper right corner of the screen, then left across the top of the screen to the beginning. Now the menu border is made.

4. Now press the F1 key to exit the line-draw function.

5. Again using the Down-arrow key, move the cursor about 1/2 inch to 1 inch from the top of the screen. With the Right-arrow key, move the cursor one position to the right. Then, using the Spacebar, space to the right about 5 spaces and type the following: 1. WordPerfect 5.1.

6. Now press the Del (delete) key enough times to return the right border segment that ran off the right side when you typed in the menu item to bring it back into alignment with the rest of the border.

   When you're finished, *do not* press the Enter key; merely press the Right-arrow key, and the cursor will return to the left edge. If you happen to press the Enter key, merely press the Backspace key to realign the borders. Then proceed with the Right arrow key.

7. Repeat step 6 for the remainder of your program items that you have created batch-file programs for.

8. When you're finished entering the information you want on your menu, use the arrow keys to move the cursor to the lower right corner, then press the Enter key. The cursor will be one line below the bottom border line in the lower left area of the screen.

9. Press the F10 key to save this file and type C:\BAT\MENU.WP. Press Enter. The file will be saved as a WordPerfect file in the BAT directory.

10. Press the Ctrl + F5 keys to save this file again. Then press the 1 key (DOS file) and press the 1 key (save) again. Then type the following: C:\BAT\MENU (don't include the WP of step 9) and press Enter. The file will again be saved, but this time as an ASCII file. This is a form the operating system (DOS) can use.

11. Now press the F7 key, the N key, and the Y key to exit WordPerfect. Then type CD\ and press Enter to be sure you're in the root directory.

12. We're going to use EDLIN again now to make another batch file. Type EDLIN MENU.BAT and Enter. The EDLIN asterisk will appear.

13. At the asterisk, type 1i and press Enter. Type TYPE \BAT\MENU and press Enter.

14. Press Ctrl+Z and then press Enter.

15. Type E and press Enter to exit EDLIN.

Now when you type MENU and press Enter, your menu will appear on your screen. If not, go back over the preceding instructions and see where a mistake has been made, correct it, and retry the program by typing MENU and pressing Enter when your current directory is the root directory.

Modifying AUTOEXEC.BAT to Find the Batch File

Once you've created the batch file to load the menu and created the menu display, you simply tell DOS to run the batch file every time you power up the computer. Follow these steps:

1. Type EDLIN AUTOEXEC.BAT and press Enter to call up the AUTO-EXEC.BAT file for modification.

2. Type L and press Enter. The AUTOEXEC.BAT file will be listed on your display.

3. Add a final instruction to the file as follows:
   Type a number one greater than the last number shown on the list and type the letter i immediately following, then press Enter.

4. Type TYPE \BAT\MENU and press Enter.

5. Type Ctrl+Z and press Enter. Then type L and press Enter. The file will be relisted, and your new final command will be the last one in the list.

6. Type E and press Enter to exit EDLIN. Then type AUTOEXEC and press Enter. Your program menu will appear.

Now when you power up your computer system, the menu will appear and you can enter any of your programs merely by pressing its number key and the Enter key. This makes it simpler to use your computer system. Of course, it also gives you a little more appreciation for the people who did the programming of your applications, because what you've created here is considered a simple programming task (constructing a batch file). Imagine the thousands of workhours of designing, data entry, and testing that went into the highly complex application programs you've purchased for only a few dollars. An amazing bargain isn't it?!

Disaster Relief Efforts

Because the computer is now becoming a valuable information tool in your business, I must reiterate the necessity of protecting that information. Once your system is up and running for a while, you will certainly see the benefits of computerization. You may forget how you ran your business without a computer. Unfortunately, as time goes on you may also experience some problems, as mentioned earlier. When you use a system 12 hours a day, 7 days a week, it gets a good workout. If it doesn't function properly, your business suffers. Although computers are fairly rugged and many users experience years of trouble-free service, computers are not perfect and they do need some TLC (tender loving care).

There is one very important reason for the following discussion. *Most disasters are preventable!* When you receive hardware and software manuals, read them and follow the instructions carefully. If you have to manually "save" what you are working on, do it often. A small power surge can cause lost data. Most important . . . back up your system regularly.

Backing Up—The Best Disaster Insurance

A *backup* is a copy of files on your hard disk. Should you have a problem with it, all the files and directories that have been backed up can be copied back onto the hard disk in a short amount of time. The information on your hard disk may be backed up to floppy disks or to tape. A tape backup is a luxury, but if you can afford one, it's well worth the investment.

How often is often enough for backups? A full monthly backup (copying everything on the hard disk) is highly recommended. At the end of each day, perform an "incremental backup"—copy only the files that have been changed. Keep three sets of these daily backups, two at your place of business and one at home. Rotate the disks each day. This way, if there is a problem with any of the diskettes (or tapes), the most you will lose is one day's work. Keep several sets of full backups also (some organizations keep all of them). Diskettes and tapes should be discarded and replaced on a regular basis (annually for moderate usage or when the label begins looking soiled from use is another guideline) to be sure the quality is good.

At this point you have completed all that is necessary to purchase, install, set up, and begin using a basic business computer system. All that is left is for you and your staff to gain additional training and experience on your specific applications. And it is recommended that you provide the time and resources necessary for you and your staff to get the needed specific applications training. Because, as you can readily see by now, if the training and "hands-on" experience is not made available, the expected productivity levels will not be attained and the initial investment will be for naught. Improper use of the computer may even cause losses in time and money. Remember, your competitors are making this investment, and those that are successfully implementing their computer systems will have a competitive advantage in their respective market areas. This is a proven phenomenon and is why computers are becoming so ubiquitous throughout the business community. Computers have their faults and problems, but they certainly afford competent users a competitive edge in business.

Now let's look to the possible future growth of your system in your business and some of the questions of health hazards presented by their use to your staff.

11

Landing Your Company a LAN

"**L**AN" (local area network) is the buzzword of the 1990s (both as a noun and a verb). Everyone seems to be either hearing it or saying it. Questions need to be asked, however, before you proceed full-speed ahead with the implementation of a LAN in your office environment. What is a LAN anyway? What kinds of LANs are there? What kind of equipment do they require? Why should it be implemented? Are there disadvantages as well?

A LAN is what the words imply—it is a collection of hardware and software that electronically connects mainframes, minicomputers, micro-computers, terminals, and peripherals such as printers in such a manner that a network of information and resource sharing is created. The LAN links these resources in such a way that anyone connected to the network has potential access to all resources of the network (such as programs, printers, and data). It also gives the impression to each user that he or she is the only one using the resources. LANs can connect equipment within an office or many offices in a confined area, a single building, or an entire complex.

Other network concepts facilitate the connection of resources throughout larger areas such as a metropolitan area, called a *MAN—metropolitan area network*. Nationwide connections are called *WANs—wide area networks*—as are internationally connected networks. However, the principal concept of operation is the same—sharing resources. But the larger area networks are more apt to be connected to the public telephone communications services to transfer digital information between computers.

You need to carefully consider all the characteristics of the LAN as well as the environment it's coming into before you call the network vendor. Items to consider include the hardware (equipment), software, network configuration, and cabling required to connect the LAN, plus the staff you'll need to maintain it and use it. The material in this chapter should help you to converse knowledgeably about a vendor's proposal.

Advantages and Disadvantages of Networks

There are numerous advantages to a centralized processing (also called "server-based") network. The data is stored on a *file server*, a dedicated computer that literally "serves" data and services to those network users who request them. Because the data is centralized and stored in the file server(s) (the number depending on the size of the business) in one physical place, security is enhanced. Access rights—along with copyrights, update rights, modify-file rights, and so on—are determined ahead of time and programmed into the network's operating system. Therefore, no one without proper authorization can access or delete a file or change information.

Central Storage

Of course, someone (usually a group representative of all concerned) has to determine these rights, and they must be programmed into the system by a system administrator. Rights must be carefully allotted so people who need them have all that they need. But the data is still protected from curious or malicious eyes.

Having one physical network storage location is advantageous, in that the location chosen will be the most secure (a basement, for example). In this way there will be no worry that someone can walk into an unattended office and pilfer floppy diskettes sitting on a desk or remove a hard drive from a PC. If someone turns on an unattended network terminal, that person will be able to obtain virtually nothing.

The disadvantage of "one place" storage is that if an unauthorized person *does* obtain access, the hard drive of the server—the heart of your business—can be removed and carried out. Then, everything is gone. Yes, there will be backup tapes and copies, but someone now has everything—the keys to the kingdom of your enterprise.

Because the network is a single entity, if it goes down, work stops. Unless there is work that can be done on the local terminals, no computer work can take place. The average business network is down 30 percent of the time, for a average of 4.5 hours for each "crash." Obviously, smaller networks are more reliable and, because of their size, easier to diagnose and repair.

The ability to allow access to the same data at the same time by different people is one of the most significant advantages of a network. This causes problems as well, because not all data can be shared at the same time. For instance, two people should not alter the same record of a database at the same time, because their changes may contradict each other. In addition, software must be converted or special network versions of the programs must be purchased to run in this multiuser environment before file sharing can take place.

Although redundancy, inconsistency, and outright errors are reduced with a network, file sharing that allows this often causes some stress. People who have maintained their own databases can suddenly find it on a network where other people can also look at it and change it. There's a sense of *ownership* that accompanies data; no one likes to have it "taken away." The only answer to this dilemma is the statement that data belongs to the enterprise and not to the gatherer—easy to say, awkward to implement.

This centralized storage has the additional advantage of allowing standards to be created and enforced. No longer will two different departments, offices, or branches name the same data fields two different things, nor can they use two separate file structures. This matching is imperative in an environment where information is going to be shared or exchanged on a regular basis.

If data is to be shared with a network, it's possible to allow access to the same data at the same time by different people.

Data Reliability

Data integrity and reliability are also enhanced by having all data stored in one place. Because centralized error checking is implemented through the software by the system administrator, errors are reduced. Users at their own computers, responsible only for their own information, tend not to be sophisticated enough to include error traps in their data-handling processes—even if it does occur to the users that such traps are needed. Computerized data-checking routines are always more accurate than eye scans.

Reliability is increased with a network, because once a change is made in a file on the network, it's made throughout the system. Contrast this to changing a customer's address in records stored on various stand-alone PCs for your billing, customer service, and shipping departments. Program maintenance is reduced in the same way; if a program is changed on the central file server, the revised software is loaded for each user who signs on. No manual copying or compiling to each user is necessary.

Redundancy is eliminated when you convert to a server-based network. Because the files are stored only in one place, there are no duplicate copies to be accidentally lost or not kept up-to-date. There is also never any confusion over which listing is more current.

A final consideration for conversion is that conflicting requirements can be balanced. Knowing the overall needs of the organization compared with the needs of the individual user gives an obvious edge.

For instance, a representation of data storage could be chosen that gives fast response time to one area at the expense of less critical operations.

Because much of the data that will now become networked has been gathered and maintained by a user or department and not a systems professional, the chances are good that the data is not in the proper or most efficient format and may have to be redesigned. Again, people who have worked hard constructing these files will not like this, and the analyst/designer has extra work convincing these people of the necessary changes.

Special Software Requirements and Accessories

If custom software has been installed, it usually must be rewritten to run in the multiuser (networked) environment. This can be an important issue if it was written by a developer who is no longer with the firm or by a consultant who did not provide source code.

Also, many commercial spreadsheets and software packages must be scrapped so that the multiuser version can be installed. This isn't the only software expense that must be considered. The network will require the additional purchase of the network operating system software as well.

The most significant expense could be the hardware required to run the network. Although some existing hardware can be configured in, it's unlikely that a machine that will serve adequately as a file server will be on hand. Other hardware includes the boards that connect individual computers to the network and the media (cabling) that connects the boards to the network.

Planning the Network System

Therefore, the first step in the implementation of a LAN is deciding just who will be included. If it's not feasible to connect everyone at once, a plan must be formulated to sketch out implementation phases. Which is a priority, connecting all the offices in one building or setting up information-exchange guidelines between buildings? Which offices in the building have greater need of the network?

Some considerations are difficulty of accessing important data in a timely fashion, expenses incurred through not implementing a LAN, and security risks. For instance, the deciding factor in instituting a personal computer (PC) LAN at one facility was breach of security. Trainees with access to sensitive data were able to copy it to floppy disks to take out of the building with them—and they did.

What equipment exists in the business currently? Are there main-frames? If so, can they be cost-effectively replaced or discarded? If they represent an investment of new technology, they can and must be included in a decision to network. If there are only stand-alone PCs, you don't have to replace them. They are easily networked by means of a file server. If your company has both larger systems and PCs, the units can be connected into a near-seamless LAN.

Configuring the LAN's Topology

The configuration of the LAN, called the *topology*, can be one of several types. A point-to-point topology is just that: one computer to another computer. This isn't practical if the computers are very far apart or if either of the devices would require a link to another device at another time. Multipoint connections—more than one—are more popular.

The most common multipoint topologies for LANs are bus (also called tree), ring, and star. A *bus network*, shown in Figure 11-1, is a special case of the tree network because there's only one trunk and no branches. A tree has many "branches" or connections. With a bus/tree network, only one pair of devices can communicate at a time, because they share one communications medium (the trunk).

A *ring network*, shown in Figure 11-2, consists of one closed loop, with each connection attached to a repeating signal element (called a *token*). A person at a workstation who wishes to transmit data to another workstation or the file server waits for the token, which is continually circulating among the workstations. The token accepts the data, addresses it, delivers it, and moves on. These networks are like the old Christmas tree lights, however—if one workstation goes down, they all do—the token can no longer circulate to receive and deliver data.

The star topology illustrated in Figure 11-3 is simply a central switching network used to connect all the workstations. A dedicated path between the two devices is established for the duration of the communication.

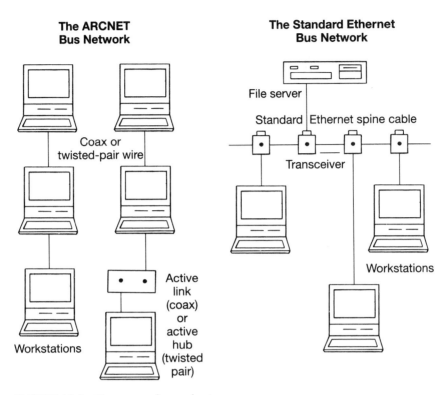

FIGURE 11-1 Bus network topologies

Another decision that enters this picture is the transmission medium necessary to connect the physical devices. It is possible to use telephone cables, twisted-pair wiring (shielded or unshielded), coaxial cabling (like cable TV), and fiber optic cable.

Telephone cables can be leased, or the standard phone lines can be used. The advantage of regular phone lines over a leased line is basically the fact that they are universally available, cheap, easy to implement, and easily rerouted. If a significant amount of traffic is generated, the leased line can be cheaper over the long haul. Cost depends primarily on the distance being connected, and installation lead time can be six weeks or longer.

Twisted-pair wiring, which is shown in Figure 11-4, consists of two spiraled copper wires. It is by far the most common transmission medium, and the medium of choice for low-cost microcomputer networks within a building. Compared with other media, though, it is limited in distance and data rate. It is also highly susceptible to interference and impulse noise. These distort a signal and can result in data loss.

**The Token Ring
Network**

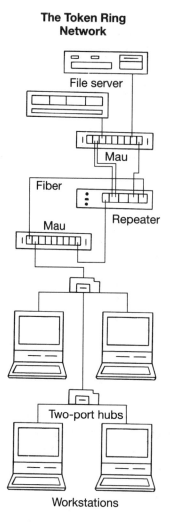

FIGURE 11-2   Ring network topology

Coaxial cable is similar to twisted pair but is constructed to allow it to operate over a wider range of frequencies. It consists of a hollow outer jacket and a single inner-wire conductor. It is perhaps the most versatile medium (it is used for cable television, for instance). It is the medium of choice for larger LANs and can support a variety of data types over distances of a single building or an entire complex of buildings. It is far less susceptible to interference than twisted pair because of its concentric design.

**The ARCNET
Star Network**

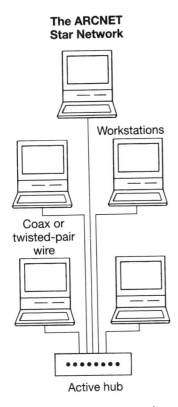

Workstations

Coax or
twisted-pair
wire

Active hub

FIGURE 11-3   Star network topology

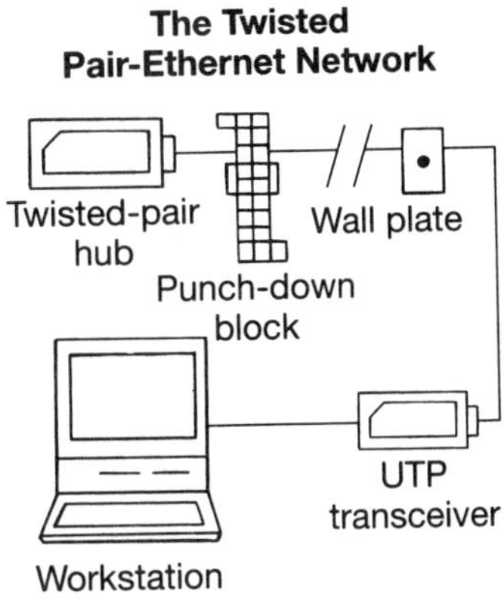

**The Twisted
Pair-Ethernet Network**

Twisted-pair
hub

Wall plate

Punch-down
block

UTP
transceiver

Workstation

FIGURE 11-4   Twisted-pair cabling as a transmission medium

Fiber optic cable is a thin, flexible medium with an insulating cover and is capable of conducting optical rays. The ultrapure glass fiber is difficult to manufacture; fibers that have higher-loss characteristics are more economical and still provide good performance. Fiber optic cable is widely used in long-distance telephone communications, and its ever-decreasing cost and clear superiority have spurred research in new areas of networking applications. Fiber optic cable is smaller in size and lighter in weight than other cable types and is very difficult to tap, because it radiates no external energy fields. This property also makes it invulnerable to interference.

It's necessary for you to go down one further level of detail before choosing a transmission medium; namely, what type of data will your company transmit? *Digital data signals* consist of discrete values—zeros and ones. Computers, by their design, generate digital data. *Analog data signals* can be likened to energy waves—voice is an analog signal.

It's possible to transmit digital data over an analog medium through a modem. This process is called *modulation*. It's also possible to transmit analog data over a digital medium through a process called *digitization*.

In addition, electric signals that pass down any medium can travel only a certain distance before the signal dissipates. Hardware "boosters" must be purchased to retransmit the signal. Analog signals require amplifiers that strengthen the signal, but still the signal has a physical limit in the distance it can travel. Digital signals require repeaters, which clean the signal and retransmit it fresh, so little data loss occurs. The greater the distance of the network, the more of these components must be purchased. It's best to know the total scope of the network initially so the components can be balanced appropriately.

Finally, knowing your equipment means knowing your personnel. No consultant or vendor can help with this. Consider the work force. Are they trained? What will it cost to train each user properly? In what order should they be trained? Will it be necessary to hire a technical trainer or establish a permanent networking position? Can current computer staff maintain the network? If not, what kind of service contract can the networking vendor provide?

Network Alternatives

There's more to PC local area networks (LANs) than the popular server-based LANs. Lesser-known LAN alternatives can save you money and time.

Although the popularity of server-based PC networks such as Novell Netware, Banyan Vines, and Microsoft LAN Manager has made server-based networks nearly synonymous with the terms "networking" and

"LAN," your networking alternatives are far more plentiful. Depending on your connectivity requirements, you can also choose from such options as peer-to-peer networks, multiuser operating systems, and zero-slot or zero-card (RS232) LANs. These alternatives are less costly, less complex, and require less maintenance than server-based LANs; some even offer additional features not available in server-based options.

Further, it is important to remember that no single networking alternative is ideal for all network situations; they each have features and limitations depending on the networking requirements of the installation. Even if you have a server-based LAN in place, these alternatives are worth considering as you work to enhance connectivity throughout your organization. By mixing and matching the available LAN alternatives, you can tailor your company-wide LAN to suit individual departments at the lowest possible cost, with the greatest ease of use. Combining multiuser and LAN technologies can offer the best of both worlds by localizing the workgroup computing environment, reducing network traffic, and improving its performance. Networks and multiuser systems should be viewed in the context of *and* rather than *either/or*.

A white paper from Digital Products, Inc. (Waltham, Massachusetts), maker of printer and peripheral sharing devices, advocates the same "mix and match" strategy with zero-slot LANs and peripheral sharing devices.

Networking Options

As stated before, a LAN is simply a group of electronically connected computers that are located in close proximity to each other, usually within a department or office building. Businesses create LANs so that their employees can leverage existing computer capabilities to communicate and to share data, expensive peripherals, and software.

Server-based LANs

Server-based LANs—LANs that link several PCs via one or more "servers"—are the most widely used type of LAN. A server is a PC on which the network operating system resides that links other workstations (also called *nodes*). The server-based LAN is centrally managed from the server, which holds the hard disk drives that store shared data and manages the shared peripherals, such as printers and modems. Individual PCs linked to a server-based LAN can (and usually do) have their own hard drive and sometimes have their own printer and other peripherals; however, other PCs on the LAN cannot use the hard drives and peripherals connected to individual PCs; they can only use the peripherals controlled by the server. (Remember that large LANs may contain several servers, each dedicated to specific functions, such as a file server, a print server, a database server, and/or a communications server.)

The most expensive of the networking alternatives costs approximately $500 to $1,400 per workstation. Server-based LANs are required for workgroups using computing-intensive applications such as CAD, desktop publishing, and statistical analysis, because these applications require the processing power of individual PCs in addition to the network links.

Major vendors of server-based networking software include Banyan (Westboro, Massachusetts), Novell, Inc. (Orem, Utah), and Microsoft Corporation (Redmond, Washington).

Peer-to-Peer Networks

A *peer-to-peer network* is a distributed, rather than centrally managed, system. In effect, any workstation functions also as a server, making the data on its hard drive and any of its peripherals available to other workstations on the LAN.

A peer-to-peer network provides many of the features of a server-based LAN on a limited scale. Most peer-to-peer networks cannot contain more than 20 workstations (most link 6 to 10 workstations), although some networks can be linked to a server-based LAN to provide for growth.

The distributed configuration of a peer-to-peer network makes it more flexible and less expensive than server-based LANs. Unlike a server-based LAN, you can share data and peripherals located on any workstation, anywhere on the LAN, not just on the server. In addition, the network doesn't rely on a single server, so if one PC goes down, the other workstations continue to work.

However, in situations where central management of the LAN is necessary, flexibility is a liability. Because any PC on a peer-to-peer network can use any other PC's hard drive, security is more cumbersome on a peer-to-peer network, and software upgrades or additions usually must be installed on several PCs.

Costs of implementing a peer-to-peer network range from $250 to $500 per workstation. The lower cost, compared to server-based LANs, results from not having to purchase a separate PC server, and the operating system software is less expensive.

Ease of installation, use, and maintenance are other advantages of this network compared to server-based LANs. Peer-to-peer systems are designed to be installed and maintained by end-users, rather than a network specialist.

Some prominent peer-to-peer network vendors include Artisoft, Inc. (Tucson, Arizona), Hayes Microcomputer Products (Atlanta, Georgia),

Invisible Software, Inc. (Foster City, California), Moses Computers (Los Gatos, California), Novell, Inc., and Webcorp (Sausalito, California).

Multiuser Operating Systems

Multiuser operating systems enable multiple users to run several different tasks simultaneously from a single 386- or 486-based PC. Like the server-based LAN, multiuser operating systems are centrally managed. The most common multiuser operating system is Multiuser DOS, a system that runs DOS software, uses DOS commands, and follows DOS conventions.

This LAN alternative, generally recommended for workgroups of 2 to 20, costs less and is easier to install and maintain than server-based systems. Because Multiuser DOS provides the power of a single 386 or 486 PC to linked workstations, the workstations need not be full stand-alone PCs; less expensive dumb terminals and older 8088 PCs can be used instead and the users will still have the processing capability of a 386, 486, or 586 PC. Also, because only one PC provides the processing power and the software for all linked workstations, you need to install software and maintain it only on the one PC. Security is ensured through the use of passwords to protect private files and by limiting users to terminals that don't include floppy drives, so users are unable to download information onto floppies.

Though individual Multiuser DOS LANs are limited to fewer than 20 workstations, many Multiuser DOS systems provide for connectivity to other Multiuser DOS LANs built around another PC, and provide for communications to server-based LANs and mainframes.

One feature of most Multiuser DOS systems that is not available in server-based or peer-to-peer systems is multitasking at the workstations. *Multitasking* allows each user to run several different DOS programs simultaneously on one PC. Much like channels on a television, users can flip from task to task without having to save work and get out every time the need arises for a quick change of application. For example, if you need to look up a figure in a spreadsheet, retrieve an address from a database, or answer an urgent E-mail message while you're in the middle of writing a document, you simply switch from the current task to another task with the touch of a "hot key."

Further, multitasking enables you to begin time-consuming tasks, such as the recalculation of a spreadsheet or data transfer via data communications, then continue working while the task is performed in the background.

Developers of Multiuser DOS include Concurrent Controls, Inc. (San Francisco, California), Digital Research (Monterey, California), Microbase, The Software Link (Norcross, Georgia), and THEOS Software Corp. (Walnut Creek, California).

Zero-Slot LANs

Zero-slot (or *zero-card*) LANs link PCs and printers with cables attached to the PC's standard serial or parallel ports, while software controls the data transfer between PCs. Of the LAN alternatives, zero-slot LANs are the least expensive but most limited means of networking. Costing between $50 and $100 per workstation, zero-slot LAN systems are an easy, inexpensive way to link a few PCs together for file and printer sharing. Products are available that can connect up to 16 PCs, though most industry analysts agree that three or four PCs should be considered maximum. Data transfer and printing are much slower than with other LAN alternatives.

Artisoft, Brown Bag Software (Campbell, California), Fifth Generation Systems, Inc. (Baton Rouge, Louisiana), Grapevine LAN Products, Inc. (Redmond, Washington), and Traveling Software, Inc. (Bothell, Washington), are a few developers of zero-slot LANs.

Selecting the Right Option for Your Business

Some questions that will help you determine which of these alternatives is best for your networking situation include:

- Why do we want a PC network?
- What tasks must be performed on the network?
- How many users do we need to network?
- Will the number of users increase in the near future?
- How much money can we spend to network?

Some reasons that business executives have for networking include sharing peripherals, maintaining a central database, sharing files, and providing E-mail. If sharing peripherals is your only or primary concern, your options include other LAN alternatives such as the following.

Additional Alternatives

Many companies or departments that think they need a LAN often don't. Eighty percent of the PC users surveyed by Creative Strategies Research International (Santa Clara, California, 1990) said peripheral sharing was their primary reason for installing a network. Fifteen percent listed file transfers as their main reason, and just five percent listed database and software sharing as their top priority. If peripheral sharing is your primary reason for networking, consider these other less expensive alternatives. Some of the alternatives also include limited data file-sharing capabilities. Alternatives that you don't want to overlook include mechanical data switches, buffered switches, and peripheral sharing devices.

Mechanical switchboxes—also called A/B or A/B/C boxes—enable you to share a single printer among two or three PCs.

Automatic switches, like switchboxes, connect several PCs to a printer, but are a "step up" in functionality from switchboxes. You can hook a few more PCs to a single printer than with the mechanical switchbox.

Buffered automatic switches are automatic switches with a memory buffer and offer the next level of capability. With it, a user can send a document to the printer while the printer is printing another document.

Printer sharing devices (controlled by a control panel switch) or *intelligent printer sharing devices* (controlled with software codes from your computer) offer the most flexible printer sharing option. Printer sharing devices are optimized so that more PCs can share a single printer than previously mentioned devices and so that multiple PCs can share multiple printers.

Peripheral sharing devices allow foreground serial file transfers between computers in addition to peripheral sharing.

Network Implementation

This chapter ends with two forms that should assist you as you install a network in your business. The implementation of a network in any organization is a serious undertaking; all aspects must be carefully considered before you make any decisions and spend your firm's funds. This top-down design consideration is an excellent start for achieving an organization's goals while getting the most from networking technology.

The LAN System Checklist will assist you in two ways:

- It will help you determine whether you really need or merely want a LAN for your business.
- If you decide to go forward with a LAN, the list will help you communicate your needs and desires to a vendor or consultant.

I strongly recommend that you obtain the services of a competent consultant (possibly recommended by your vendor or your vendor's support personnel themselves).

Merely fill in or appropriately check off the blanks you believe apply to your situation. Then take your checklist to a vendor for discussion and price quotes. You can then make a decision about whether to proceed.

Once your LAN is installed and functioning, use the LAN Fault Report Form to record as much information as possible of a fault occurrence when it happens—and they will happen. Communicate this information to all people responsible for maintaining your LAN so they can correct the problem efficiently.

Also, keep a file of these reports and review them periodically with your LAN maintenance people, with particular consideration of repeat occurrences and the frequency patterns of these occurrences. You may be able to prevent a major catastrophe in this way.

LAN SYSTEM CHECKLIST

Physical Site Layout

Number of buildings: _____

Number of floors: _____

Total distance to be covered (approximate): _____

Workstation locations: _____

Type of Cabling

Unshielded twisted pair _____   Shielded twisted pair _____

Thick coax _____   Thin coax _____

Fiber optic _____   Mixture of types _____

Physical Topology

Linear bus _____   Star-wired ring or token ring _____

Star _____   Distributed star _____

Ring _____   Tree _____

Type of Network Interface (Logical Topology)

Ethernet _____   Token Ring _____

Arcnet _____

User Information

Number of users: _____

Number of guest users: _____

Types and Number of Workstations

PC/XT	PC/AT (80286)	80386	80486	80586
_____	_____	_____	_____	_____

File Servers, Centralized Software, and Data Storage

Name	Location	Function	Type (e.g., 80286)	Server Address
_____	_____	_____	_____	_____
_____	_____	_____	_____	_____
_____	_____	_____	_____	_____
_____	_____	_____	_____	_____

Applications stored on file server(s):

Name	Location	Function	Server Address	Directory Location
_____	_____	_____	_____	_____
_____	_____	_____	_____	_____
_____	_____	_____	_____	_____
_____	_____	_____	_____	_____
_____	_____	_____	_____	_____
_____	_____	_____	_____	_____

User data stored on file server(s):

Server Name	Network Address	Directory Location
_____	_____	_____
_____	_____	_____
_____	_____	_____
_____	_____	_____

Operating Systems

Network Operating System

Name	Version	Revision	Features
_____	_____	_____	_____

Workstation Operating System(s)

Name	Version	Revision
_____	_____	_____
_____	_____	_____

_____   _____   _____

_____   _____   _____

File Server Printer(s)

Type	Model	Server Name	Address	Location
_____	_____	_____	_____	_____
_____	_____	_____	_____	_____
_____	_____	_____	_____	_____
_____	_____	_____	_____	_____
_____	_____	_____	_____	_____

Modems

Model	Baud	Location	Number of Users
_____	_____	_____	_____
_____	_____	_____	_____
_____	_____	_____	_____

Fax Boards

Model	Location	Number of Users
_____	_____	_____
_____	_____	_____
_____	_____	_____

Scanners, Plotters, and Other Shared Peripherals

Name and Model	Location	Number of Users
_____	_____	_____
_____	_____	_____

Tape Backup

Name and Model	Location
_____	_____

_____   _____

_____   _____

Uninterruptible Power Supply (UPS)

Name and
Model   Location

_____   _____

_____   _____

_____   _____

Local Printer(s)

Name and
Model   Location   Number of Users

_____ _____ _____

_____ _____ _____

_____ _____ _____

_____ _____ _____

LAN FAULT REPORT FORM

User Name: _____ Date: _____

Department: _____ Technician responding: _____
Application in use when problem occurred:

_____

Description of problem:

_____

_____

Error messages:

_____

Does problem occur in other files within the application?

Yes _____   No _____
If so, which ones?

_____

Does problem occur in other applications?

Yes _____   No _____
If so, which ones?

_____ _

Has the problem occurred with other users?

Yes _____   No _____
If so, describe the situation:

_____

_____

Has any maintenance been performed on the user's workstation in the past month?

Yes _____   No _____
If so, describe:

_____

_____

Has any software or hardware been added or upgraded at this work-station in the past month?

Yes _____   No _____
If so, describe:

_____

_____

Have any changes been made recently to the user's account?

Yes _____   No _____
If so, describe: _____

_____

Diagnostic procedures implemented: Results:

_____   _____

_____   _____

_____   _____

_____   _____

12

Planning Future Communications Systems

American business not only counts on dependable telephone communications services but also cannot survive without them. Productivity gains through computer communications (LANs, MANs, and WANs); videoconferencing; facsimile messaging; and call processing can all have one thing in common: the telephone system.

How do you ensure that your company's telephone system will be able to handle the ever-increasing demands placed on it? First, you need to know what kinds of applications your company plans to include in the system, both short term and long term. Next, find out about the adaptability of the systems that are on the market. Will they expand to meet future needs? Can your company purchase only those modules it needs currently, and incorporate more features/lines/ports as business requirements warrant them?

Management's role in the process is to consider the needs of business and what the new generation of telephone systems can bring to the mix. Three of the most important issues facing management include finding the methods to sort fact from fiction and reality from hype, discerning which of the evolving methodologies and technologies will become a de facto standard, and reconciling the budgetary implications, both near and long term.

Choosing among vendors in the telecommunications business is complicated by the fact that there are literally hundreds of vendors to choose from, all offering varying combinations of features. One of the most basic questions is whether to purchase digital or analog equipment.

Today only large companies with more than 1,000 employees really need digital equipment (for voice/data applications).

In prior years, *digital* has been more of a buzzword, but with digital price points rapidly approaching those of their analog counterparts, purchasing digital in the future, when price or growth justifies it, just makes good business sense. In addition, digital technologies are more apt to be compatible with future central office/network offerings, such as digital Centrex and ISDN.

Integrated Services Digital Network (ISDN) essentially provides end-to-end digital communications that will bring a wealth of services to businesses and residences. ISDN is still bogged down in the standards process but will someday be an important factor in telecommunications. It is a technology that, at this time, only large businesses are prepared to accept given their deep pockets and technical personnel for support, and the fact that large companies can currently offset the initial costs through volume purchases.

Experts agree that the much-touted advent of fiber optics as the total solution in networks and local distribution is still years away. Consider that many exchanges are still using analog central office switches, and that the local plant of many companies includes open wire, multiparty lines, and carrier equipment. Total fiber optics will bring a wide variety of audio and video services to the business and residential markets. Fiber optics is a transport medium of the future that will affect the way we all live.

The expense of replacing copper cannot be justified at this time for a mass changeover. Over time, fiber optics will become more prevalent, providing the user with more bandwidth to provide data and video services and perhaps the day of the video telephone.

The Economies of Scale

The priorities of the large corporation offer insights into the complexities of dealing on a large scale. Concerns of large corporations are based on economies of scale. For instance, low maintenance costs make a huge difference when you're dealing with a large number of phones and phone lines. Most of today's equipment is modular, which makes for quick installation and changes. And in today's large corporation, people change offices inside the building often.

You need to consider agreeing with your local carrier on a "point of demarcation" in the telephone circuit beyond which any problems are the phone company's problems. When your company is large, support systems become very important: on-line directory listings for use by operators and employees avoid the costly reprinting of paper directories; an integrated work order system allows for chargeback billing to departments and updates the on-line directory at the same time. The real payoff is in time saved and in data integrity.

Completing the Connection

One serious need that has never before been addressed through telephone technology is the imperative of making sure that the incoming call reaches the person, not just the person's telephone. Several approaches to that problem are being developed by vendors. For instance, local paging systems have been around for at least 30 years, but today the concept is being expanded and refined.

National satellite paging companies can now reach their subscribers anywhere in the country. You're never out of touch unless you want to be. Personal telephones (cordless and wireless) have been miniaturized to shirt-pocket size and in combination with satellite-based services can deliver your calls right to you, anywhere. This is the age of communications, with personal and business communications merging, allowing individuals freedom and accessibility at the same time. Admittedly, there are still technical details to be worked out, but the corner has been turned on personal communications.

In the event you don't *want* to carry your equipment with you, voice messaging software will hold your messages until you pick them up from wherever you may be. Voice messaging will play an ever-increasing role as in-home offices and noncommuting become more popular for environmental and practical reasons. These trends create an ever-increasing need for better communications for remote parties. And as people become more acclimated to voice mail, voice communications will be preferred and more cost effective than paper communications.

These systems will soon move into data transmission as well, thus expanding computer networking capabilities to any point on earth regardless of how remote.

As prices continue to decrease and awareness increases, businesses will be lining up for voice messaging and eventually forming longer lines for data transmission services.

Planning Ahead

As you plan your company's communications system, don't forget to check on what additional costs besides equipment and systems costs will be incurred (such as line and time charges) in using these systems. You should balance the total costs against the productivity gains to be realized.

A long-term strategy is especially important when you are dealing with a moving target, such as the European market. If your company is planning to enter Europe or expand your operations there, you'll need to ask some pointed questions. Complete service packages marketed in the United States under names such as Virtual Private Networks, Software Defined Networks, and Vnet, which use the public switched telephone network to provide "virtually private" network services, are either not available or are of limited availability abroad. In no case are they as feature-rich as those in the United States.

You'll need to formulate plans that define as clearly as possible what the network is expected to do, and timetables for how and where it will grow, both here and abroad. Your domestic and international service carrier can help with coordinating advanced services such as dynamic bandwidth management, integrated voice/data networking, and more.

Easy Access to Wiring

Through this mass of technology, one thing is clear: We are still bound to point-to-point connections to handle the power, data, and voice transmission within a given facility. So wiring connections (whether copper or optical fiber) must be considered and planned for.

Tweeds, a successful mail-order retailer of European-inspired casual clothes, recently established a new headquarters office in an old building that presented a challenging rehabilitation task. Wiring the company's crucial data and telecommunications systems in a turn-of-the-century Hudson River factory with mostly brick interior walls was no small part of that challenge. A two-piece metal raceway from the Wiremold Company (West Hartford, Connecticut) provided an easy and attractive solution, housing wiring along the brick surface.

Tweeds retained Syntech Communications, Inc. (Edgewater, New Jersey), to specify, install, and wire their phone system, a Northern Telecom (Nashville, Tennessee) Meridian SL-1, and data communications equipment.

The order center, warehouse, and MIS functions are all in Roanoke, Virginia, and continuous, reliable communications with the Edgewater, New Jersey, home office is crucial to the business. When a catalog hits customers' homes, for example, the headquarters marketing group needs to measure its effectiveness.

To do this, marketing staff print out the order data maintained on the mainframe, a Sequent (Beaverton, Oregon) S81 parallel processor, in Virginia. The inventory system is used in both places, too; order clerks check stock and availability, and home-office buyers monitor what items are hot, change price points, schedule reorders, and plan merchandising. They have a T-1 multiplexer tying the two locations together and 20 Televideo (San Jose, California) terminals in the headquarters connected with their mainframe.

The factory was wired in the following way. The main distribution frame is on the first floor, using large-capacity G-6000 raceway in the main closet and to feed intermediate distribution frames on the second and third floors. The G-6000 serves as a cable tray for panel backboards in the main closet, eliminating the need for ladder racks to run cable vertically between floors to the two smaller closets. Using a modular patch panel gave Tweeds the ability to move or add phone stations or data connectors in minutes.

Tweeds needed only 86 phones when the staff moved in, but the offices can accommodate 170 stations. The departments can add new PCs or printers, or even replace their phone system by changing wiring on the 110 punch-down terminals installed. The company also prewired for a LAN, for more networking capability than the staff is currently using. And the facilities maintenance people are especially pleased with the clear, well-labeled organization of the distribution frames.

Tweeds employees in New Jersey like the appearance of their offices. The gray raceway looks attractive against the warm red brick, and blends well with the firm's logo and interior design.

Color-coded jacks—ivory for voice wiring, black for asynchronous data, and gray for the LAN—help make changes easy. The raceway also houses the wiring for the alarm system and the night bell. The building was already wired for electricity when the communications were installed, or it too could have been in the raceway.

Particularly impressive is the way the raceway system provides phone and data connections wherever they're needed and plenty of flexibility for change and growth. The system helped achieve a unique blend of the high-tech communications that modern business needs with the charm and history of a century-old factory.

13

Protecting Your System from Computer Viruses

If you are to use a PC on a regular basis, the chances are you'll come in contact with a computer virus. In fact, according to a recent survey presented at a computer-virus conference, one in four major U.S. computer (corporate and government) users will be exposed to a virus *each month*.

The number of reported computer viruses continues to escalate. But despite such a dismal forecast, there are ways to protect yourself against the devastation that a computer virus can cause. There are preventive steps that you or your computer wizard can take to guard against infection.

Although in theory monitoring software use makes sense, in reality it's nearly impossible to do. In most cases, viruses are innocently introduced by someone using infected software that's been stored on floppy disks, including distribution disks of commercial software, or shared with other users through electronic bulletin boards. Once introduced onto a network, the virus may begin to spread, infecting and destroying existing data files, taking up valuable memory, or even causing entire systems to shut down.

What Is a Virus?

A *virus* is a program that attaches itself to other programs and then proceeds to change your data, programming instructions, or operating system. Although there are over a thousand viruses in existence (and more being born every day), most are contained in the laboratory where they are born and do not get out. Some viruses are purposely let loose as a means of sabotage or malicious mischief, and some are accidentally released.

Viruses only attach themselves to executable code (files with extensions such as .EXE, .COM, or .OVL) and are very selective of the type of environment in which they can work. For this reason, a virus that is designed for an IBM (or compatible) computer will not work on a Macintosh, minicomputer, or mainframe. The same is true for Apple viruses and Macintosh viruses.

Disease-Fighting Software and Other Combative Measures

A large number of antiviral software packages currently available can scan and detect infected programs. These scanning and filtering programs should be used with all new software programs you install. Such protection programs detect known viruses before they have a chance to spread throughout the system. If you suspect that a virus has already invaded your system, some programs can be used to identify problems and eradicate viruses.

If monitoring the software being used in a stand-alone computer is difficult, doing the same in a network environment is nearly impossible. The whole idea behind networking is sharing; sharing data, sharing peripherals, and sharing files. And, as with any type of sharing, the more you share, the less control you have.

For that reason, many information systems managers have included optical, write-once-read-many (WORM) technology into their total LAN scheme. Data recorded onto a write-once disk is permanent. A laser is used to make permanent data bubbles or pits on the surface of the media. These marks, which represent bits of data, can't be altered even by the most sophisticated computer virus.

Also, many LAN managers are using write-once optical disks for storing computer backup data. If a virus is later detected in the system, finding a clean version is as easy as accessing the optical disk. Although information recorded on write-once media can't be altered, it can be updated. Each time a file is recalled and edited, a new version of the file is created. The previous version remains somewhere on the disk. Once a virus is detected, the user need only trace the file back step-by-step until an unaffected version is found.

How Is a Virus Spread?

New viruses are being created all the time. And though studies show that heavy computer users are almost certain to come in contact with these destructive programs, many companies have few or no protective programs in place. Eliminating virus-infected programs is virtually impossible. However, with the proper planning and implementation of safeguards, the chances of contracting a virus are greatly reduced.

Viruses are spread in several ways:

- If a boot diskette has a virus on it, all computers that are booted from that diskette will be infected with the virus. Most of today's PCs have hard disks that contain the operating system, so the need for boot diskettes is greatly diminished and the temptation to share a boot diskette is greatly reduced.

- Viruses can spread if you attempt to boot from a nonsystem diskette. This happens if an infected diskette is in the A drive during bootup. Because DOS will attempt to boot from the A drive before the hard drive, some virus writers have taken advantage of the situation and made the virus act like the operating system (including issuing the message that the diskette is a nonsystem diskette) as the virus attaches itself to the operating system.

- Viruses are spread by retrieving programs from an electronic bulletin board on which users have placed infected programs. Some bulletin board operators are very careful of the programs that reside on their systems; others are not. It is impossible to tell how reliable a given bulletin board is, although you could feel safe with the large nationally advertised systems such as CompuServe and Prodigy. A user will see an impressive game/screen saver/program on the bulletin board, try it, and decide to install it. The user installs it on his or her home computer, then decides to take it to work and show it to co-workers. If the virus has connected itself to this program, then every computer that has the program stored on it can get the virus.

- Another way of getting infected is for someone to load an infected program onto a LAN server, thus spreading the virus throughout the network.

- One other very prominent source of viruses is through academia. People studying or attending computer classes—whether elementary school, universities, or commercial training facilities—can acquire computer programs in any of the above mentioned ways and bring and spread them into the work environment.

What Can Be Done to Prevent Viruses?

There are several steps you can take to avoid these plagues. The first advice is, don't panic! Just because the media has sounded a warning on viruses (recall the Michelangelo media hype) doesn't mean the whole computer world is at risk. The Michelangelo virus has been around for several years. There is also a Friday-the-13th virus, an April-Fool's virus, and many that are not date-dependent.

The best protection against viruses is to provide safeguards to ensure they're never introduced into the system. The following are a few rules that must be strictly followed to prevent or recover from viruses on your computer.

- Don't use pirated software. Not only is it illegal but it's also dangerous. Use programs from reputable companies. There have been some instances of viruses being spread from known companies, but this is not the common mode of transmission. Major software and computer developers such as Microsoft, Lotus, and Borland cannot afford the ill-will and bad press that infected disks can bring. On the other hand "bootleg software" companies have been known to intentionally infect programs.

- If you open the package for the first time and notice that the seal on the disk package has been broken, return the package to the vendor. Retailers have been known to reshrink-wrap returned software without testing it.

- Don't use software that's been downloaded from obscure bulletin boards. Although these programs may seem an inexpensive way to acquire new application programs, they often contain harmful viruses. If you use a program from a bulletin board, first download the source file and compile the program on your machine. (This implies that you have the appropriate compiler, which may not always be the case.)

- Write protect your system diskettes. On 5.25-inch floppies, attach one of the peel-off tabs (usually black or silver) that came with your box of floppies on the rectangular cutout located on the edge of the floppy. For 3.5-inch diskettes, slide the plastic tab (usually black) on the corner of the diskette so that you can see light through the slide opening. Both of these are physical devices that prevent the system from writing to your diskette.

- Back up your system regularly. Make sure you keep several sets of your backups as described previously. You may not know when your system was infected and backup diskettes can keep a virus in waiting. A rigorous program of scanning and then backing up data will help to protect against most viruses. If a virus is later detected in the system, you'll have a clean backup copy ready for use.

- Limit the access of your system to as small a group as possible. Viruses aren't created in a void; they must be introduced by someone using unauthorized or affected software.

How Do You Learn Your Computer Has a Virus?

You may not know for a period of time that your system has a virus, because the triggering conditions are not correct. Suddenly one day, a program that worked before won't work, or you get a drive error on a known good disk, or you get unknown communications errors (this last could also be a wiring problem or a loose cable between the computer and the wall), or you get a strange message on your screen.

How to Eradicate the Virus

If all the preventive measures mentioned earlier still don't keep your system disease-free, follow these steps to rid your system of the virus:

1. Stop using the computer system. Further use will only increase the damage the virus does.
2. Locate a local source of virus detection and correction software and purchase a copy, if you don't already have a copy.
3. Be sure you write protect the antiviral diskette(s) and then run the program from drive A as prescribed by the manufacturer. Do *not* back up your system until *after* your system has been disinfected. Backing up now will only cause you to create infected backup diskettes. You may try to copy data files from your older backups, provided you write-protect your diskettes first.

What about programs that reside on a hard disk? There are several manufacturers of virus scan products that have programs that reside on your hard disk and check for viruses each time a diskette is read. They generally slow down your operations while they do their scanning and for that reason they're not generally recommended.

Remember, if all you are doing is copying and transferring data diskettes, the chances of getting and transmitting a virus are very slim.

How Serious Is the Virus Threat?

Must every computer owner buy antiviral software? The answer is that there is a real threat, but it is easily exaggerated by the antiviral software firms and the news media. Your need for antiviral software depends a lot on how you use your computer systems. And though many of the programs are effective, they have downsides.

Some companies seem to play on fears; a few warn of the Maltese Amoeba virus set to erase disk files every March 15. But the independent National Computer Security Association (NCSA) in Washington, D.C., says that of the 1,000-plus viruses known to attack IBM-compatibles, fewer than 50 are common and only about 100 others have also been found "in the wild." The rest are known only to researchers.

Last year, the NCSA says, just two viruses—Jerusalem-B and Stoned—accounted for 74 percent of virus incidents in the United States. Neither wipes out whole disks, as the Michelangelo virus appeared to do. As for the dreaded Maltese Amoeba, the NCSA and others say it hasn't yet been reported in the United States. In fact, some of the worst viruses mainly flourish abroad. Mac owners face fewer viruses.

So there's no need to panic, but prudence is in order. Many computers, especially in big organizations, become infected, and most infections screw up the computer. The worst cases wipe out data or program files. Lone home users who do little disk swapping or program sharing probably don't need antiviral software. But in most other cases—especially large organizations with many computer users—antiviral software is advisable. At the very least, hard disks should be scanned for viruses every month or so, and any floppy disk from an outside source should be scanned before use.

Antiviral programs usually include a scanner, which operates on demand or when the computer starts up, looking for computer code that matches a set of "signatures" characteristic of known viruses. There's often a separate module that eradicates any viruses found. And there's normally a form of the program that can remain in memory at all times to check for viruses but, as mentioned before, these tend to slow down the system. In addition, many programs try to seek unknown viruses by looking for changes in the size and composition of program files on your hard disk, or by monitoring suspicious behavior believed common to viruses. None of these methods are foolproof.

The programs' database of virus signatures must be updated relatively often to be effective. Their memory-resident modules can goof up other software by hogging memory. And various techniques of finding unknown viruses might be rendered ineffective if the digital vandals think up new methods of infection. Two programs—Novi by Certus, of Cleveland, Ohio, and Untouchable by Fifth Generation, of Baton Rouge, Louisiana—claim such good generic virus detection that you don't need to update for new virus signatures. Novi seems to offer the more sophisticated approach, monitoring processes inside programs. The company says its generic technology has caught every new virus for four years. But if you buy these products, it would be wise to continue to scan for known viruses and to get updates, which both products allow.

If you plan to purchase a copy of this type software now, you probably wouldn't go wrong with any of four packages:

- Central Point Anti-Virus, by Central Point, Beaverton, Oregon
- Viruscan, by McAfee Associates, Santa Clara, California
- Certus's Novi
- ViruSafe by Xtree, San Luis Obispo, California

Another leading package, Norton Anti-virus, by Symantec, Santa Monica, California, is also considered good. But the NCSA gives higher marks to two lesser-known programs: Dr. Solomon's Anti-Virus Toolkit, sold by Ontrack Computer Systems, Eden Prairie, Minnesota; and Leprechaun Virus Buster, sold by Leprechaun Software, Marietta, Georgia. Some top virus busters swear by an Icelandic program that's free to home users and costs businesses just $1 a computer. Called F-Prot, it's found on database services and bulletin boards, including NCSA's (202-364-1304).

Now that we've covered the health and welfare of the computer system, let's talk about the health of the human user of the system.

14

Computer User Health Hazards and How to Prevent Them

There are two primary areas of human interaction with computer systems—the display screen or monitor and the keyboard. Other specialized equipment such as bar code readers/scanners and page scanners also require human interaction but, to date, they have not been studied for their potential effect on human health factors.

This chapter explores these primary interaction devices—the video display terminal, or VDT, and keyboard—and their potential for causing health problems. We will also suggest methods, processes, and exercises for reducing or eliminating these ill effects.

First we'll explore the monitor, then the workstation setup, and finally the keyboard and the major health problem its use engenders: carpal tunnel syndrome.

The Monitor Revolution

The display monitor has revolutionized the workplace, changing the way many people work. As a monitor user, you are in a unique position to take advantage of new opportunities and to learn new skills. Learning how to use your monitor safely and efficiently can be fun, too.

The monitor is today's "multipurpose desktop." It is quickly replacing the typewriter, calculator, telephone, filing cabinet, copier, and other office workhorses. Tasks that used to take days to complete can now be done in minutes. Office secretaries, customer service representatives, records keepers, and executives alike are discovering how monitors can increase productivity and efficiency. And, as with any new technology, the human element is the key to its success.

Ergonomics: The Human Interface

Monitors are remarkable, time-saving tools, but they require a good deal of concentration and precision to operate. You can make your monitor use less tiring and hazardous by learning the principles of *ergonomics*—how people interact safely and efficiently with machines and their working environment. Simple changes in the way you "interface" with your monitor can help prevent common health-related monitor problems. With a basic understanding of ergonomics, you can make your monitor experience fun and professionally satisfying.

Teamwork: Reaching Your Potential
Making your work with the monitor happy, healthy, and productive requires team effort. The employee and the employer can become familiar with simple, easy ways to make the interface with the monitor more comfortable and efficient. Reaching your potential can be a learning experience you'll want to share with others.

Employer's Goals
It's no secret that a good employer wants the employees to be happy, healthy, and productive, because "positive" people help make the working environment more rewarding for everyone. To make your working experience as positive as possible, the employer and employee can develop a monitor work area based on ergonomic principles. Good communication promotes positive change. With teamwork you can design a work area that helps you take full advantage of all that this new technology offers.

Employee Goals
Employee goals may be similar to those of the employer's—no doubt the employee enjoys being happy and productive, too. Reaching these goals can be as simple as improving posture, adjusting the height of a chair, or changing the angle of the display screen. Easy-to-do exercises can help relieve stress and fatigue so that you'll feel better both mentally and physically. The employee should be sure to offer ideas about how to improve the working environment. You'll be surprised how simple some solutions can be—and how important they are in making monitor work more comfortable, efficient, and rewarding.

Ergonomics is the science of suiting machines to the way people interact with them. When workplace design suits the needs and capabilities of employees, comfort and productivity are at their highest. Every individual and working situation is different, and not every factor in the workplace can be changed, but with planning and a little imagination, almost any monitor working environment can be made more efficient and comfortable. Ergonomic research has provided some general guidelines that you can follow to make your monitor experience less demanding on the eyes, body, and mind. Find ways to make your work area closer to the ideal illustrated in Figure 14-1.

Human Factors of the Workstation Environment

Good posture is essential for comfort and well-being, especially when you sit in essentially the same position several hours a day. Follow these

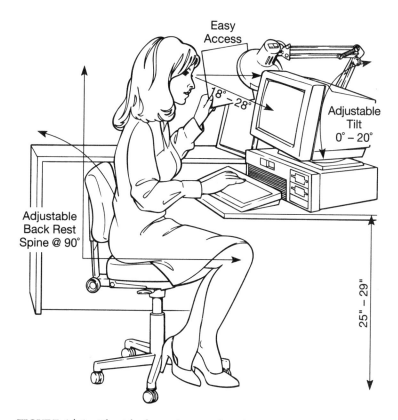

FIGURE 14-1   The ideal monitor workstation

tips to improve your posture and minimize body stress as you sit at your
PC:

- To prevent neck and back strain, keep your spine and head upright,
  and sit well back into the chair.
- Placing your feet on a footrest helps take the strain off your legs
  and back.
- Correct hand and wrist placement are important. Shoulder muscles
  can become tense when arms and hands are held too high. Hold
  arms comfortably at your side, with your upper arm and forearm at
  about a right angle. Wrists should be in line with the forearms; wrist
  problems (detailed later) can develop if they are bent at extreme
  angles.
- Good eye care can help prevent vision problems. Focusing at close
  range for long periods of time can sometimes cause blurred vision
  or eye soreness—common but temporary problems experienced by
  many people who work on jobs requiring a high degree of detail.
  To lessen the strain on eye muscles, keep your display screen at
  least 18 to 28 inches from your eyes (or farther away than you might
  hold a book). Itching and burning may be caused by dryness, so
  blink slowly now and then to help keep your eyes moist.

Design Factors of the Hardware and Office Furniture
A well-designed monitor lets the user make individual adjustments. Following are tips you can use to modify the computer's and office furniture's
design factors that can affect your health:

- For comfortable head and neck placement, the top of the screen
  should be positioned at about eye level.
- To minimize tension in shoulder muscles, the keyboard should be
  low enough so that the arms hang freely and elbows are bent at
  right angles. Detachable keyboards and desks having a split-level
  design are ideal for this. Contrast can be adjusted to a comfortable
  level—not so bright as to cause flicker or be hard on the eyes.
- A properly designed chair has a seat that curves down in the front,
  support for the lower back, and a height that can be changed to
  suit different users. Height should be adjusted to permit correct
  placement of the head, hands, and knees (you shouldn't have to
  hunch over to see the screen or bend the elbows more than 90
  degrees to reach the keys).
- Knees should be at about the same level as your hips.
- Good lighting is not always bright lighting. Reduce glare by pulling
  drapes or repositioning your display screen. Other options for adjusting light levels include hoods, glare screens, or special lighting.

Breaks That Can Revitalize You

Breaks from work can be a time for stretching muscles, relaxing the eyes, socializing, or slipping away for a quiet moment of solitude. Work area "minibreaks" can help keep your eyes, mind, and body refreshed and energized.

Scheduled Breaks

The National Institute of Occupational Safety and Health (NIOSH) suggests that monitor users take a scheduled break after every couple of hours of uninterrupted monitor work. As a small business owner, you should establish a break schedule for all computer users. Employees can make the most of break time by socializing with co-workers, stepping outside, or exercising to restore circulation and revitalize tired muscles.

Unscheduled "Downtime"

Be ready to take advantage of unscheduled downtime by doing one or more of the exercises described here.

Vision breaks: While at your workstation, you can reduce eyestrain by taking vision breaks. Simple eye "exercises" can be done for less than a minute, every 20 minutes or so. One valuable exercise is palming. Form shallow cups with the palms of your hands, then place them lightly over your closed eyes. Relax for one minute.

Changing focus is another way to give your eye muscles a chance to relax. Simply glance across the room or out the window from time to time and focus on an object at least 20 feet away.

Exercises for monitor minibreaks: Deep breathing—Breathe in slowly through the nose. Hold for 2 seconds, then exhale through the mouth. Repeat several times.

Head and neck—Turn your head slowly from one side to the other, holding each turn for a count of three. Repeat 5 to 10 times.

Upper back—With arms folded at shoulder height, push your elbows back. Hold a few seconds. Repeat 5 to 10 times.

Shoulders—Roll shoulders forward 5 times using a wide circular motion. Then roll shoulders backward 5 times. Repeat 5 to 10 times.

Wrist—Hold your hands in front of you. Raise and lower your hands to stretch the muscles in the forearm. Repeat several times.

Fingers and hands—Make a tight fist with your hands. Hold for a second. Then spread your fingers apart as far as you can. Hold for five seconds.

Lower back—While sitting, slowly bend your upper body between your knees. Hold for a few seconds, then sit up and relax.

Legs—Grasp the shin of one leg and pull slowly toward your chest. Hold for 5 seconds. Then do your other leg. Repeat several times.

PC Monitors: Today's Opportunity, Today's Health Hazard

Like other technological advances, the monitor will undoubtedly improve our lives enormously. In fact, few inventions have affected so many people so quickly. You can take full advantage of this exciting new technology by learning simple ways to make your monitor experience happier, healthier, and more productive. However, the potential risks of using monitors have made international headlines in the past several years, raising user awareness to an all-time high. Amidst both conclusive and inconclusive evidence of health hazards posed by monitors, users and vendors are taking a better-safe-than-sorry approach.

Late in 1990, the city of San Francisco passed the controversial Regulation of Video Display Terminals (VDTs)—Ord. 405-90 safety bill, which requires the city's medium- and large-size firms to provide ergonomically sound workstations for employees who spend more than 50 percent of their workday at VDTs (monitors). It also mandates alternative work for 15 minutes after every 2 hours an employee spends working on a monitor.

The passage of the San Francisco law sent a shockwave across the country. Instead of affecting only that city's employers, the law has motivated employers nationwide to comply with its standards in anticipation of future legislation. And it is thought by industry leaders that more legislation is inevitable because of "mainstream concern over computer safety." A domino effect is likely to occur from the San Francisco law until monitor safety is legislated on a national level. It will be hard to stop the tide now that it is under way.

A court test later struck down the San Francisco ordinance, as also occurred to a similar bill passed in Suffolk County, New York. The court, however, stated the state preempted the field and is responsible for regulating safety in the workplace. Thus, many people think these bills will have far-reaching effects.

Many people don't need legislators or the media to tell them about monitor health risks. They know from personal experience.

Eyestrain caused by monitor usage topped office workers' list of job-related health complaints in an annual nationwide poll conducted for Steelcase, Inc., by Louis Harris Associates. Forty-seven percent of office workers surveyed cited monitor eyestrain as a serious concern, compared with 37 percent who complained about air quality.

A survey of 5,000 optometrists conducted by Dr. James Sheedy, chief of the University of California Berkeley's VDT Eye Clinic, and supported by Optical Coating Laboratory Incorporated (OCLI) revealed that optometrists are treating more than 8 million monitor-related eyestrain cases per year in this country. It is the first optometrists' survey on monitor vision issues, according to Sheedy.

More than half of the optometrists surveyed stated that patients who use monitors have different symptoms from other patients with eye problems. Symptoms of computer-related visual stress include headaches, double vision, blurred vision beyond close range, occasional blurring of screen images, tired and red eyes, increased eye irritability, and changes in color perception.

Monitor vision symptoms are caused by physiological and spectacle design problems, as well as by environmental work station problems. Environmental factors include screen glare, inconvenient work arrangements, poor lighting, and low screen resolution.

The optometrists' poll attributed 37 percent of the cases to problems such as screen glare and poor lighting or screen resolution. Eighty-two percent of these doctors routinely recommend specific changes in the computer work environment, with nearly 70 percent recommending antiglare filters to reduce monitor glare.

Fortunately, monitor vision problems can be corrected. What are not so easy to correct are health problems resulting from monitor emissions. A major part of the problem is that no one has been able to define precisely what those health problems are.

Emission Anomaly

Although it is fairly easy to link monitor usage with vision and musculo-skeletal problems, it is much harder to determine how monitor emissions affect humans. Most electrical appliances, including computer monitors, emit electromagnetic waves. You can't see or feel electromagnetic waves but they are there, even though they're difficult to measure. But we don't know what the long-term effects of exposure to these emissions are.

Some vendors, such as Preferred Computer Service, are addressing this concern. This company offers radiation measurement products that let you assess the electric or magnetic field radiation from monitors and other electrical or electronic equipment.

Unfortunately, the few studies that have tried to determine the effects of emissions are more confusing than enlightening. Some scientific research links monitor radiation to cancer and miscarriages.

For example, the 1988 Kaiser Permanente study, conducted by researchers at the Northern California Kaiser Permanente Medical Care Program in Oakland, polled 1,583 pregnant women and found a doubling of miscarriages in those who used monitors more than 20 hours per week during their first trimester. Recently, however, the National Institute for Occupational Safety and Health (NIOSH) released a study that negated the relationship between monitor emissions and problems in pregnancy.

Then, in 1991, four international studies—sponsored by the Societe d'Exploitation Industrielle Commerciale of Geneva, Switzerland, and

Wellware of Park City, Utah—cited monitor radiation as the cause of infant mortality and cancer in laboratory animals.

Prudent Behavior

So what should a user who is concerned about radiation do? The jury is still out about the impact of radiation, so the best advice is to practice prudent avoidance. Following are several suggestions for those who wish to avoid electromagnetic emissions.

- Stay at least 28 inches away from the front and three feet away from the sides and back of a monitor. Magnetic radiation drops off with distance. (Refer to Figure 14-1.)
- Turn off monitors when they are not in use.
- Install a grounded filter on a display's screen. This helps avoid extremely low frequency (ELF) and very low frequency (VLF) electric-field (E-field) radiation.

Several companies offer filters that attenuate up to 99 percent of E-field emissions. Many filters also eliminate static charge and dust buildup.

Buyers of grounded filters should beware of vendors' exaggerated claims. Many vendors have made statements about radiation blocking that are simply not accurate. For example, some vendors say that their filters block all electromagnetic emissions. This is true only in part. The filters block only the E-field electromagnetic emissions, not the magnetic field radiation.

There is no practical way to effectively diminish magnetic fields. Magnetic waves can even penetrate walls, so add-on monitor filters or lead-lined vests won't help. Magnetic emissions have to be blocked at the source.

If you want to avoid magnetic radiation you can buy a low-emission monitor. A number of vendors now offer these monitors, including IBM, NEC Technologies, Qume, Radius, Wyse Technology, Compaq Computer, ADI Systems, ViewSonic, and Samtron Displays.

Many people are not aware that low-emission monitors are available. Manufacturers are offering low-emission displays in a low-profile way. They are fearful of casting suspicion on their installed base of monitor users.

A number of manufacturers have been stonewalling on the radiation issue for years. They point out that no scientific evidence links monitors to health problems.

They state that they believe electric and magnetic fields do not pose a health risk. However, this is a concern among users, so they encourage research and scientific investigation into the health effects of emissions.

The only existing monitor emissions and ergonomic standards are those of the 1990 Swedish National Board for Measurement and Testing (MPR). Unfortunately, the board doesn't offer a seal of authenticity for low-emission monitors, even though monitors can be tested and certified by the board.

In the absence of United States standards for monitor emissions, consumers will have to rely on manufacturers' marketing materials for emissions information. So close examination of product information is a must for buyers. Look for a statement in the data sheet.

In the near future, all new displays will have low magnetic emissions. But even if monitors meet stringent emissions guidelines, we still won't really know whether they are safe or unsafe to use.

Repetitive Strain

Possibly your job includes typing rapidly on a computer keyboard. If it does, you may touch keys up to 200,000 times a day—the equivalent of your fingers walking 10 miles. This means you continually repeat small movements in your wrists and hands, increasing the odds of *repetitive strain injury (RSI)*. This has been an office problem for years with typewriters. But with the proliferation of PCs that require heavy keyboard activity, the problem has become very visible.

Uncomfortable Computing

Awkward posture while you keyboard, poorly positioned equipment and furniture, and typing or sitting in the same position for hours can add to wear and tear on your wrists and hands. And like favorite shoes that are worn from walking, overuse of your wrists and hands can lead to uncomfortable keyboarding. The result: tired wrists and hands—and possible strains and pains—unless you take steps to prevent them.

Preventing tired wrists and hands is really a matter of taking charge of your posture and computer work environment. How? Learn the best way to hold your wrists and hands. Then practice adjusting the equipment and furniture in your work area so that you don't overwork your wrists and hands. (Again, refer to Figure 14-1.) When you have developed the right partnership between you and your workstation, your wrists and hands will usually feel fine, even at the end of a busy workday.

If your fingers do a lot of "keyboard walking," straight wrists, hands, and back posture at the keyboard are the keys to your ongoing comfort. When you've found the right position, your muscles and back are unstressed and flexible, so your wrists and hands don't have to overwork.

Each time you touch a key, nerves tell muscles and tendons in your wrists and hands they're needed to help you move your fingers. When you work with straight wrists and fingers, these nerves, muscles, and tendons stay relaxed and comfortable. So they're less likely to develop the strains and pains that may be associated with keyboarding.

Ideal posture includes sitting straight in your chair, muscles relaxed, with your body tilted slightly back. A straight wrist is a level, flat wrist. This position keeps extra pressure off muscles, tendons, and nerves in your wrist and hand. Remember:

- Flexing your wrist forward can strain muscles and tendons.
- Extending your wrist backward strains muscles and tendons.
- Twisting your wrist to the side strains nerves and tendons.

Your posture at your workstation affects the position of your wrists and hands. Why? If you lean your body forward (flexion) or backward (extension), or if you slouch, your wrists and hands adapt by becoming flexed or extended, too. This means that the nerves, muscles, and tendons that support your wrists and hands become tense and strained.

If you want to keep your wrists and hands comfortable and injury-free at the keyboard, there's no better time to start than now. To begin, check the position of your wrists, hands, and back. Then arrange your work space and use workstation props so that you can work without straining your wrists and hands.

Check your posture. At first, obtaining good posture may mean being continually aware of your posture at the keyboard. Your goal: keyboarding with straight wrists, relaxed fingers, and straight posture until it becomes second nature.

- Sit up straight, facing the computer straight-on.
- Hold your head at a slight downward tilt to avoid straining muscles in your neck and shoulders.
- Keep hands and wrists straight while keyboarding.
- Touch your keys lightly by keeping your wrists and fingers relaxed.
- Keep your feet flat and pointed toward the workstation.

Adjust your workstation—How will you know if your office furniture is adjusted to meet your needs? First, you'll be able to easily maintain a straight wrist, hand, and back posture. What else? At the end of the work day, you won't feel aches and pains.

- Adjust keyboard tray or desk height so that your wrists and hands are straight while you keyboard.
- Adjust screen height so that the top of it is at about your eye level.
- Adjust chair height and seat back so that you can keyboard with straight wrists and hands.
- Position your keyboard so that your wrists and forearms are straight.

Use workstation props—If you're unable to work comfortably with straight wrists after adjusting your furniture, try using props you've purchased or made. Props can help keep your wrists, hands, and back straight—and your muscles relaxed.

- A telephone headset helps to keep your head upright and your body straight.
- A copystand should be the same height as the screen, to keep you from straining your neck or head.
- A wrist rest can support your wrists and keep them straight.
- A lower back pad, such as a pillow or rolled-up towel, can help support your lower back.
- A mouse pad should allow the mouse to float friction-free over it, requiring little effort.

Releasing Tension

Your wrists and hands talk. When they're tense from repeated strain, they communicate stiffness and soreness. You can release tension build-up by exercising at least once every hour—even while you're at your desk. And when you're at home, avoid repeating wrist and hand motions you do at work.

In your wrists and hands:

- Stretching—place your hands out in front of you. Then spread your fingers as far apart as possible. Hold for five seconds. Relax. Repeat five times.
- Rotating—rotate your wrists, keeping your fingers relaxed and your elbows still. First turn your palms up, then rotate them down. Repeat five times.
- Shaking—let your hands dangle from your wrists. Then shake your hands, first up and down, then sideways. Repeat until tension in your hands is gone.

In your torso:

- Reaching—place your arms over your head. With your fingers stretched, reach toward the ceiling. Hold for five seconds, then relax. Repeat five times.
- Rolling—using a wide circular motion, roll your shoulders forward five times. Then roll your shoulders backward five times. Repeat cycle five times.
- Shifting—while you sit, move around in your chair. Slouch and slump, look away from the screen, dangle your arms. Repeat as often as necessary.

At work:

- Walk to the printer to retrieve work you've printed out.
- Be sure to take any breaks that are recommended by your company's policy.
- Exercise your legs by rotating your ankles, whenever possible.
- Extend your legs while sitting to increase circulation.
- Force a yawn to relax facial muscles and release tension in other parts of your body.

At home:

- Be physical by getting involved with a favorite activity, such as playing ball.
- Stretch and relax your hands and body whenever you get a free moment.
- Exercise aerobically by walking or swimming.

See your doctor if you have ongoing discomfort in your wrists, hands, eyes, torso, or lower extremities.

Carpal Tunnel Syndrome

Carpal tunnel syndrome (CTS) is a common and troublesome condition that interferes with the use of the hand. It is caused when too much pressure is put on a nerve that runs through your wrist. A variety of anatomical abnormalities may be responsible for this vise-like pressure. Once symptoms of pain and tingling appear, the condition frequently worsens and permanent nerve damage may occur. However, CTS is highly treatable if diagnosed early.

The Symptoms: Progressive Pain and Numbness

The pain, numbness, and tingling of CTS can happen anywhere and anytime, at home or at work. But most often symptoms begin by waking you up at night. Shaking or massaging the hand may work temporarily, but if ignored, CTS gets progressively worse. The pain increases, the grip weakens, and you may begin dropping things. Fortunately, appropriate treatment is available.

It's always best to prevent a condition, and CTS is no exception. But if you do notice symptoms, don't wait for them to become unbearable. The earlier you have professional diagnosis and treatment, the more successful the outcome will be.

At home or on the job, there are steps you can take that may help decrease the risk of developing or worsening the symptoms of CTS. Before you learn about prevention, however, learn the terminology of the disease.

Early diagnosis of CTS means you get relief sooner. It also minimizes the possibility of permanent nerve damage, discomfort, and disability.

Treatment usually begins with a splint, medication, or both. If symptoms don't subside, your physician may recommend surgery.

The Carpal Tunnel

In order to understand CTS, it helps if you understand the anatomy of the carpal (meaning "wrist") tunnel. Conditions in many parts of the body can cause symptoms in the hands and fingers. In CTS, the symptoms occur because a major nerve is compressed as it passes through a narrow tunnel of bone and ligament at the wrist. The result is numbness; tingling; a feeling of pins and needles, burning, and pain in the middle and index fingers and thumb; and sometimes distress in all five fingers.

Carpal Tunnel Anatomical Terms

Carpal tunnel—At the underside and in the center of the wrist, bones and a ligament form a narrow tunnel containing tendons and a major nerve.

Carpal bones—a U-shaped cluster of eight bones at the base of the palm forms the hard, rigid floor and the two sides of the tunnel.

Transverse carpal ligament—a very strong ligament, tough as bone, lies across the arch of carpal bones, forming the roof of the tunnel.

Median nerve—this nerve conducts sensation from the hand, up the arm, to the central nervous system. When the nerve is compressed at the wrist, the hand and fingers are affected.

Motor branch—the motor branch of the median nerve controls the muscle surrounding the thumb. Damage affects the hand's ability to grasp large and small items.

Flexor tendons—the nine tendons are surrounded by a lubricating fluid (*synovia*), which allows the tendons to slide back and forth through the tunnel as the wrist and the fingers are used.

Causes of Carpal Tunnel Syndrome

With the wear and tear computer users subject their carpal tunnels to, the synovial fluid around the tendons may become thick and sticky. This condition may also be caused by the normal aging process. Either means of developing the condition results in the nerve pressing against the tunnel.

Another cause of the syndrome is a previous dislocation or fracture of the wrist, which causes bone to protrude into the tunnel. Arthritis may also be present. Consequently, the tunnel becomes too narrow and puts pressure on the nerve.

Edema (fluid retention) causes swelling of tissue in the carpal tunnel, including perhaps the nerve itself. This occurs most often during pregnancy, with the symptoms subsiding after delivery.

CTS Prevention at Home and at Work

Certain repetitive hand activities may put you at high risk for developing a variety of wrist problems such as carpal tunnel syndrome. By learning how to modify the way you use your hands, you may be able to reduce the risk. Whenever possible, keep the following pointers in mind at home and on the job, and be sure to follow your company's hand and wrist safety policies and procedures.

- Keep your wrists in neutral—avoid using your wrist in a bent (flexed), extended, or twisted position for long periods of time. Instead, try to maintain a neutral (straight) wrist position.
- Minimize repetition—even simple, light tasks may eventually cause injury. If possible, avoid repetitive movements or holding an object in the same way for extended periods of time.
- Reduce speed and force—reducing the speed with which you do a forceful, repetitive movement gives your wrist time to recover from the effort. Using power tools helps reduce the force.
- Watch your grip—gripping, grasping, or lifting with the thumb and index finger can put stress on your wrist. When practical, use the whole hand and all the fingers to grasp an object.
- Rest your hands—periodically give your hands a break by letting them rest briefly. Or you may be able to alternate easy and hard tasks, switch hands, or rotate work activities.
- Perform conditioning exercises—certain exercises strengthen the hand and arm muscles. They may help by reducing the need to compensate for these weak muscles with a poor wrist position.

Early Diagnosis: Your Medical Evaluation

Accurate diagnosis is important, because treatment for this condition is specific for CTS. The sooner you have a professional evaluation, the sooner your symptoms can be relieved, and the more likely it is that permanent nerve or muscle damage will be prevented. For your evaluation, your doctor will take a medical history followed by a physical exam; your condition may also require certain tests.

Medical History
Your doctor will need a medical history. He or she will ask you to describe your symptoms, which may feel like tingling, numbness, pins and needles, pain, or a heaviness in the hand and fingers. Your doctor will need to know if symptoms are mild, intermittent, severe, or frequent, and whether they bother you only at night, only during the day, or both.

Tests
A physical exam will help to confirm that symptoms are related to a nerve problem, and then to localize the nerve problem to the wrist. Your doctor will examine your wrists for swelling and signs of previous injury. You may be tested for decreased sensitivity to touch or to pin pricks. Other simple nerve tests include:

- Tinel's test—your doctor gently taps over the nerve with his or her fingers.
- Phalen's test—your wrist is held in a flexed position for a period of time.

After the history and exam, your doctor may order additional tests to confirm and document the diagnosis of CTS if surgery is being considered. These include standard wrist or carpal tunnel X rays; a nerve conduction test and an electromyogram are objective means of definitive diagnosis. X rays help rule out other conditions such as fracture or arthritis. Nerve conduction measures the speed of electricity along the nerve. Having an electromyogram will reveal any muscular abnormalities. Your doctor will determine what further action(s) is necessary, such as the use of splints, medications, or possibly surgery in more advanced cases.

Balancing Your Computer's Hazards with Its Advantages

Regardless of the health hazards, computer workstations, like typewriters and calculators, are here to stay. They make our work easier and more productive. Thus, we must reduce or eliminate these health risks for ourselves and employees. The equipment location and stress relieving exercises mentioned here are a start. Further studies will disclose other methods. Until then, it is to your and your employees' advantage to practice these.

Final Thoughts About Computerizing Your Small Business

Personal computers have become an important tool in many modern companies, but it's still surprisingly rare to enter the office of a chief executive and find a well-worn PC. Ironically, most senior executives simply don't use them, according to Mary E. Boone, author of the book *Leadership and the Computer* (Prima Pub., 1991), because they still aren't convinced there's a connection between what their job entails and what a PC system can do for them.

If *Leadership and the Computer* has a mission, it's to shed light on the ways in which some of this country's most creative leaders have used electronic information systems (EISs) to foster change in corporate climates. A growing number of executives embrace PCs to meet the business challenges of the 1990s.

There's *no* perfect executive system, but business leaders from widely divergent industries turn to information tools for thinking, planning, and improving across-the-board communications. These tools have the potential to be valuable, provided they are custom-designed to meet the goals of a particular executive.

Over the next few years, a gradual shift to the EIS camp will occur, though change probably will be evolutionary rather than revolutionary.

It is thought that the widespread use of these tools will depend on how well the EIS manufacturers get their message across. Executives are more open than given credit for, but they need good reasons to change.

There are thousands of things that a computer can do for you, but that knowledge is so overwhelming that you almost put it aside.

Yet a growing number are joining the ranks of the CEOs in Boone's book, convinced they must augment their traditional management approaches if they are to succeed in the 1990s. After all, leaders are being asked to work with more information than ever before. And even small and medium-size companies are now operating in the global marketplace. Business routinely demands an understanding of intricate technologies, finance, and manufacturing.

At the same time, economies are more volatile, and competitive pressures are more intense and fast acting. The fundamental trends are stretching executives' leadership abilities to the limit. The growth—perhaps the survival—of many organizations may depend on a massive increase in executives' intellectual abilities. Those abilities will, of necessity, be augmented by extensive use of the PC.

The Excitement of Today's Business Environment

This is an exciting time to be in business. Although some sociologists and psychologists may bemoan the ever-increasing dependence on computers, society thrives and productivity soars as more goods are produced with less energy.

Recall those Dark Ages when handling paper and dealing with information was the most labor-intensive segment of the business world. Increases in communication requirements added a growing cost burden to the handling of information. And the evolution began—from manual to electric to memory typewriters, to computer terminals with printers, and to personal stand-alone computers with powerful text and graphics generation and editing capabilities. Today, technology is beginning to connect PCs in complex networks, enabling users to pass work from machine to machine. Personal computers have opened a new world to office workers. Workers can recall, analyze, and produce more information than ever before. It's a revolution in information technology.

Yet no revolution comes without pain. Some vendors hold back interface capability by introducing products that work only with proprietary software and interfaces. That frustrates the forward momentum. But they can't stop it. Each time a roadblock develops to prevent the free flow of information, another innovation occurs to put us back on course.

The important point is that the direction is toward more intuitive use of the computer. To be effective in the office, we shouldn't need to figure out how the computer works. Ideally, the computer should be a natural extension of ourselves—an intuitive tool.

Users clamor for more speed, memory, power, simpler interfaces and better graphics. But there's a practical limit to the hardware capabilities that can be used by the software on the market today and what users can afford.

More high-powered computers are better suited for applications most of us would never attempt. Many people might like to have these machines but not many people are likely to buy them. Although everyone wants faster machines with higher performance, their user profile determines whether they really need that power. Although businesses can always use stand-alone word processing stations, additional memory and computing power will be essential for program switching, multitasking, and complex application programs that are inevitable when the "office of the future" becomes a reality.

Software development creates a bottleneck of sorts. Most of the programs available now are monoprocessor applications written for obsolete hardware. They're not designed for a distributed application using the new architecture.

On the other hand, software can't be developed until the hardware exists, so there's always going to be a delay between hardware and software.

The drive for more sophisticated applications requires quantitative improvements in hardware and qualitative improvements in software.

Computer speed and memory capability are doubling every 1 to 2 years, and microcomputer power grows exponentially with time. Yet we seem to soak up computer capability faster than the hardware manufacturers can build it. The only thing that consistently grows faster than hardware is our level of expectation.

Evolving microcomputers have capabilities similar to the best mainframes available today. Increasingly powerful microcomputers are becoming available at lower costs. Acceptance of electronic voice has been slow, but voice mail and voice-activated telephone systems are growing in use. And there's reason to believe that computers will soon contain voice-input capability.

It's only recently that computers have had the capability to store voice directions or explanations with data files on the same disk. When users open the file, a voice message can guide them through the data. Innovations like this will have a dramatic effect on the office of tomorrow.

Office of the Future

Let's take a look at what the office of tomorrow will probably look like.

The future office will connect a telecommunications information system to a network that can handle voice, data, graphics, and video easily and clearly. Creation, dissemination, and consumption of information will be electronically enhanced, and travel reduced using new conferencing and meeting techniques.

Most operations will be integrated, and one group in the company will be responsible for producing a seamless exchange of data between computers both inside and outside the office using hard copper wire, fiber optic cable, and wireless local area networks.

Some networks will be self-managing, yet there will be some controls on the information that passes between offices or companies. The most fundamental breakthrough will be the smooth distribution of digital information. Networking and transparent interfaces will make this possible.

The modem will be an important link. According to one leading modem supplier, faster transfer speeds will exist using dial-up lines and a universal modem that can adapt quickly to interface connections and line conditions. Modems will also be smaller and more common in portable computers.

Networks will no longer be in their infancy, and modem calls will no longer be prone to disconnect or develop line static. These networks will tie into minicomputers and mainframe computers that also control thousands of terminals and printers. They'll carry enormous amounts of data, boost productivity, and improve competitiveness. Networks will become the company's vital infrastructure.

The future network operating systems will optimize human interaction in a work group. Computers will communicate with other computers over a broad range of hardware and software designs.

Each application will automatically find and use the necessary resources, such as color graphics, a mouse, voice, interface and network connections, and printers.

Storage capacity and all the resources that are needed will be packaged in a very small footprint. The desktop computer will have a graphical-user interface (GUI) and will be networked. Its built-in multimedia capabilities will provide powerful new ways to present real information, exploiting the power of visual communications. Multimedia, handwriting, and voice recognition, electronic mail and groupware will be folded into a common package.

PCs will race data along at 100 to 300 million instructions per second (MIPs) and perform true multitasking and multiprocessing easily and cost effectively.

Each computer will contain 8M bytes of memory (upgradable to 16M bytes or more) and will easily handle large, complex application programs. The graphical user interface will be optimized for image-oriented data transfers, multitasking and networking. The graphical front end will let users deal with files, directories, and applications without having to learn about the underlying operating system.

Notebook-sized computers will be commonly used by office workers both inside the office and in the field. They'll cost less than $1,000 and contain a database, fax board, and cellular phone capability so users can receive voice mail and facsimiles. Workers will rely on these portable computers to stay in touch.

Office computers will contain a small, active program that can conduct searches of CD-ROM databases on command.

Some workers will use a wrist communications computer that will interface with desktop computers. The separation between paperwork and "real work" will gradually disappear as various types of desk work can be accomplished away from the desk.

Computer output will be visual and audible with high-resolution graphics. Professional-quality image documents will be shared as casually as people hand printed pages to each other today. Character-mode applications will be replaced by graphical interface techniques. Video and voice superimposed on written text will be typical in communication. Speech input and output will be such that users will be able to talk to computers and they will understand what we say.

Computing will be done interactively with graphics and on-line access using better human interfaces. Applications will work the way people think and function.

Desktop computer publishing will be pervasive in almost every business in the United States, with color applications and capability commonplace.

Computers will continually retrieve selected information, no longer assuming that all information is good. Information will be "grown," manufactured, bought, and sold as a commodity. The PCs that caused the information-overload problem will now solve it. Users will become information managers, preventing PCs from dumping massive quantities of indiscriminate data (noise) on their desks through on-line services, networks, and data disks.

Fewer people will quickly produce more information, but software applications will help them effectively find and deal with that information. Smart software will watch what we do with our PC and analyze data content. The PC will provide information tailored to specific interests and keep desks clear of irrelevant details. It will use the patterns it finds to filter mail, select news stories, and summarize reports. Software that can do this will be the most valuable program on computers.

The computer of the future will provide each office worker with tools that aren't lock-stepped to everything else, where individual creative energies are liberated and people can do things their own way.

The computer of the future will finally be the instrument of an office worker's dreams, in tune with human thinking and our visual, verbal, and tactile functioning.

Appendix A

Computer Purchasing Worksheet

Comparing Computers, Peripherals, Software, and Accessories

Item or Feature	Computer System Models of Computers Compared		
Dealer			
Address/Phone			
Contact's Name			
Hard Disk Size			
3.5″ Drive(s)			
5.25″ Drive(s)			
Tape Backup Drive			
Other Data Storage			
RAM (in megabytes)			
Processor Type			
Processor Speed (MHz)			
No. of Parallel Ports			
No. of Serial Ports			

No. of Game Ports   _____ _____ _____

Other Expansion Slots   _____ _____ _____

Monitor Color/Size   _____ _____ _____

Graphics Adapter   _____ _____ _____

Warranty Terms   _____ _____ _____

TOTAL FOR COMPUTER
(Dealer's Best Price) $_____ $_____ $_____

Peripheral Prices
Models of Peripherals Compared

Item
Printer:

  Dot-Matrix $_____ $_____ $_____

  Daisy-Wheel $_____ $_____ $_____

  Laser $_____ $_____ $_____

  Receipt $_____ $_____ $_____

Item

Mouse $_____ $_____ $_____

Item

Bar Code Reader $_____ $_____ $_____

Item

Electronic Keypad $_____ $_____ $_____

Item

Cash Drawer $_____ $_____ $_____

Item
Modem:

  300 baud $_____ $_____ $_____

  1200 baud $_____ $_____ $_____

  2400 baud $_____ $_____ $_____

  9600 baud $_____ $_____ $_____

  Other: $_____ $_____ $_____

Item
Fax:

Fax Board	$_____	$_____	$_____
Fax Server	$_____	$_____	$_____
Stand-Alone	$_____	$_____	$_____
TOTAL FOR ALL PERIPHERALS	$_____	$_____	$_____

Software Features and Prices

Program/Features	*Software Packages Compared*		
Operating System:			
Single-User	_____	_____	_____
Multiuser	_____	_____	_____
User Friendliness	_____	_____	_____
Memory Required	_____	_____	_____
Disk Space Used	_____	_____	_____
Runs Applications Needed	_____	_____	_____
Price	_____	_____	_____
Program/Features Accounting:			
Performs All Accounting Tasks	_____	_____	_____
Memory Required	_____	_____	_____
Disk Space Used	_____	_____	_____
Price	_____	_____	_____
Program/Features Database:			
Maximum Size of Database Possible	_____	_____	_____
Maximum Number of Fields Allowed	_____	_____	_____
Memory Required	_____	_____	_____
Disk Space Used	_____	_____	_____
Price	_____	_____	_____

Program/Features
Desktop Publishing:

    Maximum Size of File
    Possible   _____ _____ _____

    Number of Fonts
    Supported   _____ _____ _____

    Memory Required   _____ _____ _____

    Disk Space Used   _____ _____ _____

    Price   _____ _____ _____

Program/Features
Spreadsheet:

    Maximum Size of
    Spreadsheet Possible   _____ _____ _____

    Maximum Number of
    Pages/Cells Allowed   _____ _____ _____

    Memory Required   _____ _____ _____

    Disk Space Used   _____ _____ _____

    Price   _____ _____ _____

Program/Features
Word Processing:

    Supports Your Printer(s)   _____ _____ _____

    Useful Help System   _____ _____ _____

    Number of Fonts
    Supported   _____ _____ _____

    Number of Windows
    Possible   _____ _____ _____

    Memory Required   _____ _____ _____

    Disk Space Used   _____ _____ _____

    Price   _____ _____ _____

**TOTAL FOR ALL
SOFTWARE** $_____ $_____ $_____

Accessory and Supply Prices

Item	Price
Uninterruptible Power Supply	$_____
Surge Suppressor	$_____
Voltage Regulator	$_____
Disks (per box of 10)	$_____
Printer Cartridges (laser)	$_____
Printer Ribbons (nonlaser)	$_____
Network Interface Cards	$_____
Cabling	$_____
TOTAL FOR ALL ACCESSORIES	$_____

Setup and Training Issues

Item to Cover with Vendor	Decision
Party to Install the System	_____
Installation Charges	_____
Length and Terms of Warranty	_____
On-Site Repair Versus Off-Site Repair	_____
Turnaround Time for Repairs	_____
Price of Extended Service Contract	_____
Price for Setup and Training	_____

Other Issues

How many users: _____

Can more be added? Yes _____ No _____ Cost per user $_____

Maximum number of users _____

Who installs cables? Me _____ Dealer _____

Comments: _____
Network products include terminals, cards, cables, and software.

Network price $_____

Operating system:

  Type: DOS _____ Windows NT _____ UNIX _____ OS/2 _____

  Other: _____

  Version: _____

  Comments _____

Software:

Brand _____

  Upgrade to multiuser? Yes _____ No _____ How much? _____

  Expandable? _____

  Access data? _____

  Link to accounting programs? _____

Initial training? _____

  Software support available? Yes _____ No _____

  Comments _____

Price of software $_____

Appendix B

Special Keyboard Considerations

If you experience difficulty in entering certain characters (the characters you type are not the ones that appear on the screen) when you use the SELECT procedure it may be due to the fact that your keyboard layout does not match the DOS that you are using.

Note: Once you have completed SELECT, you will have loaded the appropriate keyboard routine, and will no longer experience difficulty.

The characters that you may have a problem with include:

- The colon (:)
- The backslash (\ )
- The letter *y*

There is an alternate method to type each of these characters.
To get a colon:

1. Press and hold the Alt key.
2. Press 5 and then 8 on the numeric keypad.
3. Release all the keys.

To get the backslash:

1. Press and hold the Alt key.
2. Press 9 and then 2 on the numeric keypad.
3. Release all the keys.

To get the letter *y*:

1. Press and hold the Alt key.
2. Press 8 and then 9 on the numeric keypad.
3. Release all the keys.

During the SELECT procedure for a fixed disk, you are asked to enter a volume label for your fixed disk. Because of the reason just explained, the characters you type may not be the ones you expected. Do not enter a volume label during the SELECT procedure. Just press Enter.

After completing SELECT, you can give your fixed disk a volume label using the LABEL command as described in your *DOS Reference Manual.* It is strongly recommended that you give a fixed disk a volume label.

Appendix C

Messages

This appendix contains two sections: "device errors" (the message that DOS uses to indicate errors while reading or writing to devices on your computer) and "common error messages" in alphabetic order.

The first word of the description of each message is the name of the program or command that generated the message.

Device Error Messages

When an error is detected while reading or writing to any of the devices (such as disk drives and printers) on your system, DOS displays a message in the following format:

```
<type> error reading <device>
Abort, Retry, Ignore?
```

or

```
<type> error writing <device>
Abort, Retry, Ignore?
```

Warning: ——————————————————————————————

If either of these messages appears when you're using a diskette drive, do not change diskettes before you respond with A, R, or I.

The computer now waits for you to respond. If you know what caused the problem, you can take corrective action before you actually choose a response. The computer waits until one of the following responses is made. Enter:

- A for abort. The system ends the program that requested the diskette (or disk) read or write and returns to DOS.
- R for retry. The system tries the diskette (or disk) read or write operation again.
- I for ignore. The current program is terminated.

To recover from an error condition, the responses are generally made in the following order:

1. R to retry the operation because the error may not occur again.
2. A to abort the program.
3. I to abort the current program, if possible, and return you to the calling program.

In these messages, <device> is the name of the device in error, such as PRN for printer, or B: for the B drive, and <type> is one of the following error types:

Data

The computer (or DOS) was not able to read or write the data correctly.
Action: Try to correct the error by choosing Retry several times. Choose Abort if you want to end the program. This message usually means a diskette has developed a defective spot.

General Failure

An error of a type not described elsewhere in this list has occurred.
Action: Choose Retry or Abort. This problem requires further investigation by a programmer. If this is a purchased program, contact the dealer you purchased it from.

No Paper

The indicated printer either is out of paper or is not switched on.
Action: Switch on the printer, press the ONLINE switch, or add paper and retry.

Non-DOS Disk

The file allocation table contains invalid information.

Action: The diskette needs to be reformatted, but you can try running CHKDSK to see whether any corrective action is possible. Copy files to another diskette before reformatting. Files are lost forever once you format the diskette. For more information about CHKDSK refer to the *DOS Reference Manual.*

Not Ready

The named device is not ready and cannot accept or transmit data.

Action: Check that the diskette drive door is closed and choose Retry for your response if this is the problem.

Read Fault

DOS was unable to successfully read the data from the device.

Action: Make sure the diskette has been properly inserted in the drive. Then choose Retry.

Sector Not Found

The sector containing the data could not be located on the diskette.

Action: This problem usually occurs when a defective spot develops on the diskette. The diskette needs to be reformatted (copy all files from it first).

Seek

The fixed disk or diskette drive was unable to locate the proper track on the disk.

Action: Make sure the diskette has been properly inserted in the drive. Try a different drive.

Write Fault

DOS was unable to successfully write the data to the device.

Action: Make sure the diskette has been properly inserted in the drive. If this is not the problem, choose Retry. If you get the same message, choose Abort and retry the command with a new diskette.

Write Protect

An attempt was made to write on a write-protected diskette.

Action: Investigate carefully whether you want to write on a write-protected diskette. If you do, remove or reposition the write-protect tab.

Note: This message may appear if you attempt to use a double-sided diskette in a single-sided drive.

Common Error Messages

This section contains an alphabetic list of some of the more common DOS messages you may get on your screen. (The remainder of the DOS messages are in the *DOS Reference Manual*.) Note that the first term (capitalized) in the explanation is the command being used that sensed the error condition.

Attempted write-protect violation

FORMAT. The diskette being formatted cannot be written on because it is write-protected.

Action: You are prompted to insert a new diskette and press any key to restart formatting.

Bad command or filename

DOS. The command just entered is not a valid command to DOS.

Action: You should check your spelling and reenter the command. If the command name is correct, check to see that the default or specified drive contains the external command or batch file you are trying to run.

Compare error(s) on drive x, track xx, side xx

DISKCOMP. One or more locations on the indicated track and side contain differing information between the diskettes being compared.

Action: This message informs you that there is a difference between diskettes. If you want an exact copy of a diskette, use DISKCOPY.

Cannot DISKCOMP to or from a network drive

DISKCOMP. You cannot use the DISKCOMP command to compare files that are on a network drive or on a drive that is on your computer but is currently being shared on the network.

Action: Use the COMP command instead of DISKCOMP.

Cannot DISKCOPY to or from a network drive

DISKCOPY. You cannot use the DISKCOPY command to copy files to or from a network drive or on a drive that is on your computer but is currently being shared on the network.

Action: Use the COPY *.* command instead of DISKCOPY. You can also use COPY command to copy individual files instead of the whole diskette.

Cannot FORMAT a network drive

FORMAT. You can't use the FORMAT command to format a network drive or a drive that is on your computer but is currently being shared on the network.

Action: Stop attempting the FORMAT. No further action required.

Drive types or diskette types not compatible

DISKCOMP or DISKCOPY. The source and target diskettes or drives are not compatible.

Action: Refer to the DISKCOMP or DISKCOPY commands in the *DOS Reference Manual* for the allowable combinations.

Duplicate filename or file not found

RENAME. You tried to rename a file to a filename that already exists on the diskette, or the file to be renamed could not be found on the specified (or default) drive. RENAME is warning you that you are using the same name for two files, or else it cannot find the file you are trying to rename.

Action: Check whether you typed the filename and drive correctly. Take a second look at the filename you want to change and reenter the command.

File cannot be copied onto itself

COPY. You tried to copy a file and place the copy (with the same name as the original) in the same directory and on the same disk as the original file.

Action: Change the name given to the copy, put it in a different directory, or put it on another diskette.

File creation error

DOS and commands. An unsuccessful attempt was made to add a new filename to the directory or to replace a file that was already there.

Action: If the file was already there, it is possible that the file is marked "read only" and cannot be replaced. Otherwise, run CHKDSK to determine whether the directory is full or if some other condition caused the error.

File not found

DOS and commands. A file named in a command or command parameter does not exist on the diskette in the specified (or default) drive.

Action: Retry the command using the correct filename, diskette, and drive.

Format failure

FORMAT. A disk error was encountered while formatting the target diskette.

Action: The diskette is unusable. Retry the command using another diskette.

Insert disk with \COMMAND.COM in drive A: and strike any key when ready

DOS. DOS is attempting to reload the command processor, but COMMAND.COM is not in the drive that DOS was started from.

Action: Insert the DOS diskette in the indicated drive and press any key.

Invalid COMMAND.COM in drive x

DOS. While trying to reload the command processor, the copy of COMMAND.COM on the diskette was found to be an incorrect version.

Action: You need to insert the correct DOS diskette in drive x.

Invalid media or track 0 bad-disk unusable

FORMAT. FORMAT was unable to format track 0 on the specified media. This error occurs if

- Track 0 is unusable. Track 0 is where the boot record, file allocation table, and directory must reside. If track 0 is bad, the disk is unusable.

- The diskette type and drive type are incompatible. You tried to format a double-sided diskette in a high capacity drive, or a high-capacity diskette in a double-sided drive.

Action: For the first case, obtain another disk and retry the FORMAT command. For the second case, retry the FORMAT command specifying the /4 parameter.

Invalid number of parameters

Commands. You have specified too few or too many parameters for the command you entered.

Action: Correct the command you entered and try again.

Non-system disk or disk error Replace and strike any key when ready

Startup. There is no entry for IBMIO.COM or IBMDOS.COM in the directory; or a disk read error occurred while you were starting up the system.

Action: Insert a DOS diskette in drive A and restart your system.

Target diskette may be unusable

DISKCOPY. This message follows an unrecoverable read, write, or verify error message. The copy on the target diskette may be incomplete because of the unrecoverable I/O error.

Action:

- If the error is on the target diskette, get a fresh target diskette.
- If the error is on the source diskette, copy all the files from the source diskette to another diskette. Then reformat the source diskette.

Glossary

Adapter (Add-on) card A card that is installed in an expansion slot located within the central processing unit (CPU) of a computer. These cards may be used to enhance the power or to connect peripheral devices to the computer. For example, monitor cards, serial cards, parallel cards, or memory adapters.

Address The location of an individual cell of a spreadsheet, usually given in A1 address style (A1, A2, A3, and so on) or R1C1 address style (R1C1, R1C2, or R1C3). Also known as a *reference. See also* column heading and row heading.

ANSI.SYS A configuration file that, when referred to in CONFIG.SYS, enables you to customize your keyboard, screen, and cursor location.

Application software Software that allows the computer to perform specific tasks. Spreadsheet, word processing, and accounting programs are some examples of application software.

ASCII An acronym for American Standard Code for Information Interchange. It is a standard character set and coding scheme using unique, 7-bit values (8 bits with parity check) to represent letters, numbers, spaces, symbols, and special control codes.

AUTOEXEC.BAT A batch file that contains initial instructions that DOS carries out once it completes its startup procedures. You can use this file to have your computer perform any initial operation automatically.

Backup An additional copy of work created on a computer for safe-keeping.

Batch file   A text file that contains a sequence of commands supported by a batch command language. It automatically executes a series of DOS commands after you type one command at the DOS prompt.

Baud rate   A measure of the speed at which a modem can send and receive data—specifically, the number of events, or signal changes, that occur each second. Because an event can contain more than one bit, a modem's baud rate and bps are not always the same. *See also* bps.

Bidirectional   A method of data communication that allows data flow in both directions between the host computer and the keyboard.

BIOS   Pronounced "bye-ose." Short for Basic Input/Output System. The set of routines in a PC's ROM chip that allows DOS to communicate with the computer hardware.

Boot   A slang term meaning to turn on the computer. A cold boot occurs when you turn power on to the computer. A warm boot occurs when the computer is already powered on and you reset it by pressing Ctrl+Alt+Del keys together or press the "reset" switch on the CPU if available. Also, the process of starting up a computer.

Bps (bits per second)   A measure of the speed at which a modem can send and receive data—specifically, the number of bits that can be transferred each second. Often confused with baud rate. *See also* baud rate.

Break Code   The scan code produced when a key is released. Also referred to as an "up" scan code.

Break Function   The secondary function of the Pause key. To enable the Break function, press and hold the Ctrl key, then press the Pause key. Typically, Ctrl+Pause ends the current application and returns you to the DOS prompt.

Buffer   The section of RAM memory that DOS uses to store the keystrokes that compose the last command you issued. Once you issue a new command, the previous command is overwritten.

Caps Lock   A key that enables or disables the uppercase letters function. Caps Lock affects only the alpha characters of the keyboard. The Caps Lock LED indicates whether the function is enabled (LED on) or disabled (LED off).

Cell   The basic unit of a spreadsheet. Cells are formed by the intersection of rows and columns and can hold data, formulas, or both.

Central processor unit (CPU)   The part of a computer that contains the main components of the system; RAM, microprocessor, adapter cards, hard disk, floppy disk, and so on.

Column heading   A heading that identifies a vertical group of spreadsheet cells. The heading is placed at the top of the cells. Column headings are usually labeled in A1 style (A, B, C) or R1C1 style (C1, C2, C3 or 1, 2, 3). *See also* row heading.

Command syntax   The order of commands and/or symbols that you must use to issue a DOS command.

CONFIG.SYS   Known also as a *configuration file*, this text file contains a set of commands that inform DOS of the specifics of your computer and provide the instructions needed to further customize it. DOS uses this file to customize your system each time you start (boot) your computer.

Conventional memory   The first 640K bytes of memory. It can be used by DOS without special programs or drivers.

Cursor   The point at which information can be given to the computer and where the next entered character will appear on the screen (usually a flashing underline character).

Data   Information stored on the computer's hard disk or floppy disks.

Default drive   Refers to the particular drive (hard or floppy) that DOS (or any other program) will access automatically without any intervention from the user.

DIN connector (5-pin)   Provides the interface between the keyboard and an IBM-compatible computer. It contains data and clock signals and ground and power voltages.

Disk Operating System (DOS)   Usually referred to as the "operating system." It controls the computer's operation. It allows the system to read application software, accept input from the keyboard or other devices, and transfer information for storage purposes. The operating system also controls basic system maintenance functions.

Diskette/floppy disk   A flexible disk that holds information that can be read by the computer.

DOS   An acronym for Disk Operating System. This is the master program that tells your computer to perform the essential tasks needed to interact successfully with you and the application software you use.

Download   To receive a file by modem. *See also* upload.

Duplex   The communication mode in which data travels in both directions at the same time between two computers. One-way communication is called *simplex*, and two-way communication taking place in only one direction at a time is called *half-duplex*.

EDLIN   A DOS command that enables you to create and edit DOS text files.

E-mail (electronic mail)   The transmission of messages from one computer to another by way of an electronic network. This network can be either a local area network (LAN) or a larger communications network, such as CompuServe or GEnie.

Enhanced Keyboard A 101-key keyboard introduced by IBM in 1986 that recognizes additional scan codes not previously used.

Expansion slots Connections located within the CPU of a computer used to hold adapter cards.

FAT An acronym for File Allocation Table. The area on a floppy or hard disk where DOS keeps a map of available disk space and the addresses of all files stored.

Field Each individual piece of information kept within a record.

File A collection of related records. Currently you probably have a file cabinet that contains all of your customer or inventory records. A disk-based version of this is how your computer system keeps records. You will have a file of customers as well as a file of inventory items. A "file drawer" containing all of your customer records is a subdirectory.

Format To prepare a diskette for use. All diskettes must be formatted before you can use them the first time. Warning: This process erases any information previously saved.

Formula A statement that describes a mathematical calculation. Formulas in spreadsheets are linked to individual cells, though they often refer to data and formulas in other cells, allowing a user to perform what if calculations.

Function A spreadsheet calculation tool that enables you to perform decision-making and value-returning operations automatically. For example, SUM is a function that sums a group of numbers. IF is a function that permits you to test a value and take action based on the result of that test.

Function keys Special keys located across the top of the enhanced keyboard (F1 through F12) that perform functions specific to the software being used.

Hard disk Used to store information. Unlike floppy diskettes this cannot be removed.

Hardware Physical parts of a computer system.

Input To enter information into the computer via the keyboard or bar code reader.

Kilobyte (K byte) A unit of measure equal to 1,024 bytes. Used as a measure of low-density diskette storage.

Label (text) A spreadsheet text string often used as a column or row heading.

LED An acronym for light emitting diode. The Enhanced Keyboard usually contains three LEDs that show the status of the Num Lock, Caps Lock, and Scroll Lock keys. Also, the diskettes and CPU have LEDs indicating the device status. Each LED illuminates when the controlling function is active.

Macro A series of commands recorded and saved for future playback. Use of macros can improve the speed and accuracy of spreadsheet, word processing, and other programs. Also, a set of keystrokes or commands mapped (assigned) to a key, combination of keys, or other executable element.

Make code The scan code produced when a key is pressed. Also referred to as a "down" scan code.

Megabyte (MB) One million bytes. Used as a measure of storage.

Memory disk A space in your computer's random access memory (RAM) set aside as an ultrahigh-speed disk drive. The memory disk acts like a physical disk drive. You place files on it and retrieve files from it.

Microcomputer (personal computer) Small computer that uses a microprocessor as the central processing unit.

Microprocessor The integrated circuit chip that monitors, controls, and executes the machine language instructions.

MNP (Micom Network Protocol) A set of error-correction and data-compression standards that was developed by Micom and made available to other modem manufacturers.

Modem (modulator/demodulator) A device that allows a computer to send information over a standard telephone line.

MS-DOS Pronounced "em-ess-doss." Short for Microsoft Disk Operating System. The most popular PC operating system. It oversees your PC's disk input and output, video support, keyboard control, program execution, and file maintenance.

Multiuser A computer system or software package designed for use by two or more people. In a multiuser system, computers are hooked together to share data and peripherals. A multiuser system includes a host computer (or file server) and one or more stations. All stations share the same hard disk and may share other devices such as printers.

Num Lock A key that enables or disables the numeric keypad. When the numeric keypad is enabled, the Num Lock LED is ON and the keypad is used to enter numbers. When numeric mode is disabled, the LED is OFF and the keypad is placed into cursor control mode.

Operating system A set of programs that controls the computer's operation. It enables the system to read application software, accept input from the keyboard or other devices, and transfer information for storage purposes.

Parity An extra bit that a modem sends with each character to check the accuracy of that character. Common types of parity are even parity, odd parity, no parity, space parity, and mark parity.

Password A secret code entered into the computer via the keyboard that enables the authorized user to gain access to certain features of the program or computer. A password keeps certain information private and restricts access to only those authorized to use or update that information.

Peripheral An add-on device for a computer, such as a printer, bar code reader, or modem.

Pipe a command modifier that causes the output of one command to be redirected to the next command as input. The pipe symbol in a command line is ¦.

Program disk A diskette that contains a software program. Usually the program is transferred to the hard disk and the original diskettes are stored.

Prompt The symbol displayed on the screen that indicates the computer is ready to receive an instruction. Usually this is a blinking underline or a solid square.

RAM An acronym for Random Access Memory. The area of memory within your computer that is used for temporary memory storage. Once you turn off your computer or reboot, all of the memory contained in RAM is lost. Data can be written to (stored) as well as read from (retrieved) this memory area.

Record Unit of information within a file. For example, one customer's history is a record within a file of customers.

Redirection A command modifier used to tell DOS to redirect the resulting information to an output device. DOS outputs information resulting from any command to your monitor screen as a default. The redirection symbol in the command line is >.

Reset To restart the computer when the computer is already on by pressing the Ctrl+Alt+Del key combination. Also called a warm boot.

Restore To replace hard disk data that has been lost or damaged. After a hard disk has been backed up, the information can be restored to the hard disk if it is lost or damaged.

ROM An acronym for Read Only Memory. This area of memory contains files of instructions used by operating systems such as DOS. You cannot access these files to change or erase them. Data (instructions) can only be read from this memory area. These instructions are not erased when you turn off your computer or when you reboot.

Root directory   The largest single category of file organization used in reference to both hard drives and floppy disks. Think of the root directory as a large desk with many drawers. You can put your file folders directly on top of the desk and save them there, or you can place your folders into each drawer. These drawers are subdirectories.

Row heading   A heading that identifies a horizontal group of cells in a spreadsheet. The heading is placed to the left of the cells. Row headings are usually labeled in A1 style (1, 2, 3) or R1C1 style (R1, R2, R3 or 1, 2, 3). *See also* column heading.

Scan code   A numerical value that uniquely identifies each key on the keyboard. Each key is represented by a "down" scan code, generated when the key is pressed, and a corresponding "up" scan code, generated when the key is released.

Scroll Lock   A key that enables or disables the Scroll Lock function. When Scroll Lock is active, the Scroll Lock LED is ON.

Scrolling   To move data on the screen up or down, so that parts of the document outside the screen area, or window, move into view.

Serial data   Data that is transmitted in sequence, one bit at a time, rather than an entire byte (group of 8 bits) at a time (a process known as parallel data transfer).

Shell   A program that provides the user with a means to control the operating system. DOS shell programs are usually add-on programs designed to make it easier to use MS-DOS.

Software   A set of instructions (program) and/or data encoded onto such media as floppy disks and hard disks. Software tells the computer what to do and/or provides the information desired by the user.

Standard Keyboard   An 83-key keyboard introduced by IBM in 1981 for the IBM PC or an 84-key keyboard for the IBM AT.

Stop bit   The bit that signals the end of a character during an online transmission. The data bits that make up a character are usually followed by 1, 1.5, or 2 stop bits.

Subdirectory   A directory that is contained within a larger directory, like a drawer is contained within a desk. Subdirectories are often used as organizational tools for data storage within larger directories.

Synchronous   A method of data communication in which a group of characters is sent as a continuous stream of bits. The characters—data bits—are sent at a fixed rate, with the transmitter and receiver synchronized (clock controlled). This eliminates the need for start and stop bits.

System program   A set of instructions contained in one or more files that directs the performance and responses of an operating system, such as DOS.

TSR   An abbreviation for terminate and stay resident. A program that stays in memory but remains hidden until you activate it by pressing a hot key. Also known as a *memory-resident program*.

Upload   To send a file by modem. *See also* download.

Volume label   The name you give your floppy disk when you format it for use. You can also assign a volume label to your hard drive(s).

Warm boot   To restart your computer by using the Ctrl+Alt+Del key sequence (or the reset switch on some computers). You do a warm boot while your computer is still powered on.

Wildcard   A keyboard character that's used to represent one or more characters. DOS wildcards are the question mark (?), which can be used to represent any single character, and the asterisk (*), which can be used to represent one or more characters.

Worksheet   A spreadsheet document in which you can store, manipulate, calculate, and analyze data.

Index

Accounting, 38–39
Adapter card, 251
Add-on card, 111–16, 251
Address, 251
American Small Business Association, 36–37
Amiga, 28–29
ANSI.SYS, 251
Apple, 27, 29, 56
Applications, 13, 27
  making accessible, 178–83
  installing, 116–19, 159–77
  learning, 162–63
  software, 29–39, 251
ARCNET
  bus network, 189
  star network, 191
ASCII, 17, 251
Atari, 28–29
AUTOEXEC.BAT, 62, 151–58, 181–82, 251

Backup programs, 39, 84, 117–18, 182–83, 251
Bar code printing software, 38, 71–72
Bar code readers/scanners, 71–72
Batch file, 181–82, 252
Baud rate, 252
Bidirectional, 252
BIOS (basic input/output system), 252
Bit, 17
Bookkeeping, 9
Boone, Mary E., 230
Boot, 252
Bootleg software, 40–42
BPS (bits per second), 252
Break code, 252
Break function, 252
Buffer, 252
Bulletin board systems (BBSs), 19, 36–37
Business
  advantages of computer for, 1–10, 23–25, 230–34
  employees and computers, 97–99
  functions to computerize, 22–23
  purchasing worksheet, 235–40
  work patterns changed by computers, 25–26
  work space and computers, 99–101

See also Accounting; Computers, purchasing
Byte, 17

Cables, 89, 101–2, 189–92
Cabling, 64–65
CAD (Computer-Aided Design), 2–3
Caps lock, 109, 252
Carpal tunnel syndrome (CTS), 226–29
Cash drawers, 72
Cell, 252
Central processor unit (CPU), 15, 57–58, 102–6
  defined, 252
  installing add-ons in, 111–16
Check writing software, 39
Clubs, computer, 19
Coaxial cable, 190
Column heading, 252–53
Command syntax, 253
Commodore, 28–29
Communications system
  installing, 170–77
  planning for future, 203–7
  systems for, 36, 75
  See also E-mail; Fax machine; Modem
Computer-Aided Design (CAD), 2–3
Computers
  advantages of, 1–10, 23–25, 230–34
  sample configurations for, 93–97
  components of, 14–17
  fears of, 11
  and health hazards from, 215–29
  installing, 101–19
  planning for, 7–8, 42–55
  purchasing, 14, 18–20, 40–42, 90–92, 196–97, 235–40
  selecting, 21–55 setting up, 90–92, 93–119
  preparing staff for, 97–98
  support, 19
  terminology for, 17–18, 124–42, 251–58
  understanding, 10–14
  user health hazards, 215–34
  warranty and service, 18
  preparing work space for, 99–101
CONFIG.SYS, 62, 151–58, 253
Conventional memory, 253

259

Installation, 101–19
  applications, 159–77
  modem, 170–77
Integrated Services Digital Network
    (ISDN), 204
Inventory management, 4, 9, 10
ISDN, 204

K byte (kilobyte), 254
Keyboards, 63
  enhanced, 254
  installing, 104–5
  special considerations, 241–42 standard,
    257
  understanding, 107–10
  See also Keypad
Keypad, electronic, 72
Kilobyte (K-byte), 254

Label (text), 254
LAN
  See Local area network
Laser printers, 16, 70
Laser scanners, 71–72
LED (light emitting diode), 255
Letters, generating, 6
Line regulator/conditioner, 88–89
Local area network (LAN), 37, 56, 63–68,
    184–202, 203–7, 209–10
  advantages and disadvantages, 185–87
  alternatives, 192–97 implementation,
    197–98
  multiuser operating systems, 195–96
  peer-to-peer networks, 194–95 planning
    the system, 187–92
  server-based, 193–94
  system checklist, 198–202
  zero-slot, 196 *See also*
    Communications; Metropolitan area
    network; Networks; Peripherals; Wide
    area network

Macintosh
  See Apple
Macro, 255
Magnetic strip reader, 84
Mailing labels, generating, 6
Make code, 255
Megabyte (MB), 255
Megahertz (MHz), 11
Memory, 17, 61–62, 253, 255
  See also Storage
Memory disk, 255
Menu, 18
  batch file, 178–79, 181–82
  display, 179–81
Messages, 243–50
  See also Terminology

Metropolitan area network (MAN), 184
Micom Network Protocol (MNP), 255
Microcomputer, 255
Microprocessor, 15, 57–58, 255
Microsoft, 26, 28
Microsoft Windows, 29
MNP (Micom Network Protocol), 255
Modem, 16–17, 36, 72–75, 232–33, 255
  and fax machines, 77–79
  installing, 170–77
Monitors, 15, 63, 104
  and health hazards, 215–26
Motherboard, 57, 115
Mouse, 63, 111
MS-DOS, 255
  See also DOS
Multidmedia products, 12
Multitasking systems, 28, 63–68, 195
Multiuser operating systems, 63–68, 195,
    255

Network interface cards (NICS), 65
Networks, 203–7, 232–33
  See also Communications; Local area
    networks
Num lock, 109, 255

Office space
  See Workstation
On-line credit card processing, 38
Operating system, 13, 27–28, 53, 255–56
Option, 18
OS/2, 28

Parcel shipping programs, 39
Parity, 256
Password, 256
Peer-to-peer networks, 194–95
Peripherals, 28–29, 53, 56, 63, 69–92
  defined, 256
  connecting, 110–16, 170–77
  sharing devices, 197
  See also Fax machines; Modem;
    Printers
Pipe, 256
Portfolio management software, 38
Postcards, generating, 6
Power, 105–6
  See also Uninterruptible power supply
Printers, 16, 29, 69–71
  connecting, 110–11
  and fax machines, 77
  sharing devices, 197
Productivity, 9
Profit margin, 4–6
Program disk, 256
Prompt, 256